Third Edition

LEADERSHIP
THEORY AND PRACTICE

Peter G. Northouse
University of Western Michigan

SAGE Publications
International Educational and Professional Publisher
Thousand Oaks ▪ London ▪ New Delhi

For information:

Sage Publications, Inc.
2455 Teller Road
Thousand Oaks, California 91320
E-mail: order@sagepub.com

Sage Publications Ltd.
6 Bonhill Street
London EC2A 4PU
United Kingdom

Sage Publications India Pvt. Ltd.
B-42 Panchsheel Enclave
New Delhi 110 017 India

Printed in the United States of America

Library of Congress Cataloging-in-Publication Data

Northouse, Peter Guy.
Leadership: Theory and practice / Peter G. Northouse.— 3rd ed.
　　p. cm.
Includes bibliographical references and indexes.
ISBN 0-7619-2566-X (pbk.)
　 1. Leadership. 2. Leadership—Case studies. I. Title.
HM1261.N67 2003
303.3´4—dc21

　　　　　　　　　　　　　　　　　　　　　　　2002156650

This book is printed on acid-free paper.

03　 04　 05　 06　 10　 9　 8　 7　 6　 5　 4　 3　 2　 1

Acquisitions Editor:	Al Bruckner
Editorial Assistant:	MaryAnn Vail
Copy Editor:	Kate Peterson
Production Editor:	Diane S. Foster
Typesetter:	C&M Digitals (P) Ltd.
Proofreader:	Scott Oney
Indexer:	Molly Hall
Cover Designer:	Michelle Lee

Contents

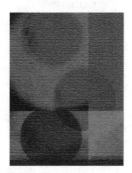

To Laurel, Scott, and Lisa

Preface

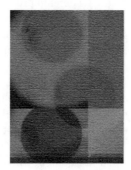

Effective leadership is in high demand. In particular, there is a call for strong ethical leadership. This interest has resulted in a burgeoning of academic programs in leadership studies throughout the country. Courses in leadership, ethics and leadership, and community leadership are being integrated into academic curricula at all levels.

These trends in leadership are extraordinary and striking, and they provide the background for the development of this third edition of *Leadership: Theory and Practice*. This edition is written with the same objective as the prior editions: to bridge the gap between the often-simplistic popular approaches to leadership and the more abstract theoretical approaches. Like previous editions, this edition reviews and analyzes a selected number of leadership theories, giving special attention to how each theoretical approach could be applied in real-world organizations. In essence, the purpose is to explore how an understanding of leadership theory can inform and direct the way leadership is practiced.

This edition features a new chapter, "Skills Approach," which focuses on the essential competencies leaders need to achieve effective performance. This skills chapter was added for three reasons: (1) The skills approach is emerging in the research literature as an important leadership theory; (2) the skills approach offers a unique perspective—leadership can be learned; and (3) the skills approach offers a valuable pragmatic perspective on the leadership process. The central argument made in the chapter is that a leader's effectiveness can be explained by three competencies: problem-solving skills, social judgment skills, and knowledge. Together these skills form the heart of effective leadership.

Although this edition retains many special features from the previous editions, it has been expanded to include more leadership topics and research findings. This edition features a well-developed instructor's manual including chapter overviews, lists of concepts and terms, questions for study and discussion, activities for use in class, writing assignments, and a test bank of true-or-false and multiple-choice questions. This manual facilitates classroom preparation and instruction, and it assists with student evaluation. In addition to the instructor's manual, this edition also includes a complete set of chapter outlines and a sophisticated set of PowerPoint slides to accompany the outlines. Furthermore, this edition includes many new research sources, innovative models, new case studies, new figures and tables, additional research-based applications, and expanded discussions of current issues in leadership research.

SPECIAL FEATURES

Although this text presents and analyzes a wide range of leadership research, every attempt has been made to present the material in a clear, concise, and interesting manner. Reviews of the first two editions of the book indicated that clarity was one of its major strengths. In addition to the writing style, several other features in the book help make it user-friendly.

- Each chapter follows the same format and is structured to include theory first and then practice.
- Each chapter includes a discussion of the strengths and criticisms of the approach and assists the reader in determining the relative merits of each approach.
- Each chapter includes an application section that discusses the practical aspects of the approach and how it could be used in today's organizational settings.
- Three case studies are provided in each chapter to illustrate common leadership issues and dilemmas. Thought-provoking questions follow each case study, assisting readers to interpret the case.

- A leadership instrument/questionnaire is provided in each of the chapters to help the reader apply the approach to his or her own leadership style or setting.
- Figures and tables illustrate the content of the theory and make the ideas more meaningful.

Through these special features, every effort has been made to make this text substantive, understandable, and practical.

AUDIENCE

This book provides both an in-depth presentation of leadership theory and a discussion of how it applies to real situations. As such it is intended for undergraduate and graduate classes in leadership studies, business, business communication, educational leadership, management, communication, small groups, organizational communication, political and military science, training and development for leadership, and health services. It is particularly well suited as a supplementary text for core organizational behavior courses or as an overview text within MBA curricula. This book would also be useful as a text in continuing education, in-service training, and other leadership development programs.

Acknowledgments

I would like to express my appreciation to many individuals who contributed to the development of the third edition of *Leadership: Theory and Practice*. First, I would like to thank the people at Sage Publications, including my editor, Al Bruckner. A special thanks goes to MaryAnn Vail, whose time and energy gave this project momentum and ensured its success. For their very capable work during the production phase, I would like to thank my copy editor, Kate Peterson, and my production editor, Diane Foster. In their own unique ways, each of these people made valuable contributions to this edition.

Second, this edition has been strengthened by the contributions of three people who revised their individual chapters for the third edition. These include Julie Indvik (California State University, Chico), who revised the chapter on women and leadership; Susan Kogler Hill (Cleveland State University), who revised the team leadership chapter; and Ernest Stech, who provided a revised version of the psychodynamic approach to leadership.

For the comprehensive reviews of the second edition, I would like to thank the following reviewers:

- Kristin Backhaus, SUNY at New Paltz
- Daniel Gutmore, Seton Hall University
- Marcy Meyer, Ball State University
- P. C. Wu, The University of West Florida

- Lora Warner, University of Wisconsin at Green Bay
- J. Patrick Murphy, DePaul University
- Dayle Smith, University of San Francisco
- Stuart E. Gothold, University of Southern California
- Tamsen Murray and Joseph Grana, Hope International University
- Vicki Goodwin, University of North Texas
- Tracey Manning, The College of Notre Dame of Maryland
- Janet Cooper Jackson, Chapman University
- Mary Jane Kuffner Hirt, Indiana University of Pennsylvania
- Brenda L. Bryant, Mary Baldwin College

Their critiques have helped to maintain the book's quality and keep the book current with the field.

Next, I am grateful to Michael Mumford for his thorough review and feedback on the new leadership skills chapter. In addition, I am appreciative of the work of Angelo Caravaggio in developing a skills case study.

A special acknowledgment goes to Joan Kmenta, for her competent editorial assistance when called upon. She has been involved in editing every edition of the book and her work is par excellence.

Finally, I would like to thank the many undergraduate and graduate students whom I have taught through the years. Their ongoing feedback has been helpful in clarifying my thinking about leadership and in encouraging me to make plain the practical implications of leadership theories.

Introduction

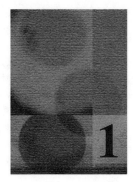

In the six years since the first edition of this book was published, the public's fascination with leadership has grown exponentially. Bookstores have been flooded with books about leaders. People are captivated by the idea of leadership, and they seek more information on how to become effective leaders. Many individuals believe that leadership is a way to improve how they present themselves to others. Corporations want individuals who have leadership ability because they believe these individuals provide special assets to their organizations. Academic institutions throughout the country are creating programs in leadership studies. Generally, leadership is a highly sought after and highly valued commodity.

In addition to popular books, there are also many publications about leadership in the research literature. A review of the scholarly studies on leadership shows that there is a wide variety of different theoretical approaches to explain the complexities of the leadership process (e.g., Bass, 1990; Bryman, 1992; Gardner, 1990; Hickman, 1998; Rost, 1991). Some researchers conceptualize leadership as a trait, or as a behavior, while others view leadership from a political perspective, or from a humanistic viewpoint. Leadership has been studied using both qualitative and quantitative methods in many contexts, including small groups, therapeutic groups, and large organizations. Collectively, the research findings on leadership from all of these areas provide a picture of a process that is far more sophisticated and complex than the often simplistic view presented in some of the popular books on leadership.

The present book will treat leadership as a complex process having multiple dimensions. Based on the research literature, this text will provide an in-depth description and application of many different approaches to leadership. The emphasis in the text will be on how theory can inform the practice of leadership. In the book, we will describe each theory and then explain how the theory can be used in real situations.

LEADERSHIP DEFINED

There are a multitude of ways to finish the sentence "Leadership is. . . . " In fact, as Stogdill (1974) pointed out in a review of leadership research, there are almost as many different definitions of *leadership* as there are people who have tried to define it (p. 7). It is much like the words *democracy, love,* and *peace.* Although each of us intuitively knows what he or she means by such words, the words can have different meanings for different people. As soon as we try to define leadership, we immediately discover that leadership has many different meanings.

In the past 50 years, there have been as many as 65 different classification systems developed to define the dimensions of leadership (Fleishman et al., 1991). One such classification system, directly related to our discussion, is the scheme proposed by Bass (1990, pp. 11–20). He suggested that some definitions view leadership as the *focus of group processes.* From this perspective, the leader is at the center of group change and activity and embodies the will of the group. Another group of definitions conceptualizes leadership from a *personality perspective,* which suggests that leadership is a combination of special traits or characteristics that individuals possess and that enable them to induce others to accomplish tasks. Other approaches to leadership have defined it as an *act* or *behavior*—the things leaders do to bring about change in a group.

In addition, leadership has been defined in terms of the *power relationship* that exists between leaders and followers. From this viewpoint, leaders have power and wield it to effect change in others. Others view leadership as an *instrument of goal achievement* in helping group members achieve their goals and meet their needs. This view includes leadership that transforms followers through vision setting, role modeling, and individualized attention. Finally, some scholars address leadership from a *skills perspective.* This viewpoint stresses the capabilities (knowledge and skills) that make effective leadership possible.

Despite the multitude of ways that leadership has been conceptualized, the following components can be identified as central to the phenomenon of leadership: (a) Leadership is a process, (b) leadership involves influence, (c) leadership occurs within a group context, and (d) leadership involves goal attainment. Based on these components, the following definition of leadership will be used in this text. *Leadership is a process whereby an individual influences a group of individuals to achieve a common goal.*

Defining leadership as a *process* means that it is not a trait or characteristic that resides in the leader, but is a transactional event that occurs between the leader and his or her followers. *Process* implies that a leader affects and is affected by followers. It emphasizes that leadership is not a linear, one-way event but rather an interactive event. When leadership is defined in this manner, it becomes available to everyone. It is not restricted to only the formally designated leader in a group.

Leadership involves *influence;* it is concerned with how the leader affects followers. Influence is the sine qua non of leadership. Without influence, leadership does not exist.

Leadership occurs in *groups.* Groups are the context in which leadership takes place. Leadership involves influencing a group of individuals who have a common purpose. This can be a small task group, a community group, or a large group encompassing an entire organization. Leadership training programs that teach people to lead themselves are not considered a part of leadership within the definition that is set forth in this discussion.

Leadership includes attention to *goals.* This means that leadership has to do with directing a group of individuals toward accomplishing some task or end. Leaders direct their energies toward individuals who are trying to achieve something together. Therefore, leadership occurs and has its effects in contexts where individuals are moving toward a goal.

Throughout this text, the people who engage in leadership will be referred to as *leaders* and those individuals toward whom leadership is directed will be referred to as *followers.* Both leaders and followers are involved together in the leadership process. Leaders need followers and followers need leaders (Burns, 1978; Heller & Van Til, 1983; Hollander, 1992; Jago, 1982). Although leaders and followers are closely linked, it is the leader who often initiates the relationship, creates the communication linkages, and carries the burden for maintaining the relationship.

In our discussion of leaders and followers, attention will be directed toward follower issues as well as leader issues. As Burns (1978) has pointed out, discussions of leadership are sometimes viewed as elitist because of the implied power and importance frequently ascribed to leaders in the leader-follower relationship. Leaders are not above followers or better than followers. Leaders and followers need to be understood in relation to each other (Hollander, 1992) and collectively (Burns, 1978). They are in the leadership relationship together—two sides of the same coin (Rost, 1991).

LEADERSHIP DESCRIBED

In addition to definitional issues, it is also important to discuss several other questions pertaining to the nature of leadership. In the following section, we will address questions such as how leadership as a trait differs from leadership as a process; how appointed leadership differs from emergent leadership; and how the concepts of power, coercion, and management differ from leadership.

Trait Versus Process Leadership

We have all heard statements such as "He is born to be a leader" or "She is a natural leader." These statements are commonly expressed by people who take a trait perspective toward leadership. The trait perspective suggests that certain individuals have special innate or inborn characteristics or qualities that make them leaders, and it is these qualities that differentiate them from nonleaders. Some of the personal qualities used to identify leaders include unique physical factors (e.g., height), personality features (e.g., extroversion), and ability characteristics (e.g., speech fluency) (Bryman, 1992). In Chapter 2, we will discuss a large body of research that has examined these qualities.

To describe leadership as a trait is quite different from describing it as a process (see Figure 1.1). The trait viewpoint conceptualizes leadership as a property or set of properties possessed in varying degrees by different people (Jago, 1982). This suggests that it resides in select people and restricts leadership to only those who are believed to have special, usually inborn, talents. The process viewpoint suggests it is a phenomenon that resides in the context and makes leadership available to everyone. As process, leadership can be observed in leader behaviors (Jago, 1982), and it is something that can be

Figure 1.1   *The Different Views of Leadership*

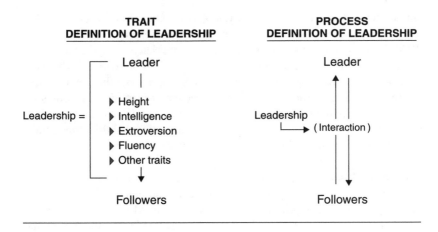

learned. The process definition of leadership is consistent with the definition of leadership that we have set forth in this chapter.

Assigned Versus Emergent Leadership

Some people are leaders because of their formal position within an organization, whereas others are leaders because of the way other group members respond to them. These two common forms of leadership are called *assigned leadership* and *emergent leadership*. Leadership that is based on occupying a position within an organization is assigned leadership. Team leaders, plant managers, department heads, directors, and administrators are all examples of assigned leadership.

Yet the person assigned to a leadership position does not always become the real leader in a particular setting. When an individual is perceived by others as the most influential member of a group or organization, regardless of the individual's title, the person is exhibiting emergent leadership. The individual acquires emergent leadership through other people in the organization who support and accept that individual's behavior. This type of leadership is not assigned by position, but rather it emerges over a period of time through communication. Some of the positive communication behaviors that account for successful leader emergence include being verbally involved, being informed, seeking others' opinions, initiating new ideas, and being firm but not rigid (Fisher, 1974).

In addition to communication behaviors, researchers have also found that personality plays a role in leadership emergence. For example, Smith and Foti (1998) found that certain personality traits were related to leadership emergence in a sample of 160 male college students. Those individuals who were more dominant, more intelligent, and more confident about their own performance (general self-efficacy) were more frequently identified as leaders by other members of their task group. Although it is uncertain whether these findings apply to women as well, Smith and Foti suggested that these three traits could be used for identifying individuals perceived to be emergent leaders.

The leadership approaches we discuss in the subsequent chapters of this book apply equally to assigned leadership and emergent leadership. When an individual is engaged in leadership, that individual is a leader, whether or not the individual was assigned to be the leader or the individual emerged as the leader. This book will focus on the leadership process that occurs when any individual is engaged in influencing other group members in their efforts to reach a goal.

Leadership and Power

The concept of power is related to leadership because it is part of the influence process. Power is the capacity or potential to influence. People have power when they have the ability to affect others' beliefs, attitudes, and courses of action. Ministers, doctors, coaches, and teachers are all examples of individuals who have the potential to influence us. When they do, they are using their power, the resource they draw on to effect change in us.

In organizations, there are two major kinds of power: *position power* and *personal power.* Position power refers to the power a person derives from a particular office or rank in a formal organizational system. Vice presidents or department heads have more power than staff personnel because of the position they have in the organization. Personal power refers to the power a leader derives from followers. When leaders act in ways that are important to followers, it gives leaders power. For example, some managers have power because their subordinates find them to good role models. Others have power because they are viewed as highly competent or considerate by their subordinates. In both cases, these managers' power is ascribed to them based on how they are seen in their relationships with others.

The most widely cited research on power is French and Raven's (1959) work on the bases of social power. In their work, power was conceptualized from the framework of a dyadic relationship that included both the person influencing and the person being influenced. French and Raven identified five common and important types of power: (a) reward, (b) coercive, (c) legitimate, (d) referent, and (e) expert. Each of these types of power increases a leader's capacity to influence the attitudes, values, or behaviors of others.

In discussions of leadership, it is not unusual that leaders are described as wielders of power, as individuals who dominate others. In these instances, power is conceptualized as a tool that leaders use to achieve their own ends. Contrary to this view of power, Burns (1978) emphasized power from a relationship standpoint. For Burns, power is not an entity that leaders use over others to achieve their own ends, but instead it occurs in relationships and should be used by leaders and followers to benefit their collective goals.

In this text, our discussions of leadership will treat power as a relational concern for both leaders and followers. We will pay attention to how leaders work with followers to reach common goals.

Leadership and Coercion

Coercion is one of the specific kinds of power that are available to leaders. Coercion involves the use of force to effect change. It means influencing others to do something by manipulating the penalties and rewards in their work environment. Coercion frequently involves the use of threats, punishment, and negative reward schedules. Classic examples of leaders who used coercion are Adolf Hitler in Germany, Jim Jones in Guyana, and David Koresch in Waco, Texas, each of whom used power and restraint to force his followers to engage in extreme behaviors.

It is important to distinguish between coercion and leadership because it allows us to separate out from our examples of leadership the behaviors of individuals such as Hitler, Jones, and Koresch. In our discussions of leadership, coercive people will not be used as models of what ideal leadership is about. Our definition suggests that leadership is reserved for those individuals who influence a group of individuals toward a common goal. Leaders who use coercion are interested in their own goals and seldom are interested in the wants and needs of subordinates. Using coercion runs counter to working with followers to achieve a common goal.

Leadership and Management

Leadership is a process that is similar to management in many ways. Leadership involves influence, as does management. Leadership requires working with people, which management requires as well. Leadership is concerned with effective goal accomplishment and so is management. In general, many of the functions of management are activities that are consistent with the definition of leadership we set forth in the beginning of this chapter.

But leadership is also different from management. While the study of leadership can be traced back to Aristotle, management emerged around the turn of the 20th century with the advent of our industrialized society. Management was created as a way to reduce chaos in organizations and to make them run more effectively and efficiently. The primary functions of management, first identified by Fayol (1916), were planning, organizing, staffing, and controlling. These functions are still representative of the field of management today.

In a book that compared the functions of management with the functions of leadership, Kotter (1990) argued that the functions of the two are quite dissimilar (see Figure 1.2). The overriding function of management is to provide order and consistency to organizations, whereas the primary function of leadership is to produce change and movement. Management is about seeking order and stability; leadership is about seeking adaptive and constructive change.

As illustrated in Figure 1.2, the major activities of management get played out differently than the activities of leadership. While different in scope, Kotter (1990) contended that both management and leadership are essential if an organization is to prosper (pp. 7-8). For example, if an organization has strong management without leadership, the outcome can be stifling and bureaucratic. Conversely, if an organization has strong leadership without management, the outcome can be meaningless or misdirected change for change's sake. To be effective, organizations need to nourish both competent management and skilled leadership.

There have been many scholars, in addition to Kotter, who have argued that leadership and management are distinct constructs. Bennis and Nanus (1985), for example, maintained that there is a significant difference between the two. To manage means to accomplish activities and master routines, while to lead means to influence others and create visions for change. Bennis and Nanus made the distinction very clear in their frequently

Figure 1.2 *Functions of Management versus Leadership*

MANAGEMENT "Produces Order and Consistency"	**LEADERSHIP** "Produces Change and Movement"
Planning / Budgeting ▶ Establish agendas ▶ Set time tables ▶ Allocate resources	**Establishing Direction** ▶ Create a vision ▶ Clarify big picture ▶ Set strategies
Organizing / Staffing ▶ Provide structure ▶ Make job placements ▶ Establish rules and procedures	**Aligning People** ▶ Communicate goals ▶ Seek commitment ▶ Build teams and coalitions
Controlling / Problem Solving ▶ Develop incentives ▶ Generate creative solutions ▶ Take corrective action	**Motivating and Inspiring** ▶ Inspire and energize ▶ Empower subordinates ▶ Satisfy unmet needs

SOURCE: Adapted from *A Force for Change: How Leadership Differs From Management* (pp. 3-8), by John P. Kotter, 1990, New York: Free Press.

quoted phrase "Managers are people who do things right and leaders are people who do the right thing" (p. 221).

Rost (1991) has also been a proponent of distinguishing between leadership and management. He contended that leadership is a multidirectional influence relationship and management is a unidirectional authority relationship. While leadership is concerned with the process of developing mutual purposes, management is directed toward coordinating activities in order to get a job done. Leaders and followers work together to create real change, while managers and subordinates join forces to sell goods and services (Rost, 1991, pp. 149-152).

Approaching the issue from a narrower viewpoint, Zaleznik (1977) has gone so far as to argue that leaders and managers themselves are distinct— they are basically different types of people. He contended that managers are reactive and prefer to work with people to solve problems but do so with low emotional involvement. They act to limit choices. Zaleznik suggested that leaders, on the other hand, are emotionally active and involved. They seek to shape ideas instead of responding to them, and act to expand the available options to long-standing problems. Leaders change the way people think about what is possible.

Although there are clear differences between management and leadership, or managers and leaders, there is also a considerable amount of overlap (Yukl, 1989). When managers are involved in influencing a group to meet its goals, they are involved in leadership. When leaders are involved in planning, organizing, staffing, and controlling, they are involved in management. Both processes involve influencing a group of individuals toward goal attainment. For purposes of our discussion in this book, we will focus on the leadership process. In our examples and case studies, we will treat the roles of managers and leaders similarly and not emphasize the differences between them.

PLAN OF THE BOOK

This book is user-friendly. It is based on substantive theories but written to emphasize practice and application. Each chapter in the book follows the same format. The first section of each chapter briefly describes the leadership approach and discusses various research studies applicable to the approach. The second section of each chapter evaluates the approach, highlighting its strengths and criticisms. Special attention is given to how the approach contributes or fails to contribute to an overall understanding of the leadership process. The next section uses brief case studies to provide a discussion of how the approach can be applied in ongoing organizations. The final section of each chapter provides a leadership questionnaire with a discussion of how the questionnaire measures the reader's leadership style. Each chapter ends with a summary and references.

SUMMARY

Leadership is a topic with universal appeal, and in the popular press and academic research literature there is much written about leadership. Despite the abundance of writing on the topic, leadership has presented a major challenge to practitioners and researchers interested in understanding the nature of leadership. It is a highly valued phenomenon that is very complex.

Through the years, leadership has been defined and conceptualized in many ways. The component common to nearly all of the classifications is that leadership is an influence process that assists groups of individuals toward goal attainment. Specifically, in this book, leadership is defined as a process whereby an individual influences a group of individuals to achieve a common goal.

Because leaders and followers are both a part of the leadership process, it is important to address issues that confront followers as well as those that confront leaders. Leaders and followers need to be understood in relation to each other.

In prior research, many studies have focused on leadership as a trait. The trait perspective suggests that certain people in our society have special inborn qualities that make them leaders. This view restricts leadership to only those who are believed to have special characteristics. In contrast, the approach in this text suggests that leadership is a process that can be learned and that it is available to everyone.

Two common forms of leadership are assigned and emergent. Assigned leadership is based on having a formal title or position within an organization. Emergent leadership results from what one does and how one acquires support from followers. Leadership, as a process, applies to individuals in both assigned roles and emergent roles.

Related to leadership is the concept of power, the potential to influence. There are two kinds of power: position and personal. Position power, which is much like assigned leadership, refers to the power an individual derives from having an office in a formal organizational system. Personal power comes from followers. It is given to leaders because followers believe leaders have something of value. Treating power as a shared resource is important because it de-emphasizes the idea that leaders are power wielders.

Leadership and coercion are not the same. Coercion involves the use of threats and punishment to induce change in followers for the sake of the leader. Coercion runs counter to leadership because it does not treat leadership as a process that includes followers, and it does not emphasize working with followers to achieve common goals.

Leadership and management are different concepts that have a considerable amount of overlap. They are different in that management traditionally focuses on the activities of planning, organizing, staffing, and controlling, whereas leadership emphasizes the general influence process. According to some researchers, management is concerned with creating order and stability, while leadership is about adaptation and constructive change. Other researchers go so far as to argue that managers and leaders are different types of people, managers being more reactive and less emotionally involved, and leaders being more proactive and more emotionally involved. The overlap between leadership and management is centered on how they both involve influencing a group of individuals in goal attainment.

In this book, we will discuss leadership as a complex process. Based on the research literature, we will describe selected approaches to leadership and assess how they can be employed to improve leadership in real situations.

REFERENCES

Bass, B. M. (1990). *Bass and Stogdill's handbook of leadership: A survey of theory and research.* New York: Free Press.

Bennis, W. G., & Nanus, B. (1985). *Leaders: The strategies for taking charge.* New York: Harper & Row.

Bryman, A. (1992). *Charisma and leadership in organizations.* London: Sage.

Burns, J. M. (1978). *Leadership.* New York: Harper & Row.

Fayol, H. (1916). *General and industrial management.* London: Pitman.

Fisher, B. A. (1974). *Small group decision making: Communication and the group process.* New York: McGraw-Hill.

Fleishman, E. A., Mumford, M. D., Zaccaro, S. J., Levin, K. Y., Korotkin, A. L., & Hein, M. B. (1991). Taxonomic efforts in the description of leader behavior: A synthesis and functional interpretation. *Leadership Quarterly, 2*(4), 245-287.

French, R. P., Jr., & Raven, B. (1959). The bases of social power. In D. Cartwright (Ed.), *Studies in social power.* Ann Arbor, MI: Institute for Social Research.

Gardner, J. W. (1990). *On leadership.* New York: Free Press.

Heller, T., & Van Til, J. (1983). Leadership and followership: Some summary propositions. *Journal of Applied Behavioral Science, 18,* 405-414.

Hickman, G. R. (Ed.). (1998). *Leading organizations: Perspectives for a new era.* Thousand Oaks, CA: Sage.

Hollander, E. P. (1992). Leadership, followership, self, and others. *Leadership Quarterly, 3*(1), 43-54.

Jago, A. G. (1982). Leadership: Perspectives in theory and research. *Management Science, 28*(3), 315-336.

Kotter, J. P. (1990). *A force for change: How leadership differs from management.* New York: Free Press.

Rost, J. C. (1991). *Leadership for the twenty-first century.* New York: Praeger.

Smith, J. A., & Foti, R. J. (1998). A pattern approach to the study of leader emergence. *Leadership Quarterly, 9*(2), 147-160.

Stogdill, R. M. (1974). *Handbook of leadership: A survey of theory and research.* New York: Free Press.

Yukl, G. A. (1989). *Leadership in organizations* (2nd ed.). Englewood Cliffs, NJ: Prentice Hall.

Zaleznik, A. (1977, May-June). Managers and leaders: Are they different? *Harvard Business Review, 55,* 67-78.

Trait Approach

DESCRIPTION

Of interest to scholars throughout the 20th century, the trait approach was one of the first systematic attempts to study leadership. In the early part of the 20th century, leadership traits were studied to determine what made certain people great leaders. The theories that were developed were called "great man" theories because they focused on identifying the innate qualities and characteristics possessed by great social, political, and military leaders (e.g., Mohandas Gandhi, Abraham Lincoln, and Napoleon). It was believed that people were born with these traits and only the "great" people possessed them. During this time, research concentrated on determining the specific traits that clearly differentiated leaders from followers (Bass, 1990; Jago, 1982).

In the mid-20th century, the trait approach was challenged by research that questioned the universality of leadership traits. In a major review in 1948, Stogdill suggested that no consistent set of traits differentiated leaders from nonleaders across a variety of situations. An individual with leadership traits who was a leader in one situation might not be a leader in another situation. Rather than being a quality that individuals possessed, leadership was reconceptualized as a relationship between people in a social situation (Stogdill, 1948). Personal factors related to leadership continued to be important, but researchers contended that these factors were to be considered as relative to the requirements of the situation.

In recent years, there has been a resurgence in interest in the trait approach in explaining how traits influence leadership (Bryman, 1992). For example, based on a new analysis of much of the previous trait research, Lord, DeVader, and Alliger (1986) found that personality traits were strongly associated with individuals' perceptions of leadership. Similarly, Kirkpatrick and Locke (1991) have gone so far as to claim that effective leaders are actually distinct types of people in several key respects. Further evidence of renewed interest in the trait approach can be seen in the current emphasis given by many researchers to visionary and charismatic leadership (see Bass, 1990; Bennis & Nanus, 1985; Nadler & Tushman, 1989; Zaleznik, 1977).

In short, the trait approach is alive and well. It began with an emphasis on identifying the qualities of great persons; next, it shifted to include the impact of situations on leadership; and most currently, it has shifted back to reemphasize the critical role of traits in effective leadership.

Although the research on traits spanned the entire 20th century, a good overview of this approach is found in two surveys completed by Stogdill (1948, 1974). In his first survey, Stogdill analyzed and synthesized more than 124 trait studies that were conducted between 1904 and 1947. In his second study, he analyzed another 163 studies that were completed between 1948 and 1970. By taking a closer look at each of these reviews, a clearer picture can be obtained of how individuals' traits contribute to the leadership process.

Stogdill's first survey identified a group of important leadership traits that were related to how individuals in various groups became leaders. His results showed that the average individual in the leadership role is different from an average group member in the following ways: (a) intelligence, (b) alertness, (c) insight, (d) responsibility, (e) initiative, (f) persistence, (g) self-confidence, and (h) sociability.

The findings of Stogdill's first survey also indicated that an individual does not become a leader solely because he or she possesses certain traits. Rather, the traits that leaders possess must be relevant to situations in which the leader is functioning. As stated earlier, leaders in one situation may not necessarily be leaders in another situation. Findings showed that leadership was not a passive state but resulted from a working relationship between the leader and other group members. This research marked the beginning of a new approach to leadership research that focused on leadership behaviors and leadership situations.

Stogdill's second survey, published in 1974, analyzed 163 new studies and compared the findings of these studies to the findings he had reported in his first survey. The second survey was more balanced in its description of the role of traits and leadership. While the first survey implied that leadership is determined principally by situational factors and not personality factors, the second survey argued more moderately that both personality and situational factors were determinants of leadership. In essence, the second survey validated the original trait idea that the leader's characteristics are indeed a part of leadership.

Similar to the first survey, Stogdill's second survey also identified traits that were positively associated with leadership. The list included the following 10 characteristics: (a) drive for responsibility and task completion, (b) vigor and persistence in pursuit of goals, (c) venturesomeness and originality in problem solving, (d) drive to exercise initiative in social situations, (e) self-confidence and sense of personal identity, (f) willingness to accept consequences of decision and action, (g) readiness to absorb interpersonal stress, (h) willingness to tolerate frustration and delay, (i) ability to influence other persons' behavior, and (j) capacity to structure social interaction systems to the purpose at hand.

Mann (1959) conducted a similar study that examined more than 1,400 findings regarding personality and leadership in small groups, but he placed less emphasis on how situational factors influenced leadership. Although tentative in his conclusions, Mann suggested that personality traits could be used to discriminate leaders from nonleaders. His results identified leaders as strong in the following traits: intelligence, masculinity, adjustment, dominance, extroversion, and conservatism.

Lord et al. (1986) reassessed the findings put forward by Mann (1959), using a more sophisticated procedure called meta-analysis. Lord and coworkers found that intelligence, masculinity, and dominance were significantly related to how individuals perceived leaders. From their findings, the authors argued strongly that personality traits could be used to make discriminations consistently across situations between leaders and nonleaders.

Yet another review argues for the importance of leadership traits: Kirkpatrick and Locke (1991) contended that "it is unequivocally clear that leaders are not like other people" (p. 59). From a qualitative synthesis of earlier research, Kirkpatrick and Locke postulated that leaders differ from nonleaders on six traits: drive, the desire to lead, honesty and

Table 2.1 *Studies of Leadership Traits and Characteristics*

Stogdill (1948)	Mann (1959)	Stogdill (1974)	Lord, DeVader, and Alliger (1986)	Kirkpatrick and Locke (1991)
Intelligence	Intelligence	Achievement	Intelligence	Drive
Alertness	Masculinity	Persistence	Masculinity	Motivation
Insight	Adjustment	Insight	Dominance	Integrity
Responsibility	Dominance	Initiative		Confidence
Initiative	Extroversion	Self-confidence		Cognitive ability
Persistence	Conservatism	Responsibility		Task knowledge
Self-confidence		Cooperativeness		
Sociability		Tolerance		
		Influence		
		Sociability		

integrity, self-confidence, cognitive ability, and knowledge of the business. According to these writers, individuals can be born with these traits, they can learn them, or both. It is these six traits that make up the "right stuff" for leaders. Kirkpatrick and Locke contended that leadership traits make some people different from others, and this difference needs to be recognized as an important part of the leadership process.

Table 2.1 provides a summary of the traits and characteristics that were identified by researchers from the trait approach. It illustrates clearly the breadth of traits related to leadership. Table 2.1 also shows how difficult it is to select certain traits as definitive leadership traits; some of the traits appear in several of the survey studies, whereas others appear in only one or two studies. Regardless of the lack of precision in Table 2.1, however, it represents a general convergence of research regarding which traits are leadership traits.

What, then, can be said about trait research? What has a century of research on the trait approach given us that is useful? The answer is an extended list of traits that would-be leaders might hope to possess or wish to cultivate if they want to be perceived by others as leaders. Some of the traits that are central to this list include the following: intelligence, self-confidence, determination, integrity, and sociability (see Table 2.2).

Table 2.2 *Major Leadership Traits*

> ▶ Intelligence
> ▶ Self-confidence
> ▶ Determination
> ▶ Integrity
> ▶ Sociability

Intelligence

Intelligence or intellectual ability is positively related to leadership. Having strong verbal ability, perceptual ability, and reasoning appears to make one a better leader. Although it is good to be bright, the research also indicates that a leader's intellectual ability should not vary too much from that of his or her subordinates. In situations where the leader's IQ is very different from that of the followers, it can have a counterproductive impact on leadership. Leaders with higher abilities may have difficulty in communicating with followers because they are preoccupied or because their ideas are too advanced to be accepted by their followers.

In the next chapter, which addresses leadership from a skills perspective, intelligence is identified as a trait that significantly contributes to a leader's acquisition of complex problem-solving skills and social judgment skills. Intelligence is described as having a positive impact on an individual's capacity for effective leadership.

Self-Confidence

Self-confidence is another trait that helps an individual to be a leader. Self-confidence is the ability to be certain about one's competencies and skills. It includes a sense of self-esteem and self-assurance and the belief that one can make a difference. Leadership involves influencing others, and self-confidence allows the leader to feel assured that his or her attempts to influence are appropriate and right.

Determination

Many leaders also exhibit determination. Determination refers to the desire to get the job done and includes characteristics such as initiative, persistence, dominance, and drive. Individuals with determination are willing to assert themselves, they are proactive, and they have the capacity to persevere in the face of obstacles. Being determined includes showing dominance at times and in certain situations where followers need to be directed.

Integrity

Integrity is another of the important leadership traits. Integrity is the quality of honesty and trustworthiness. Individuals who adhere to a strong set of principles and take responsibility for their actions are exhibiting integrity. Leaders with integrity inspire confidence in others because they can be trusted to do what they say they are going to do. They are loyal, dependable, and not deceptive. Basically, integrity makes a leader believable and worthy of our trust.

In our society, integrity has received a great deal of attention in recent years. For example, as a result of the impeachment proceedings during the Clinton presidency, people are demanding more honesty of their public officials. Similarly, as a result of the scandals in the corporate world (e.g., Enron and WorldCom), people have become skeptical of leaders who are not highly ethical. In the educational arena, new K-12 curricula are being developed throughout the country to teach character, values, and ethical leadership (cf. the Character Counts! program developed by the Josephson Institute of Ethics in California, Web site: http://www.charactercounts.org/; or the Pillars of Leadership program taught at the J. W. Fanning Institute for Leadership in Georgia, Web site: http://www.fanning.uga.edu/philosophy_pillars.htm). In short, society is demanding greater integrity of character in its leaders.

Sociability

A final trait that is important for leaders is sociability. Sociability refers to a leader's inclination to seek out pleasant social relationships. Leaders who show sociability are friendly, outgoing, courteous, tactful, and diplomatic. They are sensitive to others' needs and show concern for their well-being. Social leaders have good interpersonal skills and create cooperative relationships with their followers.

Although our discussion of leadership traits has focused on five major traits (i.e., intelligence, self-confidence, determination, integrity, and sociability), this list is not all-inclusive. There are other traits indicated in Table 2.1 that are associated with effective leadership. Yet the five traits we have identified contribute substantially to whether or not an individual is going to be a leader.

HOW DOES THE TRAIT APPROACH WORK?

The way the trait approach works is very different from the other approaches discussed in subsequent chapters because the trait approach focuses exclusively on the leader, and not on the followers or the situation. This makes the trait approach theoretically more straightforward than other approaches. In essence, the trait approach is concerned with leaders and their traits. It is concerned with what traits leaders exhibit and who has these traits.

The trait approach does not lay out a set of hypotheses or principles about what kind of leader is needed in a certain situation or what a leader should do, given a particular set of circumstances. Rather, this approach emphasizes that having a leader with a certain set of traits is crucial to having effective leadership. It is the leader and his or her personality that is central to the leadership process.

The trait approach suggests that organizations will work better if the people in managerial positions have designated leadership profiles. To find the right people, it is common for organizations to use personality assessment instruments. The assumption behind these procedures is that selecting the "right" people will increase organizational effectiveness. Organizations can specify the characteristics or traits that are important to them for particular positions and then use personality assessment measures to determine whether or not an individual fits their needs.

The trait approach is also used for personal awareness and development. By analyzing their own traits, managers can gain an idea of their strengths and weaknesses, and they can get a feel for how others see them within the organization. A trait assessment can help managers to determine if they have the qualities to move up or to move to other positions in the company. It gives individuals a clearer picture of who they are as leaders and how they fit into the organizational hierarchy. In areas where their traits are lacking, leaders can try to make changes in what they do or where they work to increase the potential impact of their given traits.

At the end of the chapter, a leadership instrument is provided that can be used to assess your leadership traits. This instrument is typical of the kind of personality tests that companies use to assess individuals' leadership potential. As you will find out by completing this instrument, trait measures are a good way to assess your own abilities.

STRENGTHS

The trait approach has several identifiable strengths. First, the trait approach is intuitively appealing. It fits clearly with our notion that leaders are the individuals who are "out front" and "leading the way" in our society. The image in the popular press and community at large is that leaders are a special kind of people—people with gifts who can do extra-ordinary things. The trait approach is consistent with this perception because it is built on the premise that leaders are different and their differ-ence resides in the special traits they possess. People have a need to see their leaders as gifted people, and the trait approach fulfills this need.

A second strength of the trait approach is that it has a century of research to back it up. No other theory can boast of the breadth and depth of studies conducted on the trait approach. The strength and longevity of this line of research give the trait approach a measure of credibility not afforded other approaches. Out of this abundance of research has emerged a body of data that points to the important role of various personality traits in the leadership process.

Another strength, more conceptual in nature, results from the way the trait approach highlights the leader component in the leadership process. Leadership is composed of leaders, followers, and situations, but the trait approach is devoted only to the first of these, leaders. Although this is also a potential weakness, by focusing exclusively on the role of the leader in leadership the trait approach has been able to provide us with a deeper and more intricate understanding of how the leader and his or her personality are related to the leadership process.

Last, the trait approach has given us some benchmarks for what we need to look for if we want to be leaders. It identifies what traits we should have and whether the traits that we do have are the best traits. Based on the find-ings of this approach, personality and assessment procedures can be used to offer invaluable information to supervisors and managers about their strengths and weaknesses and ways to improve their overall leadership effectiveness.

CRITICISMS

In addition to its strengths, the trait approach also has several weaknesses. First and foremost is the failure of the trait approach to delimit a definitive list of leadership traits. Although an enormous number of studies have been conducted over the past 100 years, the findings from these studies have been ambiguous and uncertain at times. Furthermore, the list of traits that has emerged appears endless. This is obvious from Table 2.1, which illustrates a multitude of traits, and these are only a sample of the many leadership traits that were studied.

Another criticism is that the trait approach has failed to take situations into account. As Stogdill (1948) pointed out more than 50 years ago, it is difficult to isolate a set of traits that are characteristic of leaders without factoring situational effects into the equation as well. People who possess certain traits that make them leaders in one situation may not be leaders in another situation. Some people may have the traits that help them emerge as leaders but may not have the traits that allow them to maintain their leadership over time. In other words, the situation influences leadership, and it is therefore difficult to identify a universal set of leadership traits in isolation from the context in which the leadership occurs.

A third criticism, derived from the prior two criticisms, is that this approach has resulted in highly subjective determinations of the "most important" leadership traits. Because the findings on traits have been so extensive and broad, there has been much subjective interpretation of the meaning of the data. This subjectivity is readily apparent in the many self-help, practice-oriented management books. For example, one author might identify ambition and creativity as crucial leadership traits; another might identify power and achievement. In both cases, it is the author's subjective experience and observations that are the basis for the identified leadership traits. These books may be helpful to readers because they identify and describe important leadership traits, but the methods used to generate these lists of traits are weak. In our culture, people want to know a set of definitive traits of leaders. To respond to this need, authors have set forth lists of traits, even if the origins of these lists are not grounded in strong reliable research.

Research on traits can also be criticized for failing to look at traits in relationship to leadership outcomes. This research has emphasized the identification of traits, but it has not addressed how leadership traits affect group members and their work. In trying to ascertain universal leadership traits, researchers have focused on the link between specific traits and leader emergence, but they have not tried to link leader traits with other outcomes such as productivity or employee satisfaction. For example, trait research does not provide data on whether leaders who might have high intelligence and strong integrity have better results than leaders without these traits. The trait approach is weak in describing how leaders' traits affect the outcomes of groups and teams in organizational settings.

A final criticism of the trait approach is that it is not a useful approach for training and development for leadership. Even if definitive traits could be identified, teaching new traits is not an easy process because traits are not easily changed. For example, it is not reasonable to send managers to a training program to raise their IQ or to train them to become introverted or extroverted people. The point is that traits are relatively fixed psychological structures, and this limits the value of teaching and leadership training.

APPLICATION

Despite its shortcomings, the trait approach provides valuable information about leadership. It can be applied by individuals at all levels and in all types of organizations. Although a definitive set of traits is not provided by the trait approach, the approach does provide direction regarding which traits are good to have if one aspires to take a leadership position. By taking personality tests and other similar questionnaires, individuals can gain insight into whether or not they have select traits deemed important for leadership, and they can pinpoint their strengths and weaknesses.

As we discussed previously, managers can use information from the trait approach to assess where they stand within their organization and what they need to do to strengthen their position. Trait information can suggest areas in which their personal characteristics are very beneficial to the company, and areas in which they may wish to get more training to enhance their overall approach. Using trait information, managers can develop a deeper understanding of who they are and how they will affect others in the organization.

CASE STUDIES

In the following section, three case studies (Cases 2.1, 2.2, and 2.3) are provided to illustrate the trait approach and to help you understand how the trait approach can be used in making decisions in organizational settings. The settings of the cases are diverse—from directing a research department to running an office supply business to being head of recruitment for a large bank—but all of the cases deal with trait leadership. At the end of each case, you will find questions that will help in analyzing the cases.

CASE 2.1

Choosing a New Director of Research

Sandra Coke is vice president for research and development at Great Lakes Foods (GLF), a large snack food company that has approximately 1,000 employees. As a result of a recent reorganization, Sandra must choose an individual to be the new director of research. The director will report directly to Sandra and will be responsible for developing and testing new products. The research division of GLF employs about 200 individuals. The choice of directors is important because Ms. Coke is receiving pressure from the president and board of GLF to improve the company's overall growth and productivity.

Sandra has identified three candidates for the position. Each candidate is at the same managerial level. She is having difficulty choosing one of them because each of the individuals has very strong credentials. Alexa Smith is a longtime employee of GLF who started part-time in the mailroom while in high school, and after finishing school worked in as many as 10 different positions throughout the company to become manager of new-product marketing. Performance reviews of Alexa's work have repeatedly described her as being very creative and insightful. In her tenure at GLF, Alexa has developed and brought to market four new product lines. Alexa is also known throughout GLF as being very persistent about her work; when she starts a project she stays with it until it is finished. It is this quality that probably accounts for the success of each of the four new products with which she has been involved.

A second candidate for the new position is Kelsey Metts, who has been with GLF for 5 years and is presently manager of quality control for established products. Kelsey has a reputation of being very bright. Before joining GLF, she received her MBA at Harvard, graduating at the top of her class. People talk about Kelsey as the kind of person who will be president of her own company someday. Kelsey is also very personable. On all of her performance reviews, she received extra-high scores on sociability and human relations skills. There isn't a supervisor in the company who doesn't have positive things to say about how comfortable it is to work with Kelsey Metts. Since joining GLF, Kelsey has been instrumental in bringing two new product lines to market.

Thomas Santiago, the third candidate, has been with GLF for 10 years and is frequently consulted by upper management regarding strategic planning and corporate direction setting. Thomas has been very involved in establishing the vision for GLF and is a company person all the way. He believes in the values of GLF, and he actively promotes its mission. The one quality that stands out above the rest in Thomas's performance reviews is his honesty and integrity. Employees who have worked under his supervision consistently report that they feel they can trust Thomas to be fair and consistent with them. Thomas is highly respected at GLF. In his tenure at the company, Thomas has been involved in some capacity with the development of three new product lines.

The challenge confronting Sandra Coke is to choose the best person for the newly established director's position. Because of the pressures she feels from upper management, Sandra knows she must select the best leader for the new position.

Questions

Based on the information provided about the trait approach in Tables 2.1 and 2.2,

1. Which candidate should Ms. Coke select?
2. In what ways is the trait approach helpful in this type of selection?
3. In what ways are the weaknesses of the trait approach highlighted in this case?

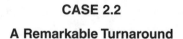

CASE 2.2

A Remarkable Turnaround

Carol Baines was married for 20 years to the owner of the Baines Company until he lost his life in a tragic car accident. After his death, Carol decided not to sell the business but to try to run it herself. Before the accident, her only involvement in the business was in informal discussions with her husband over dinner, although she has a college degree in business, with a major in management.

Baines Co. was one of three office supply stores in a city with a population of 200,000 people. The other two stores were owned by national chains. Baines Co. was not a large company; it employed only five people. Baines Co. had stable sales of about $200,000 a year, serving mostly the smaller companies in the city. The firm had not grown in a number of years and was beginning to feel the pressure of the advertising and lower prices of the national chains.

For the first 6 months, Carol spent her time familiarizing herself with the employees and the operations of the company. Next, she did a citywide analysis of those companies that had reason to purchase office supplies. Based on her understanding of Baines's capabilities and her assessment of the potential market for their products and services, Carol developed a specific set of short-term and long-range goals for the company. Behind all of her planning, Carol had a vision that Baines could be a viable, healthy, and competitive company. She wanted to carry on the business that her husband had started, but more than that, she wanted it to grow.

Over the first 5 years, Carol invested significant amounts of money in advertising, sales, and services. These efforts were well spent because the company began to show rapid growth immediately. Because of the growth, another 20 individuals were hired at Baines.

The expansion at Baines was particularly remarkable because of another major hardship Carol had to confront. Carol was diagnosed with breast cancer a year after her husband died. The treatment for her cancer included 2 months of radiation therapy and 6 months of strong chemotherapy. Although the side effects included losing her hair and being very tired, Carol continued to manage the company throughout the ordeal. In spite of her difficulties, Carol was successful. Under the strength of her leadership, the growth at Baines continued for 10 consecutive years.

Interviews with new and old employees at Baines revealed much about Carol's leadership. Employees said that Carol was a very solid person. She cared deeply about others and was fair and considerate. They said she created a family-like atmosphere at Baines. Few employees had quit Baines since Carol took over. Carol was devoted to all the employees and she supported their interests. For example, the company has a softball team in the summer and a basketball team in the winter, and both are sponsored by Baines. Others described Carol as a strong individual. Even though she had cancer, she continued to be positive and interested in them. She did not get depressed with the cancer and its side effects, even though it was difficult. Employees said she was a model of strength, goodness, and quality.

At the age of 55, Carol turned the business over to her two sons. She continues to act as the president but does not supervise the day-to-day operations. The company is presently doing more than $3.1 million in sales, and it outpaces both of the other two chain stores in the city.

Questions

1. How would you describe Carol Baines's leadership traits?
2. How big a part did Carol's traits play in the expansion of the company?
3. Would Carol be a leader in other business contexts?

◆

CASE 2.3

Recruiting for the Bank

Pat Nelson is the assistant director of human resources in charge of recruitment for Central Bank, a large, full-service banking institution. One of Pat's major responsibilities each spring is to visit as many college campuses as he can to interview graduating seniors for credit analyst positions in the commercial lending area at Central Bank. Although the number varies, Mr. Nelson usually ends up hiring about 20 new people, most of whom come from the same schools year after year.

Pat has been doing recruitment for the bank for more than 10 years, and he enjoys it very much. However, for the upcoming spring he is feeling increased pressure from management to be particularly discriminating about who he recommends be hired. Management is concerned about the retention rate at the bank because in recent years as many as 25% of the new hires have left. Departures after the first year have meant lost training dollars as well as excess strain on the staff who remain. Although management understands that some new hires always leave, they are not comfortable with the present rate, and they have begun to question the recruitment and hiring procedures.

The bank wants to hire individuals whom they can groom for higher-level leadership positions. Although certain competencies are required at the entry level of credit analyst, the bank is equally interested in skills that will allow individuals to advance to upper management positions as their careers progress.

In the recruitment process, Pat Nelson always looks for several characteristics. First, individuals need to have strong interpersonal skills, they need to be confident, and they need to show poise and initiative. Next, because banking involves fiduciary responsibilities, individuals need to have proper ethics, including a strong sense of the importance of confidentiality. In addition, to do the work in the bank, individuals need to have strong analytical and technical skills as well as experience in working with computers. Last, individuals need to exhibit a good work ethic, and they need to show commitment and a willingness to do their job even in difficult circumstances.

Pat is relatively certain that he has been selecting the right people to be leaders at Central Bank, yet upper management is telling him to reassess his hiring criteria. Although he feels he that has been doing the right thing, he is starting to question himself and his recruitment practices.

Questions

Based on ideas described in the trait approach,

1. Do you think Pat Nelson is looking for the right characteristics in the people he hires?
2. Could it be that the retention issue raised by upper management is unrelated to Pat's recruitment criteria?
3. If you were Pat, would you change your approach to recruiting?

———————————————◆———————————————

LEADERSHIP INSTRUMENT

There are a wide variety of questionnaires that are used by organizations for measuring individuals' personality characteristics. In many organizations, it is common practice to use standard personality measures such as the Minnesota Multiphasic Personality Inventory or the Myers-Briggs Type Indicator™. These measures provide valuable information to the individual and the organization about the individual's unique attributes for leadership and where the individual could best serve the organization.

In this section, the Leadership Trait Questionnaire (LTQ) is provided as an example of a measure that can be used to assess your personal leadership characteristics. The LTQ quantifies the perceptions of the individual leader and selected observers, such as subordinates or peers. It measures an individual's traits and points the individual to those areas in which he or she may have special strengths or weaknesses.

By taking the LTQ, you can gain an understanding of how trait measures are used for leadership assessment. You can also obtain an assessment of your own leadership traits.

Leadership Trait Questionnaire (LTQ)

Instructions: The purpose of this questionnaire is to measure personal characteristics of leadership. The questionnaire should be completed by the leader and five individuals who are familiar with the leader.

For each adjective listed below, indicate the degree to which you think the adjective describes the leader. Please select one of the following responses to indicate the strength of your opinion.

Key: 5 = Strongly agree 4 = Agree 3 = Neutral 2 = Disagree 1 = Strongly disagree

1. Articulate—Communicates effectively with others.	1	2	3	4	5
2. Perceptive—Discerning and insightful.	1	2	3	4	5
3. Self-confident—Believes in oneself and one's ability.	1	2	3	4	5
4. Self-assured—Secure with self, free of doubts.	1	2	3	4	5
5. Persistent—Stays fixed on the goal(s), despite interference.	1	2	3	4	5
6. Determined—Takes a firm stand, acts with certainty.	1	2	3	4	5
7. Trustworthy—Acts believable, inspires confidence.	1	2	3	4	5
8. Dependable—Is consistent and reliable.	1	2	3	4	5
9. Friendly—Shows kindness and warmth.	1	2	3	4	5
10. Outgoing—Talks freely, gets along well with others.	1	2	3	4	5

Scoring Interpretation

The scores you received on the LTQ provide information about how you see yourself and how others see you as a leader. The chart allows you to see where your perceptions are the same as others and where they differ from others.

The example below provides ratings for the first three characteristics, which help explain how the questionnaire can be used. For example, on the characteristic Articulate, the leader rated himself or herself significantly higher than the observers. On the second characteristic, Perceptive, the leader rated himself or herself substantially lower than others. On the Self-confident characteristic, the leader was quite close to others' ratings of his or her leadership.

There are no best ratings on this questionnaire. The purpose of the instrument is to give you a way to assess your strengths and weaknesses and to evaluate areas where your perceptions are congruent with others and where there are discrepancies.

———————————◆———————————

EXAMPLE RATINGS

	R1	R2	R3	R4	R5	AVE	SELF	DIF
1. Articulate	4	3	5	2	5	3.8	5	-1.2
2. Perceptive	3	5	5	5	4	4.4	3	+1.4
3. Self-confident	4	4	5	4	4	4.2	4	+0.2
4. Self-assured								
5. Persistent								
6. Determined								
7. Trustworthy								
8. Dependable								
9. Friendly								
10. Outgoing								
Total								

SUMMARY

The trait approach has its roots in leadership theory that suggested that certain people were born with special traits that made them great leaders. Because it was believed that leaders and nonleaders could be differentiated by a universal set of traits, throughout the 20th century researchers were challenged to identify the definitive traits of leaders.

Around the middle of the 20th century, several major studies questioned the basic premise that a unique set of traits defined leadership. As a result, attention shifted to incorporating the impact of situations and of followers on leadership. Researchers began to study the interactions that occur between leaders and their context instead of focusing only on leaders' traits. More recently, there are signs that trait research has come full circle, because there is a renewed interest in focusing directly on the critical traits of leaders.

From the multitude of studies that have been conducted through the years on individuals' personal characteristics, it is clear that many traits contribute to leadership. Some of the important traits that are consistently identified in many of these studies are intelligence, self-confidence, determination, integrity, and sociability. These traits, more than many of the others, are characteristic of the people we call leaders.

On a practical level, the trait approach is concerned with which traits leaders exhibit and who has these traits. Organizations employ personality assessment instruments to identify how individuals will fit within their organizations. The trait approach is also used for personal awareness and development, as it allows managers to analyze their strengths and weaknesses and to gain a clearer understanding of how they should try to change to enhance their leadership.

There are several advantages to viewing leadership from the trait approach. First, it is intuitively appealing because it fits clearly into the popular idea that leaders are special people who are out front, leading the way in society. Second, there is a great deal of research that validates the basis of this perspective. Third, by focusing exclusively on the leader, the trait approach provides an in-depth understanding of the leader component in the leadership process. Last, it has provided some benchmarks against which individuals can evaluate their own personal leadership attributes.

On the negative side, the trait approach has failed to delimit a definitive list of leadership traits. In analyzing the traits of leaders, the approach has failed to take into account the impact of situations. In addition, the approach has resulted in subjective lists of the most important leadership traits, which are not necessarily grounded in strong, reliable research. Furthermore, the trait approach has not adequately linked the traits of leaders with other outcomes such as group and team performance. Last, this approach is not particularly useful for training and development for leadership because individuals' personal attributes are relatively stable and fixed, and therefore their traits are not amenable to change.

REFERENCES

Bass, B. M. (1990). *Bass and Stogdill's handbook of leadership: A survey of theory and research.* New York: Free Press.

Bennis, W. G., & Nanus, B. (1985). *Leaders: The strategies for taking charge.* New York: Harper & Row.

Bryman, A. (1992). *Charisma and leadership in organizations.* London: Sage.

Jago, A. G. (1982). Leadership: Perspectives in theory and research. *Management Science, 28*(3), 315-336.

Kirkpatrick, S. A., & Locke, E. A. (1991). Leadership: Do traits matter? *The Executive, 5,* 48-60.

Lord, R. G., DeVader, C. L., & Alliger, G. M. (1986). A meta-analysis of the relation between personality traits and leadership perceptions: An application of validity generalization procedures. *Journal of Applied Psychology, 71,* 402-410.

Mann, R. D. (1959). A review of the relationship between personality and performance in small groups. *Psychological Bulletin, 56,* 241-270.

Nadler, D. A., & Tushman, M. L. (1989). What makes for magic leadership? In W. E. Rosenbach & R. L. Taylor (Eds.), *Contemporary issues in leadership* (pp. 135-139). Boulder, CO: Westview.

Stogdill, R. M. (1948). Personal factors associated with leadership: A survey of the literature. *Journal of Psychology, 25,* 35-71.

Stogdill, R. M. (1974). *Handbook of leadership: A survey of theory and research.* New York: Free Press.

Zaleznik, A. (1977, May-June). Managers and leaders: Are they different? *Harvard Business Review, 55,* 67-78.

Skills Approach

DESCRIPTION

Similar to the trait approach, which we discussed in the previous chapter, the skills approach takes a leader-centered perspective on leadership. However, in the skills approach we shift our thinking from a focus on personality characteristics, which are usually viewed as innate and relatively fixed, to an emphasis on skills and abilities that can be learned and developed. While personality certainly plays an integral role in leadership, the skills approach suggests that knowledge and abilities are needed for effective leadership.

Researchers have studied leadership skills directly or indirectly for a number of years (cf. Bass, 1990, pp. 97-109). However, the impetus for research on skills was a classic article published by Robert Katz in the *Harvard Business Review* in 1955, titled "Skills of an Effective Administrator." Katz's article appeared at a time when researchers were trying to identify a definitive set of leadership traits. Katz's approach was an attempt to transcend the trait problem by addressing leadership as a set of developable *skills*. More recently, a renewed interest in the skills approach has emerged. Beginning in the early 1990s, a multitude of studies have been published that contend that a leader's effectiveness depends on the leader's ability to solve complex organizational problems. This research has resulted in a comprehensive skills-based model of leadership that was advanced by Mumford and his colleagues (Mumford, Zaccaro, Harding, Jacobs, & Fleishman, 2000; Yammarino, 2000).

In this chapter, our discussion of the skills approach will be divided into two parts. First, we will discuss the general ideas set forth by Katz regarding three basic administrative skills: technical, human, and conceptual. Second, we will discuss the recent work of Mumford and colleagues that has resulted in a new skills-based model of organizational leadership.

THREE-SKILL APPROACH

Based on field research in administration and his own firsthand observations of executives in the workplace, Katz (1955) suggested that effective administration (i.e., leadership) depends on three basic personal skills: technical, human, and conceptual (p. 34). Katz argued that these skills are quite different from traits or qualities of leaders. *Skills* imply what leaders *can accomplish* whereas traits imply who leaders *are* (i.e., their innate characteristics). Leadership skills are defined in this chapter as the ability to use one's knowledge and competencies to accomplish a set of goals or objectives. This chapter shows that these leadership skills can be acquired and leaders can be trained to develop them.

Technical Skill

Technical skill is having knowledge about and being proficient in a specific type of work or activity. It requires competencies in a specialized area, analytical ability, and the ability to use appropriate tools and techniques (Katz, 1955). For example, in a computer software company, technical skill might include knowing software language and programming, the company's software products, and how to make these products function for clients. Similarly, in an accounting firm, technical skill might include understanding and having the ability to apply generally accepted accounting principles to a client's audit. In both of these examples, technical skills involve a "hands on" activity with a basic product or process within an organization. Technical skills play an essential role in producing the actual products a company is designed to produce.

As illustrated in Figure 3.1, technical skill is most important at lower levels of management and becomes less important in middle and upper levels of management. For leaders at the highest level, such as chief executive officers (CEOs), presidents, and senior officers, technical competencies are not as essential. Individuals at the top level depend on skilled subordinates to handle technical issues of the physical operation.

Figure 3.1 *Management Skills Necessary at Various Levels of an Organization.*

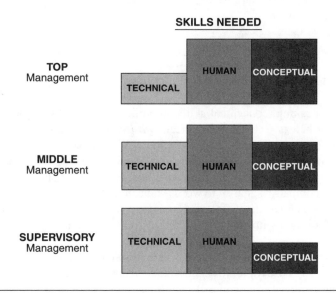

SOURCE: Adapted from "Skills of an Effective Administrator," by R. L. Katz, 1955, *Harvard Business Review.*

Human Skill

Human skill is having knowledge about and being able to work *with people*. It is quite different from technical skill, which has to do with working *with things* (Katz, 1955). Human skills are "people skills." They are the abilities that help a leader to work effectively with subordinates, peers, and superiors to successfully accomplish the organization's goals. Human skills allow a leader to assist group members in working cooperatively as a group to achieve common goals. For Katz, it means being aware of one's own perspective on issues and, at the same time, being aware of the perspective of others. Leaders with human skills adapt their own ideas to those of others. Furthermore, they create an atmosphere of trust where employees can feel comfortable and secure, and where they can feel encouraged to become involved in the planning of things that will affect them. To be a leader with human skills means being sensitive to the needs and motivations of others, and taking into account others' needs in one's decision making. In short, human skill is the capacity to get along with others as you go about your work.

In Figure 3.1, human skills are important in all three levels of management. Although managers at lower levels may communicate with a far greater number of employees, human skills are equally important at middle and upper levels as well.

Conceptual Skill

Broadly speaking, conceptual skills are abilities to work with ideas and concepts. Whereas technical skills deal *with things* and human skills deal *with people,* conceptual skills involve the ability to work *with ideas.* A leader with conceptual skills is comfortable talking about the ideas that shape an organization and the intricacies involved. He or she is good at putting the company's goals into words and can understand and express the economic principles that affect the company. A leader with conceptual skills works easily with abstractions and hypothetical notions.

Conceptual skills are central to creating a vision and strategic plan for an organization. For example, it would take conceptual skills for a CEO in a struggling manufacturing company to articulate a vision for a line of new products that would successfully steer the company into profitability. Similarly, it would take conceptual skill for the director of a nonprofit health organization to create a strategic plan that could compete success-fully with for-profit health organizations in a market with scarce resources. The point of these examples is that conceptual skill has to do with the mental work of shaping the meaning of organizational or policy issues— understanding what a company stands for and where it is or should be going.

In Figure 3.1, conceptual skill is most important at the top management levels. In fact, when upper-level managers do not have strong conceptual skills, they can jeopardize the whole organization. As you move down to middle and lower management levels, conceptual skills become less important.

Summary of the Three-Skill Approach

To summarize, the three-skill approach includes technical, human, and conceptual skills. It is important for leaders to have all three skills, but depending on where they are in the management structure, some skills are more important than others.

Katz's work in the mid-1950s set the stage for conceptualizing leadership in terms of skills, but it was not until the mid-1990s that an empirically based skills approach received recognition in leadership research. In the next section, the comprehensive skills-based model of leadership is presented.

SKILLS MODEL

Beginning in the early 1990s, a group of researchers, with funding support from the U.S. Army and Department of Defense, set out to test and develop a comprehensive theory of leadership based on problem-solving skills in organizations. The studies were conducted over a number of years using a sample of more than 1,800 Army officers, representing six grade levels, from second lieutenant to colonel. The project used a variety of new measures and tools to assess the skills of these officers, their experiences, and the situations in which they worked.

The main goal of the researchers was to explain the underlying elements of effective performance. They addressed questions such as these: What accounts for why some leaders are good problem solvers and others are not? What specific skills do high-performing leaders exhibit? How do leaders' individual characteristics, career experiences, and environmental influences affect their job performance? As a whole, researchers wanted to identify the leadership factors that create exemplary job performance in an actual organization.

Based on the extensive findings from the project, Mumford and colleagues formulated a skills-based model of leadership (Mumford, Zaccaro, Harding, et al., 2000). The model is characterized as a *capability* model because it examines the relationship between a leader's knowledge and skills (i.e., capabilities) and the leader's performance (p. 12). Leadership capabilities can be developed over time through education and experience. Unlike the "great person" approach (discussed in Chapter 2), which implies that leadership is reserved only for the "gifted few," the skills approach suggests that many individuals have the potential for leadership. If people are capable of learning from their experiences, they can acquire leadership. The skills approach can also be distinguished from those leadership approaches we will discuss in subsequent chapters, which focus on behavioral patterns of leaders (e.g., the style approach, transformational leadership, or leader-member exchange theory). Rather than emphasizing *what leaders do,* the skills approach frames leadership *as the capabilities*

Figure 3.2 *Three Components of the Skill Model*

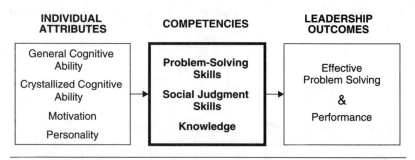

SOURCE: Adapted from the Influence of Leader Characteristics on Leader Performance in "Leadership Skills for a Changing World: Solving Complex Social Problems," by M. D. Mumford, S. J. Zaccaro, F. D. Harding, T. O. Jacobs, and E. A. Fleishman, *Leadership Quarterly, 11*(1), 23, 2000.

(knowledge and skills) that make effective leadership possible (Mumford, Zaccaro, Harding, et al., 2000, p. 12).

Mumford's group's skills-based model is composed of five different components: competencies, individual attributes, leadership outcomes, career experiences, and environmental influences. A portion of the model, illustrating three of these components, appears in Figure 3.2. This portion of the model is essential to understanding the overall skills-based leadership model.

Competencies

As can be observed in the middle box in Figure 3.2, problem-solving skills, social judgment skills, and knowledge are at the heart of the skills model. These three competencies are the key factors that account for effective performance.

Problem-Solving Skills

What are problem-solving skills? According to Mumford, Zaccaro, Harding, et al. (2000), problem-solving skills refer to a leader's creative ability to solve new and unusual, ill-defined organizational problems. The skills include being able to define significant problems, gather problem information, formulate new understandings about the problem, and generate prototype plans for problem solutions. These skills do not function in a vacuum but are carried out in an organizational context. Problem-solving skills demand that leaders understand their own leadership capacities as they apply to the unique problems and possible solutions to those problems within their organization (Mumford, Zaccaro, Connelly, & Marks, 2000).

Being able to construct solutions plays a special role in problem solving. In considering solutions to organizational problems, skilled leaders need to attend to the time frame for constructing and implementing a solution, short-term and long-term goals, career goals and organizational goals, and external issues, which all could impinge on the solution (Mumford, Zaccaro, Harding, et al., 2000, p. 15).

To clarify what is meant by problem-solving skills, consider the following hypothetical situation. Imagine that you are the director of human resources for a medium-sized company and you have been informed by the president that you have to develop a plan to reduce the company's health care costs. In deciding what you will do, you could demonstrate problem-solving skills in the following ways. First, you identify the full ramifications for employees of changing their health insurance coverage. What is the impact going to be? Second, you need to gather information about how benefits can be scaled back. What other companies have attempted a similar change and what were their results? Third, you need to find a way to teach and inform the employees about the needed change. How can you frame the change in such a way that it is clearly understood?

Fourth, you need to create possible scenarios for how the changes will be instituted. How will the plan be described? Fifth, you will need to look closely at the solution itself. How will implementing this change affect the company's mission and your own career? Last, are there issues in the organization (e.g., union rules) that may infringe on the implementation of these changes?

As illustrated by this example, the process of dealing with novel, ill-defined organizational issues is complex and demanding for leaders. In many ways, it is like a puzzle that needs to be solved. For leaders to solve such puzzles, the skills-based model suggests that problem-solving skills are essential.

Social Judgment Skills

In addition to problem-solving skills, effective leadership performance also requires social judgment skills (see Figure 3.2). In general, social judgment skills refer to the capacity to understand people and social systems (Zaccaro, Mumford, Connelly, Marks, & Gilbert, 2000, p. 46). They enable leaders to *work with others* to solve problems and to marshal support to implement change within an organization. Social judgment skills are the people skills that are necessary to solve unique organizational problems.

Conceptually, social judgment skills are similar to Katz's (1955) early work on the role of human skills in management. In contrast to Katz's work, Mumford and colleagues have delineated social judgment skills into the following: perspective taking, social perceptiveness, behavioral flexibility, and social performance.

Perspective taking means understanding the attitudes that *others* have toward a particular problem or solution. It is empathy applied to problem solving. Perspective taking means being sensitive to other people's perspectives and goals—being able to understand their point of view on different issues. Included in perspective taking is knowing how other constituencies within an organization view a problem and its possible solutions. According to Zaccaro, Gilbert, Thor, and Mumford (1991), perspective-taking skills can be likened to *social intelligence.* They are concerned with knowledge about people, the social fabric of organizations, and the interrelatedness of each of them.

Social perceptiveness refers to having insight and awareness into how others within the organization function. What is important to others? What motivates them? What problems do they face and how do they react to change? Social perceptiveness means understanding the unique needs, goals, and demands of different organizational constituencies (Zaccaro et al., 1991). A leader with social perceptiveness has a keen sense of how employees will respond to any proposed change within the organization. In a sense, you could say it allows the leader to "take the pulse" of employees on any issue at any time.

In addition to understanding others accurately, social judgment skills also involve reacting to others with flexibility. *Behavioral flexibility* is the capacity to change and adapt one's behavior in light of an understanding of others' perspectives in the organization. Being flexible means one is not locked into a singular approach to a problem. One is not dogmatic but rather maintains an openness and willingness to change. As the circumstances of a situation change, a flexible leader changes to meet the new demands.

Social performance includes a wide range of leadership competencies. Based on an understanding of employees' perspectives, leaders need to be able to effectively communicate their own vision to others. Skill in persuasion and communicating change is essential to do this. When there is resistance to change or interpersonal conflict about change, leaders need to function as mediators. To this end, skill in conflict resolution is an important aspect of social performance competency. In addition, social performance sometimes requires that leaders coach subordinates, giving them direction and support as they move toward selected organizational goals. In all, social performance includes many related skills that may come under the umbrella of being a "good communicator."

To review, social judgment skills are about being sensitive to how your ideas fit in with others. Can you understand others and their unique needs and motivations? Are you flexible and can you adapt your own ideas to others? Last, can you work with others even when there are resistance and conflict? Social judgment skills are the people skills required to advance change in an organization.

Knowledge

As shown in the model (see Figure 3.2), the third aspect of the competencies component is knowledge. Knowledge is inextricably related to the application and implementation of problem-solving skills in organizations. It directly influences a leader's capacity to define complex organizational problems and to attempt to solve them (Mumford, Zaccaro, Harding, et al., 2000). *Knowledge* refers to the accumulation of information and the mental structures used to organize that information. Such a mental structure is called a *schema* (a summary, a diagrammatic representation, or an outline). Knowledge results from having developed an assortment of complex schemata for learning and organizing data.

For example, all of us take various kinds of facts and information into our minds. As we organize that information into categories or schemata, the information becomes more meaningful. Knowledge emerges from the facts *and* the organizational structures we apply to them. People with a lot of knowledge have more complex organizing structures than individuals with less knowledge. These knowledgeable people are called experts.

Consider the following baseball example. A baseball expert knows a lot of facts about the game; he or she knows the rules, strategies, equipment, players, and much, much more. The expert's knowledge about baseball includes the facts, but it also includes the complex mental structures used in organizing and structuring those facts. That person knows not only the season and lifetime statistics for each player but also his quirks, his injuries, the personality of the manager, the strengths and weaknesses of available substitutes, and so on. The expert knows baseball because she or he comprehends the complexities and nuances of the game. Like experts on baseball, the same is true for leadership in organizations. Leaders with knowledge know much about the products, the tasks, people, organization, and all the different ways these elements are related to each other. A knowledgeable leader has many mental structures with which to organize the facts of organizational life.

Knowledge has a positive impact on how leaders engage in problem solving. It is knowledge and expertise that make it possible for people to think about complex systems issues and identify possible strategies for appropriate change. Furthermore, this capacity allows people to use prior cases and incidents in order to plan for needed change. It is knowledge that allows people to use the past to constructively confront the future.

To summarize, the skills model is comprised of three competencies: problem-solving skills, social judgment skills, and knowledge. Collectively, these three components are positively related to effective leadership performance (see Figure 3.2).

Individual Attributes

Returning to Figure 3.2, the box on the left identifies four individual attributes that have an impact on leadership skills and knowledge: general cognitive ability, crystallized cognitive ability, motivation, and personality. These attributes play an important role in the skills model. Complex problem solving is a very difficult process and becomes more difficult as people move up in the organization. The following attributes support people as they apply their leadership competencies.

General Cognitive Ability

General cognitive ability can be thought of as a person's intelligence. It includes perceptual processing, information processing, general reasoning skills, creative and divergent thinking capacities, and memory skills. General cognitive ability is linked to biology and not to experience.

Sometimes described as fluid intelligence, it is a type of intelligence that usually grows and expands up through early adulthood and then begins to decline with age. In the skills model, intelligence is described as having a positive impact on the leader's acquisition of complex problem-solving skills and the leader's knowledge.

Crystallized Cognitive Ability

Crystallized cognitive ability refers to intellectual ability that is learned or acquired over time. It is the store of knowledge we get through experience. We learn more and increase our capacities over a life span—increasing our leadership potential (e.g., problem-solving skills, conceptual ability, and social judgment skills). In normally functioning adults, this type of cognitive ability grows continuously and does not typically fall off in adulthood. It includes being able to comprehend complex information and learn new skills and information, as well as being able to communicate to others in oral and written forms (Connelly et al., 2000, p. 71). Stated another way, crystallized cognitive ability is acquired intelligence—the ideas and mental abilities people learn through experience. Because it stays relatively stable over time, this type of intelligence is not diminished as people get older.

Motivation

Motivation is listed as the third attribute in the model. While the model does not purport to explain the many ways that motivation may affect leadership, it does suggest three aspects of motivation that are particularly essential to developing leadership skills (Mumford, Zaccaro, Harding, et al., 2000, p. 22). First, leaders must be willing and motivated to tackle complex organizational problems. It is the critical first step. For leadership to occur, a person wants to lead. Second, leaders must be willing to express dominance—to exert their influence, as we discussed in Chapter 1. In influencing others, the leader must take on the responsibility of dominance because the influence component of leadership is inextricably bound to asserting dominance. Third, leaders must be committed to the social good of the organization. "The social good" is a broad term that can refer to a host of outcomes. However, in the skills model it refers to the leader's willingness to take on the responsibility of trying to advance the overall human good and value of the organization. Taken together, these three aspects of motivation (willingness, dominance, and social good) prepare people to become leaders.

Personality

Personality is the fourth individual attribute in the skills model. Placed where it is in the model, this attribute reminds us that our personality has an impact on the development of our leadership skills. For example, openness, tolerance for ambiguity, and curiosity may affect a leader's motivation to try to solve some organizational problem. Or, in conflict situations, traits such as confidence and adaptability may be beneficial to a leader's performance. The skills model hypothesizes that any personality characteristic that helps people to cope with complex organizational situations is most likely related to leader performance (Mumford, Zaccaro, Harding, et al., 2000).

Leadership Outcomes

In the box on the right in Figure 3.2, effective problem solving and performance represent the outcomes of leadership. These outcomes are strongly influenced by the leader's competencies (i.e., problem-solving skills, social judgment skills, and knowledge). When leaders exhibit these competencies, they increase their chances of problem solving and overall performance.

Effective Problem Solving

As we discussed earlier, the skills model is a *capability model,* designed to explain why some leaders are good problem solvers and others are not. Problem solving is the keystone in the skills approach. In the model (Figure 3.2), problem-solving skills, as competencies, lead to effective problem solving as a leadership outcome. The criteria for good problem solving are determined by the originality and the quality of expressed solutions to problem situations. Good problem solving involves creating solutions that are logical, effective, and unique and that go beyond given information (Zaccaro et al., 2000).

Performance

In the model, performance outcomes refer to how well the leader has done her or his job. To measure performance, standard external criteria are employed. If the leader has done well and been successful, the leader's evaluations will be positive. Leaders who are effective receive good annual performance reviews, get merit raises, and are recognized by superiors and

Figure 3.3 *Skills Model of Leadership*

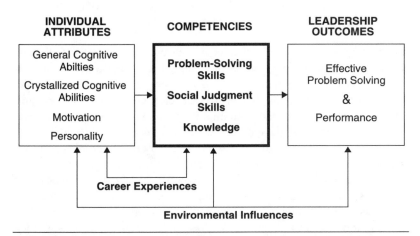

SOURCE: Adapted from the Influence of Leader Characteristics on Leader Performance in "Leadership Skills for a Changing World: Solving Complex Social Problems," by M. D. Mumford, S. J. Zaccaro, F. D. Harding, T. O. Jacobs, and E. A. Fleishman, *Leadership Quarterly, 11*(1), 23, 2000.

subordinates as competent leaders. In the end, performance refers to the degree to which a leader has successfully performed the duties to which he or she has been assigned.

Taken together, effective problem solving and performance are the two ways to assess leadership effectiveness using the skills model. Furthermore, good problem solving and good performance go hand in hand. A full depiction of the comprehensive skills model appears in Figure 3.3. It contains two other components, not depicted in Figure 3.2, that contribute to overall leadership performance: career experiences and environmental influences.

Career Experiences

As you can see in Figure 3.3, career experiences have an impact on the characteristics and competencies of leaders. The skills model suggests that the experiences acquired in the course of leaders' careers influence their knowledge and skills to solve complex problems. Mumford, Zaccaro, Harding, et al. (2000) point out that leaders can be helped by the following: (1) challenging job assignments, (2) mentoring, (3) appropriate training, and (4) hands-on experience in solving new and unusual problems (p. 24). In addition, the authors think that career experiences can positively affect the individual characteristics of leaders. For example, certain on-the-job assignments could enhance a leader's motivation or enhance her or his intellectual ability.

In the first section of this chapter, we discussed Katz's (1955) work, which notes that conceptual skills are essential for upper-level administrators. This is consistent with Mumford, Zaccaro, Harding, et al.'s (2000) skills model that contends that leaders develop competencies over time. Career experience helps leaders to improve their skills and knowledge over time. Leaders learn and develop higher levels of conceptual capacity if the kinds of problems they confront are progressively more complex and long term as they ascend the organizational hierarchy (Mumford, Zaccaro, Connelly, & Marks, 2000). Similarly, upper-level leaders, as opposed to first-line supervisors, develop new competencies because they are required to address problems that are more novel and more poorly defined and that demand more human interaction. As these individuals move through their careers, the need for higher levels of problem-solving and social judgment skills becomes increasingly important (Mumford & Connelly, 1991).

So the skills and knowledge of leaders are shaped by their career experiences as they address increasingly complex problems in the organization. This notion of developing leadership skills is unique and quite different from other leadership perspectives. If we say, "Leaders are shaped by their experiences," then it means leaders are not "born" to be leaders (Mumford, Zaccaro, Harding, et al., 2000). Leaders can develop their abilities through experience, according to the skills model.

Environmental Influences

The final component of the skills model is environmental influences, which is illustrated at the bottom of Figure 3.3. Environmental influences represent factors in a leader's situation that lie outside the leader's competencies, characteristics, and experiences. For example, an aging factory or one lacking in high-speed technology could have a major impact on the nature of problem-solving activities. Another example might be the level of skill of subordinates. If a leader's subordinates are highly competent, they will definitely have an impact on the group's problem solving and performance. Similarly, if a task is particularly complex or a group's communication is poor, the leader's performance will be affected.

The skills model does not provide an inventory of specific environmental influences. Instead, it acknowledges the existence of these factors and recognizes that they are indeed influences that can affect a leader's performance. In other words, environmental influences are a part of the skills model but not usually under the control of the leader.

Summary of the Skills Model

In summary, the skills model frames leadership by describing five components of leader performance. At the heart of the model are three competencies: *problem-solving skills, social judgment skills,* and *knowledge.* These three competencies are the central determinants of effective problem solving and performance, although individual attributes, career experiences, and environmental influences all have an impact on leader competencies. Through job experience and training, leaders can improve their abilities to become better problem solvers and more effective leaders.

HOW DOES THE SKILLS APPROACH WORK?

The skills approach is primarily descriptive—it *describes* leadership from a skills perspective. Rather than providing prescriptions for success in leadership, the skills approach provides a structure for understanding the nature of effective leadership. In the previous section, we discussed the skills perspective based on the work of Katz (1955) and Mumford, Zaccaro, Harding, et al. (2000). What does each of these bodies of work suggest regarding the structure and functions of leadership?

The three-skill approach of Katz suggests that the importance of certain leadership skills varies depending on where leaders are in a management hierarchy. For leaders operating at lower levels of management, technical and human skills are most important. When individuals move into middle management, it becomes important that they have all three skills—technical, human, and conceptual. At the upper management levels, it is paramount for individual leaders to exhibit conceptual and human skills. Although the various skill requirements change across management levels, the one skill that needs to be present at each level is effective "human" or interpersonal skills.

Mumford and colleagues provide a similar but far more complex picture of how skills relate to the manifestation of effective leadership. Their skills model contends that leadership outcomes are the direct result of a leader's competencies in problem-solving skills, social judgment skills, and knowledge. Each of these competencies includes a large repertoire of abilities and each can be learned and developed. In addition, the model illustrates how individual attributes such as general cognitive ability, crystallized cognitive ability, motivation, and personality do influence the leader's competencies. And finally, the model describes how career experiences and environmental influences play a direct or indirect role in leadership performance.

The skills approach works by providing a *map* for how to reach effective leadership in an organization: Leaders need to have problem-solving skills, social judgment skills, and knowledge. Workers can improve their capabilities in these areas through training and experience. Although each leader's personal attributes affect his or her skills, it is the leader's *skills* themselves that are most important in addressing organizational problems.

STRENGTHS

The skills approach contributes positively to our understanding about leadership in several ways. First, it is a leader-centered model that stresses the importance of developing particular leadership skills. It is the first approach to conceptualize and create a structure of the process of leadership around *skills*. While the early research on skills highlighted the importance of skills and the value of skills across different management levels, the later work placed learned skills at the center of effective leadership performance at *all* management levels.

Second, the skills approach is intuitively appealing. To describe leadership in terms of skills makes leadership available to everyone. Unlike personality traits, skills are competencies that individuals can learn or develop. It is like playing a sport such as tennis or golf. Even without natural ability in these sports, individuals can improve their games with practice and instruction. The same is true with leadership. When leadership is framed as a set of skills, it becomes a process that people can study and practice to become better at performing their jobs.

Third, the skills approach provides an expansive view of leadership that incorporates a wide variety of components, including problem-solving skills, social judgment skills, knowledge, individual attributes, career experiences, and environmental influences. Each of these components can further be subdivided into several subcomponents. The result is a picture of leadership that encompasses a multitude of factors. Because it includes so many variables, the skills approach can capture many of the intricacies and complexities of leadership not found in other models.

Last, the skills approach provides a structure that is very consistent with the curricula of most leadership education programs. Leadership education programs throughout the country have traditionally taught classes in creative problem solving, conflict resolution, listening, and teamwork, to name a few. The content of these classes closely mirrors many of the components in the skills model. Clearly, the skills approach provides a structure that helps to frame the curricula of leadership education and development programs.

CRITICISMS

As with all approaches to leadership, the skills approach also has certain weaknesses. First, the breadth of the skills approach seems to extend beyond the boundaries of leadership. For example, by including motivation, critical thinking, personality, and conflict resolution, the skills approach addresses more than just leadership. Another example of the model's breadth is including two types of intelligence (i.e., general cognitive ability and crystallized cognitive ability). Although both areas are studied widely in the field of cognitive psychology, they are seldom addressed in leadership research. By including so many components, the skills model of Mumford and others becomes more general and less precise in explaining leadership performance.

Second, related to the first criticism, the skills model is weak in predictive value. It does not explain specifically how variations in social judgment skills and problem-solving skills affect performance. The model suggests that these components are related, but it does not describe just how that works, with any precision. In short, the model can be faulted because it does not explain *how* skills lead to effective leadership performance.

In addition, the skills approach can be criticized for claiming *not* to be a trait model when in fact a major component in the model includes individual attributes, which are trait-like. Although Mumford and colleagues describe cognitive abilities, motivation, and personality variables as factors contributing to competencies, these are also factors that are typically considered to be trait variables. The point is that the "individual attributes" component of the skills model is trait driven, and that shifts the model away from being strictly a "skills" approach to leadership.

The final criticism of the skills approach is that it may not be suitably or appropriately applied to other contexts of leadership. The skills model was constructed by using a large sample of military personnel and observing their performance in the armed services. This raises an obvious question: Can the results be generalized to other populations or organizational settings? While some research suggests these Army findings can be generalized to other groups (Mumford, Zaccaro, Connelly, & Marks, 2000), more research is needed to address this criticism.

APPLICATION

Because the skills approach is a relatively new theoretical formulation, it is an approach that has not been widely used in applied leadership settings. For example, there are no "training packages" designed specifically to teach people leadership skills from this approach. Although there have been many programs designed to teach leadership skills from a general "self-help" orientation, few of these programs are based on the conceptual frameworks set forth in this chapter.

Despite the lack of formal training programs, the skills approach offers valuable information about leadership. The approach provides a way to delineate the skills of the leader, and leaders at all levels within an organization can use it. In addition, this approach helps us to identify our strengths and weaknesses in regard to these technical, human, and conceptual skills. By taking a skills inventory like the one provided at the end of this chapter, individuals can gain further insight into their own leadership competencies. Their scores allow them to learn about areas in which they may wish to seek further training to enhance their overall contributions to their organization.

From a wider perspective, the skills approach may be used in the future as a template for the design of extensive leadership development programs. This approach provides the evidence for teaching leaders the important aspects of listening, creative problem solving, conflict resolution skills, and much more.

CASE STUDIES

The following three case studies (Cases 3.1, 3.2, and 3.3) provide leadership situations that can be analyzed and evaluated from the skills perspective. The first case involves the principal investigator of a federally funded research grant. The second case takes place in a military setting and describes how a lieutenant colonel handles the downsizing of a military base. In the third case, we learn about how the owner of an Italian restaurant has created his own recipe for success.

As you read each case, try to apply the principles of the skills approach to the leaders and their situations. At the end of each case are questions that will assist you in analyzing the case.

CASE 3.1

A Strained Research Team

Dr. Adam Wood is the principal investigator on a 3-year, $1 million federally funded research grant to study health education programs for older populations, called the Elder Care Project. Unlike previous projects where Dr. Wood worked alone or with one or two other investigators, on this project Dr. Wood has 11 cohorts. His project team is made up of two coinvestigators (Ph.D.s), four intervention staff (M.A. degrees), and five general staff members (B.A. degrees).

One year into the project, it became apparent to Dr. Wood and the team that the project is underbudgeted and has too few resources. Team members are spending 20% to 30% more of their time on the project than the project has been budgeted to pay them. Regardless of the resource strain, all of the team members are committed to the project—they believe in its goals and the importance of its outcomes.

Dr. Wood is known throughout the country as the foremost scholar in this area of health education research. He is often called on to serve on national review and advisory boards. His publication record is second to none. In addition, his colleagues in the university know Dr. Wood as a very competent researcher. People come to Dr. Wood for advice on research design and methodology questions. They also come to him for questions about theoretical formulations. He has a reputation as someone who can see the "big picture" on research projects.

In spite of his research competence, there are problems on Dr. Wood's research team. Dr. Wood worries there is a great deal of work to be done but that the members of the team are not devoting sufficient time to the Elder Care Project. Dr. Wood is frustrated because many of the day-to-day research tasks of the project are falling in his lap. He entered a recent research meeting, threw his notebook down on the table, and said, "I wish I'd never taken this project on. It's taking way too much of my time. The rest of you aren't pulling your fair share."

Team members felt exasperated at Dr. Wood's comments. While they respect his competence, they find his leadership style frustrating. His negative comments at staff meetings are having a demoralizing effect on the research team. In spite of their hard work and devotion to the project, Dr. Wood seldom compliments or praises their efforts. Team members believe that they have spent more time than anticipated on the project and have received less pay or "credit" than expected. The project is sucking away a lot of staff energy, yet Dr. Wood does not seem to understand it or acknowledge it. The research staff is starting to feel burned out, but members realize that they need to keep trying because they are under time constraints from the federal government to do the work promised.

Recently, the team needed to develop a pamphlet for the participants in the Elder Care Project, but the pamphlet costs were significantly more than was budgeted in the grant. Dr. Wood was very adept at finding out where they might find "small pockets" of money to help cover those costs. While team members were pleased that he was able to obtain the money, they were sure he would use this as just another example of how he was the one doing most of the work on the project.

Questions

1. Based on the skills approach, how would you assess Dr. Wood's leadership and his relationship to the members of the Elder Care Project team? Will the project be successful?
2. Does Dr. Wood have the skills necessary to be an effective leader of this research team?
3. The skills model describes three important competencies for leaders: problem-solving skills, social judgment skills, and knowledge. If you were to coach Dr. Wood using this model, what type of things would you address with him?

CASE 3.2

A Shift for Lieutenant Colonel Adams

Lieutenant Colonel Adams was an aeronautical engineer in the Air Force who was recognized as an accomplished officer and rose quickly through the ranks of lieutenant, captain, and major. In addition, he successfully completed a number of professional development courses in the Air Force and received a master's degree in engineering. In the earlier part of his service, his career assignments required overseeing small 15- to 20-person shifts that were responsible for the routine maintenance schedules for squadron and base aircraft. As he progressed in rank, he moved to engineering projects, which were supported by small technical staffs.

Based on his strong performance, Major Adams was promoted to lieutenant colonel earlier than his peers. Instead of moving him into another engineering position, the personnel bureau and his assignment officer decided that Lt. Col. Adams would benefit from a tour where he could expand his professional background and experience. Consequently, he was assigned to Base X as the commanding officer of the administration branch. Base X was an airbase with approximately 5,000 military and civilian personnel.

As the administration officer, Lt. Col. Adams was the senior human resources officer and the principal adviser to the base commander on all human resource issues. Lt. Col. Adams and his staff of 135 civilian and military personnel were responsible for personnel issues, food services, recreation, family support, and medical services. In addition, Lt. Col. Adams was assigned to chair the Labor-Management Relations Committee for the base.

At the end of the Cold War, as part of the declared peace dividend, the government decided to reduce the defense budget. In February, barely 6 months after taking over command of the administration branch, the federal government announced a significant reduction in the size of the military and the closure of many bases. Base X was to be closed as an airbase and reassigned to the Army. The transition was to take place within 1 year and the base was to be prepared for the arrival of the first Army troops in 2 years. As part of the reduction program, the federal government initiated voluntary retirement programs for civilian and military personnel. Those wishing to retire had until the first of April to decide.

Orders for the conversion of the airbase included the following:

- The base will continue normal operations for 6 months.

- The squadrons—complete with aircrews, equipment, and families (1,000)—must be relocated to their new bases and operational by August 1.
- The remaining base personnel strength, both civilian and military, must be reduced by 30%.
- The base must continue to provide personnel for operational missions.
- The reduction of personnel must be consistent with federal voluntary early-retirement programs.
- The base must be prepared with a support structure to accept 2,000 new soldiers expected to arrive in 2 years' time.

Lt. Col. Adams was assigned to develop a human resources plan that would meet the imposed manning levels for the entire base while ensuring that the base was still able to meet the operational tasks it had been given. Faced with this daunting task, Adams conducted an extensive review of all of the relevant orders concerning the base transformation, and he familiarized himself with all of the rules concerning the early-retirement program. After a series of initial meetings with the other base branch chiefs, he laid out a plan that could be accomplished by the established deadlines. At the same time, he chaired a number of meetings with his own staff about how to meet the mandated reductions within his own branch.

After considering the target figures for the early-retirement program, it was clear that the mandated numbers could not be reached. Simply allowing everyone who had applied for early retirement to leave was not considered an option because doing so would devastate entire sections of the base. More job cuts were required and choices had to be made as to who would stay, why, and in what areas. Lt. Col. Adams met stiff resistance in the meetings to determine what sections would bear the brunt of the additional cutbacks.

Lt. Col. Adams conducted his own independent analysis of his own branch before consulting with his staff. Based on his thorough examination of the data, he mandated further reductions within his sections. Specifically targeted were personnel in the base housing, single personnel accommodation, family services, and recreational sections. He also mandated a further 10% cut of military positions within his sections.

After meeting the mandated reduction targets, Lt. Col. Adams was informed that the federal government would accept all personnel who applied for early retirement—which was an unexpected decision. This move, when superimposed on the already mandated reductions, caused critical shortages in key areas. Within weeks of the implementation of the plan, the base commander was receiving mounting complaints from both civilian and military members over the implementation of the plan. Incidents of stress, frustration, and discontent rose dramatically. Families trying to move found support services cut back or nonexistent. The transition staff was forced to work evenings and weekends. Family support services were swamped and were asking for additional help.

Despite spending a considerable amount of overtime hours trying to address the diverse issues both basewide and within his branch, Lt. Col. Adams found himself struggling to keep his head above water. To make matters worse, the base was now having difficulty meeting its operational mission, and vital sections were critically understaffed. The base commander wanted answers. When pressed, Lt. Col. Adams stated that his plan met all of the required deadlines and targets, and the plan conformed to all of the guidelines of the early-retirement programs. "Maybe so," replied the base commander, "but you forgot about the bigger picture."

Questions

1. Based on the skills model, how would you assess Lt. Col. Adams's ability to meet the challenges of the base administration position?
2. How would you assess his ability to meet the additional tasks he faced regarding the conversion of the base?
3. If you were to coach Lt. Col. Adams on how he could improve his leadership, what would you tell him?

------------------------------◆------------------------------

CASE 3.3

Andy's Recipe

Andy Garafallo owns an Italian restaurant that sits out in the middle of a cornfield near a large midwestern city. On the restaurant's far wall is an elaborate mural of the canals of Venice. A gondola hangs on the opposite wall, up by the ceiling. Along another wall is a row of real potted lemon trees. "My ancestors are from Sicily," says Andy. "In fact, I can remember seeing my grandfather take a bite out of a lemon, just like the ones hanging on those trees."

Andy is very confident about his approach to this restaurant, and he should be, because the restaurant is celebrating its 25th anniversary. "I'm darned sure of what I want to do. I'm not trying different fads to get people to come here. People come here because they know they will get great food. They also want to support someone with whom they can connect. This is my approach. Nothing more, nothing less." While other restaurants have folded, Andy seems to have found a recipe for success.

Since opening his restaurant, Andy has had a number of managers. Currently, he has three: Kelly, Danielle, and Patrick. Kelly is a kitchen (food prep) manager who is known as very honest and dependable. She loves her work and she is efficient, good with ordering, and good with preparation. Andy really likes Kelly but is frustrated with her because she has such difficulty getting along with the sales people, delivery people, and the wait staff.

Danielle, who works out front in the restaurant, has been with Andy the longest, 6 years. Danielle likes working at Garafallo's—she lives and breathes the place. She fully buys into Andy's approach of putting customers first. In fact, Andy says she has a knack for knowing what customers need before they even ask. Although she is very hospitable, Andy says she is lousy with numbers. She just doesn't seem to catch on to that side of the business.

Patrick, who has been with Andy for 4 years, usually works out front but can work in the kitchen as well. While Patrick has a strong work ethic and is great with numbers, he is weak on the people side. For some reason, Patrick treats customers as if they are faceless, coming across as very unemotional. In addition, Patrick tends to be very "cut and dried" about things, and approaches problems with a "black and white" perspective. This has gotten him into trouble on more than one occasion. Andy wishes that Patrick would learn to lighten up. "He's a good manager, but he needs to recognize that some things just aren't that important," says Andy.

Andy's approach to his managers is that of a teacher and coach. He is always trying to help them improve. He sees part of his responsibility as teaching them every aspect of the restaurant business. Andy's stated goal is that he wants his managers to be "A" players when they leave his business to take on new jobs elsewhere. Helping people to become the best they can be is Andy's goal for his restaurant employees.

Although Andy works 12 hours a day, he spends little time analyzing the numbers. He does not think about ways to improve his profit margin by "cutting corners"—raising an item price here, or cutting the quality there. Andy says, "It's like this: The other night I got a call from someone who said they wanted to come in with a group and wondered if they could bring along a cake. I said 'yes' with one stipulation . . . I get a piece! Well the people came and spent a lot of money. Then they told me that they had actually wanted to go to another restaurant but the other place would not allow them to bring in their own cake." Andy believes very strongly in his approach. "You get business by being what you should be."

Compared with other restaurants, his restaurant is doing quite well. While many places are happy to net 5% to 7% profit, Andy's Italian restaurant nets 30% profit, year in and year out.

Questions

1. What accounts for Andy Garafallo's success in the restaurant business?
2. From a skills perspective, how would you describe the three managers: Kelly, Danielle, and Patrick? What does each of them need to do to improve his or her skills?
3. How would you describe Andy's competencies? Does Andy's leadership suggest that one does not need all three skills in order to be effective?

LEADERSHIP INSTRUMENT

There are many questionnaires that assess an individual's skills for leadership. A quick search of Web sites on the Internet provides a host of these questionnaires. Most all of them are designed to be used in training and development to give people a feel for their leadership abilities. Surveys have been used for years to help people understand and know how to improve their leadership style, but most questionnaires are not typically used in research because they have not been tested for reliability and validity. Nevertheless, they are useful as "self-help" instruments because they provide specific information to people about their leadership skills.

In this chapter, we present a comprehensive skills model that is based on many empirical studies of leaders' skills. Although the questionnaires used in these studies are highly reliable and valid instruments, they are not suited for our more pragmatic discussion of leadership in this text. In essence, they are too complex and involved. For example, Mumford and his colleagues (2000) used measures that included open-ended responses and very sophisticated scoring procedures. While critically important for validating the model, these complicated measures are less valuable as self-instructional questionnaires.

A skills inventory is provided in the next section to assist you in understanding how leadership skills are measured and what your own skills might be. Your scores on the inventory will give you a sense of your own leadership competencies. You may be strong in all three skills or stronger in some skills than in others. The questionnaire will give you a sense of your own skills profile. If you are stronger in one skill and weaker in another, this may help you determine where you want to improve in the future.

Skills Inventory

Instructions: Read each item carefully and decide whether the item describes you as a person. Indicate your response to each item by circling one of the five numbers to the right of each item.

Key:
1 = Not true 2 = Seldom true 3 = Occasionally true 4 = Somewhat true 5 = Very true

1. I enjoy getting into the details of how things work.	1 2 3 4 5
2. As a rule, adapting ideas to people's needs is relatively easy for me.	1 2 3 4 5
3. I enjoy working with abstract ideas.	1 2 3 4 5
4. Technical things fascinate me.	1 2 3 4 5
5. Being able to understand others is the most important part of my work.	1 2 3 4 5
6. Seeing the "big picture" comes easy for me.	1 2 3 4 5
7. One of my skills is being good at making things work.	1 2 3 4 5
8. My main concern is to have a supportive communication climate.	1 2 3 4 5
9. I am intrigued by complex organizational problems.	1 2 3 4 5
10. Following directions and filling out forms comes easily for me.	1 2 3 4 5
11. Understanding the social fabric of the organization is important to me.	1 2 3 4 5
12. I would enjoy working out strategies for my organization's growth.	1 2 3 4 5
13. I am good at completing the things I've been assigned to do.	1 2 3 4 5
14. Getting all parties to work together is a challenge I enjoy.	1 2 3 4 5
15. Creating a mission statement is rewarding work.	1 2 3 4 5
16. I understand how to do the basic things required of me.	1 2 3 4 5
17. I am concerned with how my decisions affect the lives of others.	1 2 3 4 5
18. Thinking about organizational values and philosophy appeals to me.	1 2 3 4 5

Scoring

The skills inventory is designed to measure three broad types of leadership skills: technical, human, and conceptual. Score the questionnaire by doing the following. First, sum the responses on items 1, 4, 7, 10, 13, and 16. This is your *technical skill* score. Second, sum the responses on items 2, 5, 8, 11, 14, and 17. This is your *human skill* score. Third, sum the responses on items 3, 6, 9, 12, 15, and 18. This is your *conceptual skill* score.

Total scores: Technical skill _____ Human skill _____ Conceptual skill _____

Scoring Interpretation

The scores you received on the skills inventory provide information about your leadership skills in three areas. By comparing the differences between your scores you can determine where you have leadership strengths and where you have leadership weaknesses. Your scores also point toward the level of management for which you might be most suited.

———————————————◆———————————————

SUMMARY

The skills approach is a leader-centered perspective that emphasizes the competencies of leaders. It is best represented in the early work of Katz (1955) on the *three-skill approach* and the more recent works of Mumford and his colleagues (Mumford, Zaccaro, Harding, et al., 2000), who initiated the development of a comprehensive *skills model of leadership*.

In the three-skill approach, effective leadership depends on three basic personal skills: technical, human, and conceptual. While all three skills are important for leaders, the importance of each skill varies in different management levels. At lower management levels, technical and human skills are most important. For middle managers, the three different skills are equally important. At upper management levels, conceptual and human skills are most important, while technical skills become less important. Leaders are more effective when there is a match between their skills and their management level.

During the 1990s, the skills model was developed to explain the capabilities (knowledge and skills) that make effective leadership possible. Far more complex than Katz's paradigm, this model delineated five components of effective leader performance: competencies, individual attributes, leadership outcomes, career experiences, and environmental influences. The leader competencies at the heart of the model are problem-solving skills, social judgment skills, and knowledge. These competencies are directly affected by the leader's individual attributes, which include the leader's general cognitive ability, crystallized cognitive ability, motivation, and personality. The leader's competencies are also affected by his or her career experiences and the environment. The model postulates that effective problem solving and performance can be explained by the leader's basic competencies and that these competencies are in turn affected by the leader's attributes, experience, and the environment.

There are several strengths in conceptualizing leadership from a skills perspective. First, it is a leader-centered model that stresses the importance of the leader's abilities, and it places learned skills at the center of effective leadership performance. Second, the skills approach describes leadership in such a way that it makes it available to everyone. Skills are competencies that we all can learn to develop and improve upon. Third, the skills approach provides a sophisticated map that explains how effective leadership performance can be achieved. Based on the model, researchers can develop complex plans for studying the leadership process. Last, this approach provides a structure for leadership education and development programs that include creative problem solving, conflict resolution, listening, and teamwork.

In addition to the positive features, there are also some negative aspects to the skills approach. First, the breadth of the model seems to extend beyond the boundaries of leadership, including, for example, conflict management, critical thinking, motivation theory, and personality theory. Second, the skills model is weak in predictive value. It does not explain how a person's competencies lead to effective leadership performance. Third, the skills model claims not to be a trait approach, but individual traits such as cognitive abilities, motivation, and personality play a large role in the model. Finally, the skills model is weak in general application because it was constructed using only data from military personnel. Until the model has been tested with other populations, such as small and large organizations and businesses, its basic tenets must still be questioned.

REFERENCES

Bass, B. M. (1990). *Bass & Stogdill's handbook of leadership: Theory, research, and managerial application* (3rd ed.). New York: Free Press.

Connelly, M. S., Gilbert, J. A., Zaccaro, S. J., Threlfall, K. V., Marks, M. A., & Mumford, M. D. (2000). Exploring the relationship of leadership skills and knowledge to leader performance. *Leadership Quarterly, 11*(1), 65-86.

Katz, R. L. (1955, January-February). Skills of an effective administrator. *Harvard Business Review.*

Mumford, M. D., & Connelly, M. S. (1991). Leaders as creators: Leader performance and problem solving in ill-defined domains. *Leadership Quarterly, 2,* 289-315.

Mumford, M. D., Zaccaro, S. J., Connelly, M. S., & Marks, M. A. (2000). Leadership skills: Conclusions and future directions. *Leadership Quarterly, 11*(1), 155-170.

Mumford, M. D., Zaccaro, S. J., Harding, F. D., Owen Jacobs, T., & Fleishman, E. A. (2000). Leadership skills for a changing world: Solving complex social problems. *Leadership Quarterly, 11*(1), 11-35.

Yammarino, F. J. (2000). Leadership skills: Introducing and overview. *Leadership Quarterly, 11*(1), 5-9.

Zaccaro, S. J., Gilbert, J., Thor, K. K., & Mumford, M. D. (1991). Leadership and social intelligence: Linking social perceptiveness and behavioral flexibility to leader effectiveness. *Leadership Quarterly, 2,* 317-331.

Zaccaro, S. J., Mumford, M. D., Connelly, M. S., Marks, M. A., & Gilbert, J. A. (2000). Assessment of leader problem-solving capabilities. *Leadership Quarterly, 11*(1), 37-64.

Style Approach

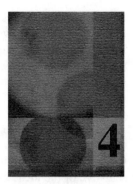

DESCRIPTION

The style approach emphasizes the behavior of the leader. This distinguishes it from the trait approach (Chapter 2), which emphasizes the personality characteristics of the leader, and the skills approach (Chapter 3), which emphasizes the leader's capabilities. The style approach focuses exclusively on what leaders do and how they act. In shifting the study of leadership to leader style or behaviors, the style approach expanded the study of leadership to include the actions of leaders toward subordinates in various contexts.

Researchers studying the style approach determined that leadership is composed of essentially two general kinds of behaviors: *task behaviors* and *relationship behaviors*. Task behaviors facilitate goal accomplishment: They help group members to achieve their objectives. Relationship behaviors help subordinates feel comfortable with themselves, with each other, and with the situation in which they find themselves. The central purpose of the style approach is to explain how leaders combine these two kinds of behaviors to influence subordinates in their efforts to reach a goal.

Many studies have been conducted to investigate the style approach. Some of the first studies to be done were conducted at Ohio State University in the late 1940s, based on the findings of Stogdill's (1948) work, which pointed to the importance of considering more than leaders' traits in leadership research. At about the same time, another group of researchers at the University of Michigan was conducting a series of studies that explored how leadership functioned in small groups. A third line of research was begun by Blake and Mouton in the early 1960s; it explored how managers used task and relationship behaviors in the organizational setting.

Although many research studies could be categorized under the heading of the style approach, the Ohio State studies, the Michigan studies, and the studies by Blake and Mouton (1964, 1978, 1985) are strongly representative of the ideas in this approach. By looking closely at each of these groups of studies, a clearer picture can be drawn of the underpinnings and implications of the style approach.

The Ohio State Studies

Because the results of studying leadership as a personality trait appeared fruitless, a group of researchers at Ohio State began to analyze how individuals acted when they were leading a group or organization. This analysis was conducted by having subordinates complete questionnaires about their leaders. On the questionnaires, subordinates had to identify the number of times their leaders engaged in certain types of behaviors.

The original questionnaire that was used in these studies was constructed from a list of more than 1,800 items describing different aspects of leader behavior. From this long list of items, a questionnaire composed of 150 questions was formulated, and it was called the Leader Behavior Description Questionnaire (LBDQ; Hemphill & Coons, 1957). The LBDQ was given to hundreds of individuals in educational, military, and industrial settings, and the results showed that certain clusters of behaviors were typical of leaders. Five years later, Stogdill (1963) published a shortened version of the LBDQ. The new form, which was called the LBDQ-XII, became the most widely used in research. A style questionnaire similar to the LBDQ appears later in this chapter. You can use this questionnaire to assess your own leadership behavior.

Researchers found that subordinates' responses on the questionnaire clustered around two general types of leader behaviors: *initiating structure* and *consideration* (Stogdill, 1974). Initiating structure behaviors were essentially task behaviors, including such acts as organizing work, giving structure to the work context, defining role responsibilities, and scheduling work activities. Consideration behaviors were essentially relationship behaviors and included building camaraderie, respect, trust, and liking between leaders and followers.

The two types of behaviors identified by the LBDQ-XII represent the core of the style approach—these behaviors are central to what leaders do: Leaders provide structure for subordinates, and they nurture them. The Ohio State studies viewed these two behaviors as distinct and independent. They were not thought of as two points along a single continuum, but as two different continua. For example, a leader could be high in initiating structure and high or low in task behavior. Similarly, a leader could be low in setting structure and low or high in consideration behavior. The degree to which a leader exhibited one behavior was not related to the degree to which she or he exhibited the other behavior.

Many studies have been done to determine which style of leadership is most effective in a particular situation. In some contexts high consideration has been found to be most effective, but in other situations high initiating structure has been found most effective. Some research has shown that being high on both behaviors is the best form of leadership. Determining how a leader optimally mixes task and relationship behaviors has been the central task for researchers from the style approach. The path-goal approach, which is discussed in Chapter 7, exemplifies a leadership theory that attempts to explain how leaders should integrate consideration and structure into the leader's style.

The University of Michigan Studies

While researchers at Ohio State were developing the LBDQ, researchers at the University of Michigan were also exploring leadership behavior, giving special attention to the impact of leaders' behaviors on the performance of small groups (Cartwright & Zander, 1960; Katz & Kahn, 1951; Likert, 1961, 1967).

The program of research at Michigan identified two types of leadership behaviors, called *employee orientation* and *production orientation.* Employee orientation describes the behavior of leaders who approach subordinates with a strong human relations emphasis. They take an interest in workers as human beings, value their individuality, and give special attention to their personal needs (Bowers & Seashore, 1966). Employee orientation is very similar to the cluster of behaviors identified in the Ohio State studies as consideration.

Production orientation refers to leadership behaviors that stress the technical and production aspects of a job. From this orientation, workers are viewed as a means for getting work accomplished (Bowers & Seashore, 1966). Production orientation parallels the initiating structure cluster found in the Ohio State studies.

Unlike the Ohio State researchers, the Michigan researchers, in their initial studies, conceptualized employee and production orientations as opposite ends of a single continuum. This suggested that leaders who were oriented toward production were less oriented to employees, and those who were employee oriented were less production oriented. As more studies were completed, however, the researchers reconceptualized the two constructs, similar to the Ohio State studies, as two independent leadership orientations (Kahn, 1956). When the two behaviors were treated as independent orientations, leaders were seen as being able to be oriented to both production and employees at the same time.

In the 1950s and 1960s, there were a multitude of studies conducted by researchers from both Ohio State and the University of Michigan to determine how leaders could best combine their task and relationship behaviors so as to maximize the impact of these behaviors on the satisfaction and performance of followers. In essence, the researchers were looking for a universal theory of leadership that would explain leadership effectiveness in every situation. The results that emerged from this large body of literature were contradictory and unclear (Yukl, 1994). Although some of the findings pointed to the value of a leader being both high-task and high- relationship oriented in all situations (Misumi, 1985), the preponderance of the research in this area was inconclusive.

Blake and Mouton's
Managerial (Leadership) Grid

Perhaps the most well-known model of managerial behavior is the Managerial Grid®, which first appeared in the early 1960s and since that time has been refined and revised several times (Blake & McCanse, 1991; Blake & Mouton, 1964, 1978, 1985). It is a model that has been used extensively in organizational training and development. The Managerial Grid, which has been renamed the Leadership Grid, was designed to explain how leaders help organizations to reach their purposes through two factors: *concern for production* and *concern for people*. Although these factors are described as leadership orientations in the model, they closely parallel the task and relationship leadership behaviors we have been discussing throughout this chapter.

Concern for production refers to how a leader is concerned with achieving organizational tasks. It involves a wide range of activities, including attention to policy decisions, new product development, process issues, workload, and sales volume, to name a few. Not limited to things, concern for production can refer to whatever it is the organization is seeking to accomplish (Blake & Mouton, 1964).

Concern for people refers to how a leader attends to the people within the organization who are trying to achieve its goals. This concern includes building organizational commitment and trust, promoting the personal worth of employees, providing good working conditions, maintaining a fair salary structure, and promoting good social relations (Blake & Mouton, 1964).

The Leadership (Managerial) Grid joins concern for production and concern for people in a model that has two intersecting axes (see Figure 4.1). The horizontal axis represents the leader's concern for results, and the vertical axis represents the leader's concern for people. Each of the axes is drawn as a 9-point scale on which a score of 1 represents *minimum concern* and 9 represents *maximum concern*. By plotting scores from each of the axes, various leadership styles can be illustrated. The Leadership Grid portrays five major leadership styles: authority-compliance (9,1), country club management (1,9), impoverished management (1,1), middle-of-the-road management (5,5), and team management (9,9).

Authority-Compliance (9,1)

The 9,1 style of leadership places heavy emphasis on task and job requirements and less emphasis on people, except to the extent that people are tools for getting the job done. Communicating with subordinates is not emphasized except for the purpose of giving instructions about the task. This style is results driven, and people are regarded as tools to that end. The 9,1 leader is often seen as controlling, demanding, hard-driving, and overpowering.

Figure 4.1 *The Leadership Grid®*

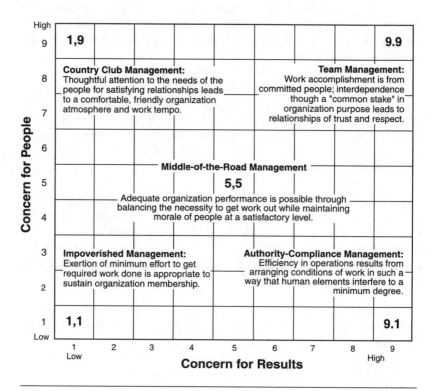

SOURCE: The Leadership Grid figure is from *Leadership Dilemmas—Grid Solutions* (p. 29), by Robert R. Blake and Anne Adams McCanse (formerly the Managerial Grid figure by Robert R. Blake and Jane S. Mouton), 1991, Houston, TX: Gulf Publishing Company. Copyright 1991 by Scientific Methods, Inc. Reproduced by permission of the owners.

Country Club Management (1,9)

The 1,9 style represents a low concern for task accomplishment coupled with a high concern for interpersonal relationships. De-emphasizing production, 1,9 leaders stress the attitudes and feelings of people, making sure the personal and social needs of followers are met. They try to create a positive climate by being agreeable, eager to help, comforting, and uncontroversial.

Impoverished Management (1,1)

The 1,1 style is representative of a leader who is unconcerned with both the task and interpersonal relationships. This type of leader goes through the motions of being a leader, but acts uninvolved and withdrawn. The 1,1 leader often has little contact with followers and could be described as indifferent, noncommittal, resigned, and apathetic.

Middle-of-the-Road Management (5,5)

The 5,5 style describes leaders who are compromisers, who have an intermediate concern for the task and an intermediate concern for the people who do the task. They find a balance or mixture between taking people into account and still emphasizing the work requirements. Their compromising style gives up some of the push for production as well as some of the attention to employee needs. To arrive at an equilibrium, the 5,5 leader avoids conflict and emphasizes moderate levels of production and interpersonal relationships. This type of leader is often described as one who is expedient, prefers the middle ground, soft-pedals disagreement, and swallows convictions in the interest of "progress."

Team Management (9,9)

The 9,9 style places a strong emphasis on both tasks and interpersonal relationships. It promotes a high degree of participation and teamwork in the organization, and satisfies a basic need in employees to be involved and committed to their work. The following are some of the phrases that could be used to describe the 9,9 leader: stimulates participation, acts determined, gets issues into the open, makes priorities clear, follows through, behaves open-mindedly, and enjoys working.

In addition to the five major styles described in the Leadership Grid, Blake and his colleagues have identified two other styles that incorporate multiple aspects of the grid.

Paternalism/Maternalism

Paternalism/Maternalism refers to a leader who uses both 1,9 and 9,1 styles but does not integrate the two (see Figure 4.2). This is the "benevolent

FIGURE 4.2 *Paternalism/Maternalism: Reward and approval are bestowed to people in return for loyalty and obedience: failure to comply leads to punishment.*

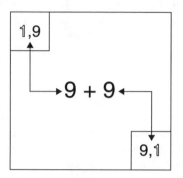

SOURCE: The Paternalism/Maternalism figure is from *Leadership Dilemmas—Grid Solutions* (p. 30), by Robert R. Blake and Anne Adams McCanse (formerly the Managerial Grid figure by Robert R. Blake and Jane S. Mouton), 1991, Houston, TX: Gulf Publishing Company. Copyright 1991 by Scientific Methods, Inc. Reproduced by permission of the owners.

dictator" who acts gracious but does so for the purpose of goal accomplishment. In essence the paternalistic/maternalistic style treats people as if they were disassociated with the task.

Opportunism

Opportunism refers to a leader who uses any combination of the basic five styles for the purpose of personal advancement (see Figure 4.3).

Blake and Mouton (1985) indicate that a person usually has a dominant grid style, which he or she uses in most situations, and a backup style. The backup style is what the leader reverts to when under pressure, when the usual way of accomplishing things does not work.

In summary, the Leadership Grid is an example of a practical model of leadership that is based on the two major leadership behaviors: task and relationship. It closely parallels the ideas and findings that emerged in the Ohio State and University of Michigan studies. It is used in consulting for organizational development throughout the world.

Figure 4.3 *Opportunism: In opportunistic management, people adapt and shift to any grid style needed to gain the maximum advantage. Performance occurs according to a system of selfish gain. Effort is given only for an advantage for personal gain.*

Opportunism

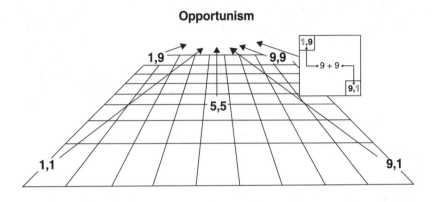

SOURCE: The Opportunism figure is from *Leadership Dilemmas—Grid Solutions* (p. 31), by Robert R. Blake and Anne Adams McCanse (formerly the Managerial Grid figure by Robert R. Blake and Jane S. Mouton), 1991, Houston, TX: Gulf Publishing Company. Copyright 1991 by Scientific Methods, Inc. Reproduced by permission of the owners.

HOW DOES THE STYLE APPROACH WORK?

Unlike many of the other approaches discussed in the book, the style approach is not a refined theory that provides a neatly organized set of prescriptions for effective leadership behavior. Rather, the style approach provides a framework for assessing leadership in a broad way, as behavior with a task and relationship dimension. The style approach works not by telling leaders how to behave, but by describing the major components of their behavior.

The style approach reminds leaders that their actions toward others occur on a task level and a relationship level. In some situations, leaders need to be more task oriented, whereas in others, they need to be more relationship oriented. Similarly, some subordinates need leaders who provide a lot of direction, whereas others need leaders who can show them a great deal of nurturance and support. The style approach gives the leader a way to look at his or her own behavior by subdividing it into two dimensions.

An example may help explain how the style approach works. Imagine two college classrooms on the first day of class and two professors with entirely different styles. Professor Smith comes to class, introduces herself, takes attendance, goes over the syllabus, explains the first assignment, and dismisses the class. Professor Jones comes to class and, after introducing herself and handing out the syllabus, tries to help the students to get to know one another by having each of the students describe a little about themselves, their major, and their favorite nonacademic activities. The leadership styles of Professors Smith and Jones are quite different. The preponderance of what Professor Smith does could be labeled task behavior, and the majority of what Professor Jones does is relationship behavior. The style approach provides a way to inform the professors about the differences in their behaviors. Depending on the response of the students to their style, the professors may wish to change their behavior to improve their teaching on the first day of class.

Overall, the style approach offers a means of assessing in a general way the behaviors of leaders. It reminds leaders that their impact on others occurs through the tasks they perform as well as in the relationships they create.

STRENGTHS

The style approach makes several positive contributions to our understanding of the leadership process. First, the style approach marked a major shift in the general focus of leadership research. Prior to the inception of the style approach, researchers treated leadership exclusively as a personality trait (see Chapter 2). The style approach broadened the scope of leadership research to include the behaviors of leaders and what they do in various situations. No longer was the focus of leadership on the personal characteristics of leaders; it was expanded to include what leaders did and how they acted.

Second, a wide range of studies on leadership style validates and gives credibility to the basic tenets of the approach. First formulated and reported by researchers from Ohio State University and the University of Michigan and subsequently in the work of Blake and Mouton (1964, 1978, 1985) and Blake and McCanse (1991), the style approach is substantiated by a multitude of research studies that offer a viable approach to understanding the leadership process.

Third, on a conceptual level, researchers from the style approach have ascertained that a leader's style is composed of primarily two major types of behaviors: task and relationship. The significance of this idea is not to be understated. Whenever leadership occurs, the leader is acting out both task and relationship behaviors; the key to being an effective leader often rests on how the leader balances these two behaviors. Together they form the core of the leadership process.

Fourth, the style approach is heuristic. It provides us with a broad conceptual map that is worthwhile to use in our attempts to understand the complexities of leadership. Leaders can learn a lot about themselves and how they come across to others by trying to see their behaviors in light of the task and relationship dimensions. Based on the style approach, leaders can assess their actions and determine how they may wish to change to improve their leadership style.

CRITICISMS

Along with its strengths, the style approach also has several weaknesses. First, the research on styles has not adequately shown how leaders' styles are associated with performance outcomes (Bryman, 1992; Yukl, 1994). Researchers have not been able to establish a consistent link between task and relationship behaviors and outcomes such as morale, job satisfaction, and productivity. According to Yukl (1994), the "results from this massive research effort have been mostly contradictory and inconclusive" (p. 75). He further points out that the only strong finding about leadership styles is that leaders who are considerate have followers who are more satisfied.

Another criticism is that this approach has failed to find a universal style of leadership that could be effective in almost every situation. The overarching goal for researchers studying the style approach appeared to be the identification of a universal set of leadership behaviors that would consistently result in effective outcomes. Because of inconsistencies in the research findings, this goal was never reached. Similar to the trait approach, which was unable to identify the definitive personal characteristics of leaders, the style approach has been unable to identify the universal behaviors that are associated with effective leadership.

A final criticism of the style approach is that it implies that the most effective leadership style is the high-high style (i.e., high task and high relationship). Even though some researchers (e.g., Blake & McCanse, 1991;

Misumi, 1985) have suggested that high-high managers are most effective, that may not be the case in all situations. In fact, the full range of research findings provides only limited support for a universal high-high style (Yukl, 1994). Certain situations may require different leadership styles; some may be complicated and require high task behavior, and others may be simple and require supportive behavior. At this point in the development of research on the style approach, it remains unclear whether the high-high style is the most preferred style of leadership.

APPLICATION

The style approach can be easily applied in ongoing leadership settings. At all levels within all types of organizations, managers are continually engaged in task and relationship behaviors. By making an assessment of their own style, managers can determine how they are coming across to others and how they could change their behaviors to be more effective. In essence, the style approach provides a mirror for managers that is helpful in answering the frequently asked question, "How am I doing as a leader?"

In training and development for leadership, many programs throughout the country are structured along the lines of the style approach. Almost all of them are designed similarly and include giving managers questionnaires that assess in some way their task and relationship behaviors toward subordinates. Participants use these assessments to improve their overall leadership style.

An example of a training and development program that deals exclusively with leader styles is Blake and Mouton's Leadership Grid (formerly Managerial Grid) seminar. Grid seminars are about increasing productivity, improving morale, and gaining employee commitment. They are offered by Scientific Methods,[1] an international organization development company. At grid seminars, through self-assessments, small-group experiences, and candid critiques, managers learn how to define effective leadership, how to manage for optimal results, and how to identify and change ineffective leadership behaviors. The conceptual framework around which the grid seminars are structured is the style approach to leadership.

In short, the style approach applies to nearly everything a leader does. It is an approach that is employed as a model by many training and development companies to teach managers how to improve their effectiveness and organizational productivity.

CASE STUDIES

On the following pages, you will find case studies (Cases 4.1, 4.2, and 4.3) that describe the leadership styles of three different managers, each of whom is working in a different organizational setting. The first case is about a maintenance director in a large hospital, the second deals with a supervisor in a small sporting goods store, and the third is concerned with the director of a design department in a large manufacturing company. At the end of each case are questions that will help you to analyze the case from the perspective of the style approach.

CASE 4.1

A Drill Sergeant at First

Mark Young is the head of the painting department in a large hospital, and 20 union employees report to him. Prior to coming on board at the hospital, he had worked as an independent contractor. At the hospital, he took a position that was newly created because the hospital believed change was needed in how painting services were provided.

Upon beginning his job, Mark did a 4-month analysis of the direct and indirect costs of painting services. His findings supported the perceptions of his administrators that painting services were inefficient and costly. As a result, Mark completely reorganized the department, designed a new scheduling procedure, and redefined the expected standards of performance.

Mark says that when he started out in his new job he was "all task," like a drill sergeant who didn't seek any input from his subordinates. From Mark's point of view, the hospital environment did not leave much room for errors, so he needed to be strict about getting painters to do a good job within the constraints of the hospital environment.

As time went along, Mark relaxed his style and was less demanding. He allocated some responsibilities to two crew leaders who reported to him, but always stayed in close touch with each of the employees. On a weekly basis, Mark was known to take small groups of workers to the local sports bar for burgers on the house. He loved to banter with the employees and could dish it out as well as take it.

Mark is very proud of his department. He says he always wanted to be a coach and that's how he feels about running his department. He enjoys working with people, and in particular he says he likes to see that glint in their eyes when they come to the realization that they've done a good job and they have done it on their own.

Because of Mark's leadership, the painting department improved substantially and is now seen by workers in other departments as the most productive department in hospital maintenance. Painting services received a customer rating of 92%, which was the highest of any service in the hospital.

Questions

1. From the style perspective, how would you describe Mark Young's leadership?
2. How did his style change over time?
3. In general, do you think he is more task oriented or more relationship oriented?
4. If he took Blake and Mouton's grid, what score do you think he would get?

CASE 4.2

Eating Lunch Standing Up

Susan Parks is the part-owner and manager of Marathon Sports, an athletic store that specializes in running shoes and accessories. The store employs about 10 people, most of whom are college students who work part-time during the week and full-time on weekends. Marathon Sports is the only store of its kind in a college town with a population of 125,000. The annual sales figures for the store have shown a 15% growth for each of the past 7 years.

Ms. Parks has a lot invested in the store, and she works very hard to make sure the store continues to maintain its reputation and pattern of growth. She works 50 hours a week at the store, where she wears many hats, including those of buyer, scheduler, trainer, planner, and salesperson. There is never a moment when Susan is not doing something. Rumor has it that she eats her lunch standing up.

Employees' reactions to Ms. Parks are strong and quite varied. Some people like her style and others do not. Those who like her style talk about how organized and efficient the store is when she is in charge. Susan makes the tasks and goals for everyone very clear. She keeps everyone busy, and when they go home at night they feel as if they have accomplished something. They like to work for Susan because she knows what she is doing. Those who do not like her style complain that she is too driven. It seems that her sole purpose for being at the store is to get the job done. She seldom, if ever, takes a break or just hangs out with the staff. These people say Susan is pretty hard to relate to and as a result it is not much fun working at Marathon Sports.

Susan is beginning to sense that employees have a mixed reaction to her leadership style. This bothers her, but she does not know what to do about it. In addition to her work at the store, Susan struggles hard to be a good spouse and mother of three children.

Questions

1. According to the style approach, how would you describe Susan Parks's leadership?
2. Why does it create such a pronounced reaction from her subordinates?
3. Do you think she should change her style?
4. Would she be effective if she changed?

CASE 4.3

Enhancing the Department's Culture

Douglas Ludwig is the director of design services at a large office furniture manufacturing company that employs about 1,200 people. The design department is made up of 80 individuals who are divided into eight working teams, all of which report to Mr. Ludwig. Douglas is relatively new to the company, having been hired away from a smaller competitor where he was vice president for research and development. His reputation as a leader at the previous company was generally favorable.

During his first year, Douglas has spent a lot of time trying to enhance the culture in his department. Unlike the previous director, who had spent a good portion of his time monitoring projects and emphasizing company goals, Douglas has involved himself with the mood, climate, and tenor of the department. To that end, Douglas has instituted a new department meeting schedule for the purpose of allowing everyone to share his or her ideas and concerns. While continuing to do the "nuts and bolts" things, Douglas has tried to promote greater esprit de corps in the department by having brown-bag lunches on Fridays. Each week, Douglas meets informally with the team leaders to get a feel for what they need and how they are doing.

Douglas is also a strong supporter of social events outside of work. In the summer, the design department held an outdoor family barbecue—the first ever for some of the older employees in the company. Over the holidays, Douglas held an open house at his residence that was catered by the company. Employees thought it was "first class" and talked about it for many months. Douglas was also instrumental in getting the company to sponsor a coed indoor soccer team, made up completely of employees from the design department.

Most, but not all, of the people in the department give Douglas Ludwig positive reviews for his first year as director. Designers and staffers alike are impressed by what a nice guy Mr. Ludwig seems to be. For years, the mood in the design department had been somewhat stale, but with Douglas's arrival some life came back into the place. People began to enjoy the new vitality in the department, and they found themselves chatting more and complaining less.

Questions

The leadership used by Douglas Ludwig is clearly one of the major types in the style approach.

1. What style is it?
2. Does it sound as if it is effective within the context of the design department at the furniture company?
3. Would you or would you not like to work for Douglas Ludwig?
4. Is there a downside to this style of leadership? If so, describe it.

———————————◆———————————

LEADERSHIP INSTRUMENT

Researchers and practitioners alike have used many different instruments to assess the styles of leaders. The two most commonly used measures have been the LBDQ (Stogdill, 1963) and the Leadership Grid (Blake & McCanse, 1991). Both of these measures provide information about the degree to which a leader acts task directed and people directed. The LBDQ was designed primarily for research and has been used extensively since the 1960s. The Leadership Grid was designed primarily for training and development, and it continues to be used today for training managers and supervisors in the leadership process.

To assist you in developing a better understanding of how leadership style is measured and what your own style might be, a leadership style questionnaire is included in this section. This questionnaire is made up of 20 items that assess two factors: *task* and *relationship.* By scoring the style questionnaire, you can obtain a general profile of your leadership behavior.

The score you receive for task refers to the degree to which you help others by defining their roles and letting them know what is expected of them. This factor describes your tendencies to be task directed toward others when you are in a leadership position. The score you receive for relationship is a measure of the degree to which you try to make subordinates feel comfortable with themselves, each other, and the group itself. It represents a measure of how people oriented you are.

Your results on the style questionnaire give you data about your task orientation and people orientation. What do your scores suggest about your leadership style? Are you more likely to lead with an emphasis on task or with an emphasis on relationship? As you interpret your responses to the style questionnaire, are there ways you could change your style to shift the emphasis you give to tasks and relationships? To gain more information about your style, you may wish to have four or five of your coworkers fill out the questionnaire based on their perceptions of you as a leader. This will give you additional data to compare and contrast to your own scores about yourself.

Style Questionnaire

Instructions: Read each item carefully and think about how often you (or the person you are evaluating) engage in the described behavior. Indicate your response to each item by circling one of the five numbers to the right of each item.

Key: 1 = Never   2 = Seldom   3 = Occasionally   4 = Often   5 = Always

1.	Tells group members what they are supposed to do.	1	2	3	4	5
2.	Acts friendly with members of the group.	1	2	3	4	5
3.	Sets standards of performance for group members.	1	2	3	4	5
4.	Helps others feel comfortable in the group.	1	2	3	4	5
5.	Makes suggestions about how to solve problems.	1	2	3	4	5
6.	Responds favorably to suggestions made by others.	1	2	3	4	5
7.	Makes his or her perspective clear to others.	1	2	3	4	5
8.	Treats others fairly.	1	2	3	4	5
9.	Develops a plan of action for the group.	1	2	3	4	5
10.	Behaves in a predictable manner toward group members.	1	2	3	4	5
11.	Defines role responsibilities for each group member.	1	2	3	4	5
12.	Communicates actively with group members.	1	2	3	4	5
13.	Clarifies his or her own role within the group.	1	2	3	4	5
14.	Shows concern for the personal well-being of others.	1	2	3	4	5
15.	Provides a plan for how the work is to be done.	1	2	3	4	5
16.	Shows flexibility in making decisions.	1	2	3	4	5
17.	Provides criteria for what is expected of the group.	1	2	3	4	5
18.	Discloses thoughts and feelings to group members.	1	2	3	4	5
19.	Encourages group members to do quality work.	1	2	3	4	5
20.	Helps group members get along.	1	2	3	4	5

Scoring

The style questionnaire is designed to measure two major types of leadership behaviors: task and relationship. Score the questionnaire by doing the following. First, sum the responses on the odd-numbered items. This is your task score. Second, sum the responses on the even-numbered items. This is your relationship score.

Total scores: Task _____   Relationship _____

Scoring Interpretation

45-50	Very high range	30-34	Moderately low range
40-44	High range	25-29	Low range
35-39	Moderately high range	10-24	Very low range

——————————————— ◆ ———————————————

SUMMARY

The style approach is strikingly different from the trait approach and skills approach to leadership because the style approach focuses on what leaders do rather than who leaders are. It suggests that leaders engage in two primary types of behaviors: task behaviors and relationship behaviors. How leaders combine these two types of behaviors to influence others is the central purpose of the style approach.

The style approach originated from three different lines of research: the Ohio State University studies, the University of Michigan studies, and the work of Blake and Mouton on the Managerial Grid.

Researchers at Ohio State developed a leadership questionnaire called the Leader Behavior Description Questionnaire (LBDQ), which identified *initiation of structure* and *consideration* as the core leadership behaviors. The Michigan studies provided similar findings but called the leader behaviors *production orientation* and *employee orientation.*

Using the Ohio State and Michigan studies as a basis, much research has been carried out to find the best way for leaders to combine task and relationship behaviors. The goal has been to find a universal set of leadership behaviors capable of explaining leadership effectiveness in every situation; however, the results from these efforts have not been conclusive. Researchers have had difficulty identifying one best style of leadership.

Blake and Mouton developed a practical model for training managers that described leadership behaviors along a grid with two axes: concern for results and concern for people. How leaders combine these orientations results in five major leadership styles: authority-compliance (9,1), country club management (1,9), impoverished management (1,1), middle-of-the-road management (5,5), and team management (9,9).

The style approach has several strengths and weaknesses. On the positive side, it has broadened the scope of leadership research to include the study of the behaviors of leaders rather than only their personal traits or characteristics. Second, it is a reliable approach because it is supported by a wide range of studies. Third, the style approach is valuable because it underscores the importance of the two core dimensions of leadership behavior: task and relationship. Fourth, it has heuristic value in that it provides us with a broad conceptual map that is useful in gaining an understanding of our own leadership behaviors.

On the negative side, researchers have not been able to associate the behaviors of leaders (task and relationship) with outcomes such as morale, job satisfaction, and productivity. In addition, researchers from the style approach have not been able to identify a universal set of leadership behaviors that would consistently result in effective leadership. Last, the style approach implies, but fails to support fully, the idea that the most effective leadership style is a high-high style (i.e., high task and high relationship).

Overall, the style approach is not a refined theory that provides a neatly organized set of prescriptions for effective leadership behavior. Rather, the style approach provides a valuable framework for assessing leadership in a broad way as assessing behavior with task and relationship dimensions. Finally, the style approach reminds leaders that their impact on others occurs along both dimensions.

NOTE

1. Scientific Methods, P.O. Box 195, Austin, TX 78767.

REFERENCES

Blake, R. R., & McCanse, A. A. (1991). *Leadership dilemmas—Grid solutions.* Houston, TX: Gulf.

Blake, R. R., & Mouton, J. S. (1964). *The Managerial Grid.* Houston, TX: Gulf.

Blake, R. R., & Mouton, J. S. (1978). *The new Managerial Grid.* Houston, TX: Gulf.

Blake, R. R., & Mouton, J. S. (1985). *The Managerial Grid III.* Houston, TX: Gulf.

Bowers, D. G., & Seashore, S. E. (1966). Predicting organizational effectiveness with a four-factor theory of leadership. *Administrative Science Quarterly, 11,* 238-263.

Bryman, A. (1992). *Charisma and leadership in organizations.* London: Sage.

Cartwright, D., & Zander, A. (1960). *Group dynamics research and theory.* Evanston, IL: Row, Peterson.

Hemphill, J. K., & Coons, A. E. (1957). Development of the Leader Behavior Description Questionnaire. In R. M. Stogdill & A. E. Coons (Eds.), *Leader behavior: Its description and measurement.* Columbus: Ohio State University, Bureau of Business Research.

Kahn, R. L. (1956). The prediction of productivity. *Journal of Social Issues, 12,* 41-49.

Katz, D., & Kahn, R. L. (1951). Human organization and worker motivation. In L. R. Tripp (Ed.), *Industrial productivity* (pp. 146-171). Madison, WI: Industrial Relations Research Association.

Likert, R. (1961). *New patterns of management.* New York: McGraw-Hill.

Likert, R. (1967). *The human organization: Its management and value.* New York: McGraw-Hill.

Misumi, J. (1985). *The behavioral science of leadership: An interdisciplinary Japanese research program.* Ann Arbor: University of Michigan Press.

Stogdill, R. M. (1948). Personal factors associated with leadership: A survey of the literature. *Journal of Psychology, 25,* 35-71.

Stogdill, R. M. (1963). *Manual for the Leader Behavior Description Questionnaire Form XII.* Columbus: Ohio State University, Bureau of Business Research.

Stogdill, R. M. (1974). *Handbook of leadership: A survey of theory and research.* New York: Free Press.

Yukl, G. (1994). *Leadership in organizations* (3rd ed.). Englewood Cliffs, NJ: Prentice Hall.

Situational Approach

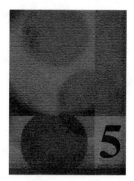

DESCRIPTION

One of the more widely recognized approaches to leadership is the situational approach, which was developed by Hersey and Blanchard (1969a) based on Reddin's (1967) 3-D management style theory. The situational approach has been refined and revised several times since its inception (see Blanchard, Zigarmi, & Nelson, 1993; Blanchard, Zigarmi, & Zigarmi, 1985; Hersey & Blanchard, 1977, 1988), and it has been used extensively in organizational leadership training and development.

As the name of the approach implies, situational leadership focuses on leadership in situations. The basic premise of the theory is that different situations demand different kinds of leadership. From this perspective, to be an effective leader requires that an individual adapt his or her style to the demands of different situations.

Situational leadership stresses that leadership is composed of both a directive and a supportive dimension, and each has to be applied appropriately in a given situation. To determine what is needed in a particular situation, a leader must evaluate her or his employees and assess how competent and committed they are to perform a given task. Based on the assumption that employees' skills and motivation vary over time, situational leadership suggests that leaders should change the degree to which they are directive or supportive to meet the changing needs of subordinates.

Figure 5.1 *Situational Leadership II*

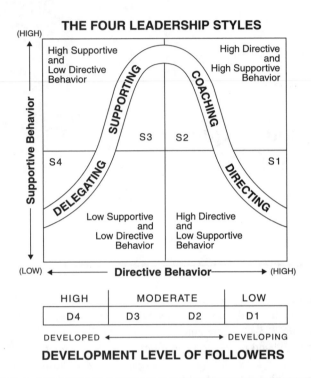

SOURCE: From *Leadership and the One Minute Manager: Increasing Effectiveness Through Situational Leadership,* by K. Blanchard, P. Zigarmi, and D. Zigarmi, 1985, New York: William Morrow. Used with permission.

In brief, the essence of situational leadership demands that a leader match his or her style to the competence and commitment of the subordinates. Effective leaders are those who can recognize what employees need and then adapt their own style to meet those needs.

The situational approach is illustrated in the model developed by Blanchard (1985) and Blanchard et al. (1985) called the Situational Leadership II (SLII) model (see Figure 5.1). The model is an extension and refinement of the original situational leadership model developed by Hersey and Blanchard (1969a).

The dynamics of situational leadership are best understood by separating the SLII model into two parts: *leadership style* and *development level of subordinates.*

Leadership Styles

Leadership style refers to the behavior pattern of an individual who attempts to influence others. It includes both *directive (task) behaviors* and *supportive (relationship) behaviors.* Directive behaviors assist group members in goal accomplishment through giving directions, establishing goals and methods of evaluation, setting time lines, defining roles, and showing how the goals are to be achieved. Directive behaviors clarify, often with one-way communication, what is to be done, how it is to be done, and who is responsible for doing it. Supportive behaviors help group members feel comfortable about themselves, their coworkers, and the situation. Supportive behaviors involve two-way communication and responses that show social and emotional support to others. Examples of supportive behaviors would be asking for input, problem solving, praising, sharing information about self, and listening. Supportive behaviors are mostly job related.

Leadership styles can be classified further into four distinct categories of directive and supportive behaviors (see Figure 5.1). The first style (S1) is a *high directive-low supportive* style, which is also referred to as a *directing* style. In this approach, the leader focuses communication on goal achievement and spends a smaller amount of time using supportive behaviors. Using this style, a leader gives instructions about what and how goals are to be achieved by the subordinates and then supervises them carefully.

The second style (S2) is called a *coaching* approach and is a *high directive-high supportive* style. In this approach, the leader focuses communication on both goal achievement and maintenance of subordinates' socioemotional needs. The coaching style requires that the leader involve himself or herself with subordinates through giving encouragement and soliciting subordinate input. However, coaching is an extension of S1 in that it still requires that the leader make the final decision on the what and how of goal accomplishment.

Style 3 (S3) is a *supporting* approach that requires that the leader take a *high supportive-low directive* style. In this approach, the leader does not focus exclusively on goals but uses supportive behaviors that bring out the employees' skills around the task to be accomplished. The supportive style includes listening, praising, asking for input, and giving feedback. A leader using this style gives subordinates control for day-to-day decisions but remains available to facilitate problem solving. An S3 leader is quick to give recognition and social support to subordinates.

Last, Style 4 (S4) is called the *low supportive-low directive* style, a *delegating* approach. In this approach, the leader offers less task input and social support, facilitating employees' confidence and motivation in reference to the task. The delegative leader lessens his or her involvement in planning, control of details, and goal clarification. After agreeing on the definition of what they are to do, this style lets subordinates take responsibility for getting the job done the way they see fit. A leader using S4 gives control over to subordinates and also refrains from intervening with unnecessary social support.

The SLII model (see Figure 5.1) illustrates how directive and supportive leadership behaviors combine for each of the four different leadership styles. As shown by the arrows on the bottom and left side of the model, directive behaviors are high in the S1 and S2 quadrants and low in S3 and S4, whereas supportive behaviors are high in S2 and S3 and low in S1 and S4.

Development Levels

A second major part of the situational leadership model is concerned with the development level of subordinates. Development level refers to the degree to which subordinates have the competence and commitment necessary to accomplish a given task or activity (Blanchard et al., 1985). Stated another way, it refers to whether a person has mastered the skills to do a specific task and whether a person has developed a positive attitude regarding the task (Blanchard et al., 1993). Employees are at a high development level if they are interested and confident in their work and they know how to do the task. Employees are at a low development level if they have little skill for the task at hand but feel as if they have the motivation or confidence to get the job done.

The levels of development are illustrated in the lower portion of the diagram in Figure 5.1. The levels describe various combinations of commitment and competence for employees on a given task. They are intended to be task specific and are not intended to be used for the purpose of labeling employees.

On a particular task, employees can be classified into four categories: D1, D2, D3, and D4, from low development to high development. Specifically, D1 employees are low in competence and high in commitment. They are new to a task and do not know exactly how to do it, but they are excited about the challenge of it. D2 employees are described as having some competence but low commitment. They have started to learn a job but they also have lost some of their initial motivation about the job. D3 represents employees who have moderate to high competence but may lack commitment. They have essentially developed the skills for the job, but they are uncertain as to whether they can accomplish the task by themselves. Finally, D4 employees are the highest in development, having both a high degree of competence and a high degree of commitment to getting the job done. They have the skills to do the job and the motivation to get it accomplished.

HOW DOES THE SITUATIONAL APPROACH WORK?

The situational approach is constructed around the idea that employees move forward and backward along the developmental continuum—a continuum that represents the relative competence and commitment of subordinates. For leaders to be effective, it is essential that they diagnose where subordinates are on the developmental continuum and adapt their leadership styles so they directly match their style to the development level of subordinates.

In a given situation, the first task for a leader is to diagnose the nature of the situation. Questions such as the following need to be addressed: What is the task that subordinates are being asked to perform? How complicated is the task? Are the subordinates sufficiently skilled to accomplish the task? Do they have the desire to complete the job once they start it? Answers to these questions will help leaders to identify correctly the specific developmental level at which their subordinates are functioning. For example, new employees who are very excited but lack understanding of job requirements would be identified as D1-level employees. Conversely, seasoned workers with proven abilities and great devotion to a company would be identified as functioning at the D4 level.

Having identified the correct development level, the second task for the leader is to adapt his or her style to the prescribed leadership style represented in the SLII model. There is a one-to-one relationship between the development level of subordinates (D1, D2, etc.) and the leader's style (S1, S2, etc.). For example, if subordinates are at the first level of development, D1, the leader needs to adopt a high directive and low supportive leadership style (S1). If subordinates are more advanced and at the second development level, D2, the leader needs to adopt a coaching style (S2). For each level of development there is a specific style of leadership that the leader should adopt.

Because subordinates move back and forth along the development continuum, it is imperative for leaders to be flexible in their leadership behavior. Subordinates may move from one development level to another rather quickly over a short period (e.g., a day or a week), as well as more slowly on tasks that may proceed over much longer periods of time (e.g., a month). Leaders cannot use the same style in all contexts; rather, they need to adapt their style to subordinates and their unique situations. Unlike the trait or contingency approaches, which argue a fixed style for leaders, the situational approach demands that leaders demonstrate a strong degree of flexibility.

STRENGTHS

The situational approach to leadership has several strengths, particularly for practitioners. The first strength is that it has stood the test in the marketplace. Situational leadership is well-known and frequently used for training leaders within organizations. Hersey and Blanchard (1993) reported that it has been a factor in training programs of more than 400 of the Fortune 500 companies. It is perceived by corporations as offering a credible model for training individuals to become effective leaders.

A second strength of situational leadership is its practicality. Situational leadership is easy to understand, intuitively sensible, and easily applied in a variety of settings. Whereas some leadership approaches provide complex and sophisticated ways to assess your own leadership behavior (e.g., Vroom and Yetton's, 1973, decision-making approach), situational leadership provides a straightforward approach that is easily used. Because it is described at an abstract level that is easily grasped, the ideas behind the approach are quickly acquired. In addition, the principles suggested by situational leadership are easy to apply across a variety of settings, including work, school, and family.

Closely akin to the strength of practicality is a third strength of situational leadership: its prescriptive value. Although many theories of leadership are descriptive in nature, the situational approach is prescriptive. It tells you what you should and should not do in various contexts. For example, if your subordinates are very low in competence, situational leadership prescribes a directing style for you as the leader. If, on the other hand, your employees appear to be competent but lack confidence, the situational approach suggests that you should lead with a supporting style. These prescriptions provide leaders with a valuable set of guidelines that can facilitate and enhance leadership.

A fourth strength of situational leadership is that it emphasizes the concept of leader flexibility (Graeff, 1983; Yukl, 1989). Situational leadership stresses that leaders need to find out about their subordinates' needs and then adapt their style accordingly. Leaders cannot lead using a single style; they must be willing to change their style to meet the requirements of the situation. Situational leadership recognizes that employees act differently when doing different tasks and that they may act differently during different stages of the same task. Effective leaders are those who can change their own style based on the task requirements and the subordinates' needs—even in the middle of a project.

Finally, situational leadership reminds us to treat each subordinate differently based on the task at hand and to seek opportunities to help subordinates learn new skills and become more confident in their work (Fernandez & Vecchio, 1997; Yukl, 1998). Overall, this approach underscores that subordinates have unique needs and are deserving of our help in trying to become better at doing their work.

CRITICISMS

Despite its extensive use in leadership training and development, situational leadership does have some limitations. The following criticisms point out several weaknesses in situational leadership and help to provide a more balanced picture of the general utility of this approach in studying and practicing leadership.

The first criticism of situational leadership is that there have been only a few research studies conducted to justify the assumptions and propositions set forth by the approach. Although many doctoral dissertations address dimensions of situational leadership, most of these research studies have not been published. The lack of a strong body of research on situational leadership raises questions concerning the theoretical basis of the approach (Fernandez & Vecchio, 1997; Graeff, 1997; Vecchio & Boatwright, 2002). Can we be sure it is a valid approach? Is it certain that this approach does indeed improve performance? Does this approach compare favorably in its impact on subordinates with other leadership approaches? It is difficult to give firm answers to these questions when the testing of this approach has not resulted in a significant amount of published research findings.

A second criticism that can be directed at situational leadership concerns the ambiguous conceptualization in the model of subordinates' development levels. The authors of the model do not make clear how commitment is combined with competence to form four distinct levels of development (Graeff, 1997; Yukl, 1989). In one of the earliest versions of the model, Hersey and Blanchard (1969b) defined the four levels of commitment (maturity) as unwilling and unable (Level 1), willing and unable (Level 2), unwilling and able (Level 3), and willing and able (Level 4). Yet in a more recent version, represented by the SLII model, development level is described as high commitment and low competence in D1, low commitment and some competence in D2, variable commitment and high competence in D3, and high commitment and high competence in D4.

The authors of situational leadership do not explain the theoretical basis for these changes in the composition of each of the development levels. Furthermore, they do not provide an explanation for how competence and commitment are weighted across different development levels. As pointed out by Blanchard et al. (1993), there is a need for further research to establish how competence and commitment are conceptualized for each development level.

Closely related to the general criticism of ambiguity about subordinates' development levels is a concern with how commitment itself is conceptualized in the model. For example, Graeff (1997) suggested the conceptualization is very unclear. Blanchard et al. (1985) stated that subordinates' commitment is composed of confidence and motivation, but it is not clear how confidence and motivation combine to define commitment. According to the SLII model, commitment starts out high in D1, moves down in D2, becomes variable in D3, and then rises again in D4. Intuitively, it would appear more logical to describe subordinate commitment as existing on a continuum moving from low to moderate to high.

The argument provided by Blanchard et al. (1993) for how commitment varies in the SLII model is that subordinates usually start out motivated and eager to learn, then they may become discouraged and disillusioned, next they may begin to lack confidence or motivation, or both, and last they become highly confident and motivated. But why is this so? Why do subordinates who learn a task become less committed? Why is there a regression in commitment at development levels 2 and 3? Without research findings to substantiate the way subordinate commitment is conceptualized, this dimension of situational leadership remains unclear.

A fourth criticism of situational leadership has to do with how the model matches leader style with subordinate development level—the prescriptions of the model. To determine the validity of the prescriptions suggested by the Hersey and Blanchard approach, Vecchio (1987) conducted a study of more than 300 high school teachers and their principals. He found that newly hired teachers were more satisfied and performed better under principals who had highly structured leadership styles, but the performance of more experienced and mature teachers was unrelated to the style their principals exhibited. In essence, the Vecchio findings suggest that in terms of situational leadership, it is appropriate to match a highly structured S1 style of leadership with immature subordinates, but it is not certain whether it is appropriate to match S2, S3, and S4, respectively, with more mature subordinates. In a replication study using university employees, Fernandez and Vecchio (1997) found similar results. Taken together, these studies fail to support the basic prescriptions suggested in the situational leadership model.

A fifth criticism of situational leadership is that it fails to account for how certain demographic characteristics (e.g., education, experience, age, and gender) influence the leader-subordinate prescriptions of the model. For example, a study conducted by Vecchio and Boatwright (2002) showed that level of education and job experience were inversely related to directive leadership and not related to supportive leadership. In other words, employees with more education and more work experience desired less structure. Interestingly, age was positively related to desire for structure—the older employees desired more structure than the younger employees. In addition, their findings indicated that female and male employees had different preferences for styles of leadership. Female employees expressed a stronger preference for supportive leadership, while male employees had a stronger desire for directive leadership. These findings indicate that demographic characteristics may affect employees' preferences for a particular leadership style. However, these characteristics are not considered in the situational leadership model.

Situational leadership can also be criticized from a practical standpoint because it does not fully address the issue of one-to-one versus group leadership in an organizational setting. For example, should a leader with a group of 20 employees lead by matching her or his style to the overall development level of the group or to the development level of individual members of the group? Carew, Parisi-Carew, and Blanchard (1990) suggested that groups go through development stages that are similar to individuals', and therefore leaders should try to match their styles to the group's development level. However, if the leader matches her or his style to the mean development level of a group, how will this affect the individuals whose development levels are quite different from their colleagues? Existing research on situational leadership does not answer this question. More research is needed to explain how leaders can adapt their styles simultaneously to the development levels of individual group members and the group as a whole.

A final criticism of situational leadership can be directed at the leadership questionnaires that accompany the model. Questionnaires on situational leadership typically ask respondents to analyze various work-related situations and select the best leadership style for each situation. The questionnaires are constructed so as to force respondents to describe leadership style in terms of the specific parameters of situational leadership (i.e., directing, coaching, supporting, and delegating) rather than in terms of other leadership behaviors. Because the best answers available to respondents have been predetermined, the questionnaires are biased in favor of situational leadership (Graeff, 1983; Yukl, 1989).

APPLICATION

As we discussed earlier in the chapter, situational leadership is used in consulting because it is an approach that is easy to conceptualize and also easy to apply. The straightforward nature of situational leadership makes it practical for managers to use.

The principles of this approach can be applied at many different levels in an organization. They can apply to how a chief executive officer (CEO) of a large corporation works with her or his board of directors, and they can also apply to how a crew chief in an assembly plant leads a small group of production workers. Middle managers can use situational leadership to direct staff meetings, and heads of departments can use this approach in planning structural changes within an organization. There is not a shortage of opportunities for using situational leadership.

Situational leadership applies during the initial stages of a project when idea formation is important, as well as during the various subsequent phases of a project when issues regarding implementation are important. The fluid nature of situational leadership makes it ideal for applying to subordinates as they move forward or go backward (regress) on various projects. Because situational leadership stresses adapting to followers, it is ideal for use with followers whose commitment and competence changes over the course of a project.

Given the breadth of the situational approach, it is applicable in virtually any type of organization, at any level, for nearly all types of tasks. It is an encompassing model with a wide range of applications.

CASE STUDIES

To assist in clarifying how situational leadership can be applied in different organizational settings, you may wish to assess Case Studies 5.1, 5.2, and 5.3. For each of the cases, ask yourself what you would do if you found yourself in a similar situation. At the end of each case, there are questions that will assist you in analyzing the context from the perspective of situational leadership.

CASE 5.1

What Style Do I Use?

Bruce Cannon is the owner of a 5-year-old small plastics company that employs about 20 people. The company is composed of essentially three areas: engineering, sales, and production. For each of these areas, there is a single manager.

Rick Nakano heads up the engineering crew. He is a seasoned engineer and is the oldest employee in the company (he is 55 years old). Rick was hired because of his engineering ability and because of his experience. Prior to joining the company, Rick worked for 20 years as an engineer for

Ford Motor Company. He is perceived by his coworkers as very competent, even-tempered, and interested in the company.

Rick has been spending most of his time in recent weeks on developing a long-range plan for the company. His goal is to develop a creative model for making decisions about future expenditures for materials, equipment, plant development, and personnel. Rick feels good about the way upper management has reacted to the first drafts of his plans.

Beth Edwards heads up the sales force, which is the smallest unit in the company. Beth is the most recent hire in the company and has 15 years of sales experience in a different product area. Beth is seen by her peers as highly motivated but not too knowledgeable regarding the nature of the product the company produces. Beth's goal is to increase the company's annual sales by 30%. However, the first-quarter sales figures indicate the rate of growth to be only 2%.

Although Beth has been upbeat since the first day she walked in the door, in recent weeks there have been problems in her department. Her sales staff talks about how little she knows about the plastics industry. In discussions about new products, Beth is often confused. In addition, she has difficulty describing the company's capabilities to outside customers because she does not seem to understand fully how a plastics company of this type functions.

Steve Lynch is the manager of production and has been with the company since its inception. Steve started out with the company just out of high school, working on the line, and moved up in the company as a result of his hard work. His goal is to streamline production and decrease costs by 10%. He knows production backward and forward but is a bit apprehensive about his new role as production manager. In fact, Steve is afraid he might fail as manager. He does not know if he is ready to have others depend on him when he has always been the one depending on others. The owner, Bruce, has great faith in Steve and has had several meetings with him to clarify his role and reassure him that he can do the work. He is certain that Steve will be an outstanding production manager.

Bruce Cannon meets weekly with each of his managers to talk about how their group is fitting in with the overall company goals. In his forthcoming weekly conference, he wants to discuss with them what new procedures they could implement within their departments to improve their long-term performance. Bruce is wondering how he should approach each of his managers.

Questions

According to the basic assumptions of situational leadership,

1. Where would you place the three managers in regard to levels of development in the SLII model (see Figure 5.1)?
2. If you were Bruce Cannon, would you act the same toward each of the three managers?
3. Which conference will be the hardest for you, and which will be the easiest? Why?

CASE 5.2

Why Aren't They Listening?

Jim Anderson is a training specialist in the human resources department of a large pharmaceutical company. In response to a recent companywide survey, Jim specifically designed for the company a 6-week training program on listening and communication skills for effective management. Jim's goals for the seminar are twofold: (a) for participants to learn new communication behaviors and (b) for participants to enjoy the seminar so they will want to attend future seminars.

The first group to be offered the program was middle-level managers in research and development. This group consisted of about 25 individuals, nearly all of whom had advanced degrees. Most of this group had attended several in-house training programs in the past, so they had a sense of how the seminar would be designed and run. Because the outcomes of previous seminars had not always been very productive, many of the managers felt a little disillusioned about coming to the seminar. As one of the managers verbalized, "Here we go again—a fancy in-house training program from which we will gain nothing."

Because Jim recognized that the managers were very experienced, he did not put many restrictions on attendance and participation. He used a variety of presentation methods and actively solicited involvement from the managers in the seminar. Throughout the first two sessions, he went out of his way to be friendly with the group. He gave them frequent coffee breaks during the sessions, and during these breaks he promoted socializing and networking.

During the third session, Jim became aware of some difficulties with the seminar. Rather than the full complement of 25 managers, attendance had dropped to only about 15 managers. Although the starting time was established at 8:30, attendees had been arriving as late as 10:00. During the afternoon sessions, some of the managers were leaving the sessions to return to their offices at the company.

As he approached the fourth session, Jim was apprehensive about why things had been going poorly. He had become quite uncertain about how he should approach the group. Many questions were running through his mind. Had he treated the managers in the wrong way? Had he been too easy regarding attendance at the sessions? Should he have said something about the managers skipping out in the afternoon? Weren't the participants taking the seminar seriously? Jim was certain that the content of the seminars was innovative and substantive, but he just could not figure out what he could change to make the program more successful. He sensed that his style was not working for this group, but he didn't have a clue as to how he should change what he was doing to make the sessions better.

Questions

According to the SLII model (see Figure 5.1),

1. What style of leadership is Jim Anderson using to run the seminars?
2. At what level are the managers?
3. From a leadership perspective, what is Jim doing wrong?
4. What specific changes could Jim implement to improve the seminars?

---◆---

CASE 5.3

Getting the Message Across

Ann Caldera is the program director of a college campus radio station (WCBA) that is supported by the university. WCBA has a long history and is seen favorably by students, faculty, the board of trustees, and the people in the community.

Ann does not have a problem getting students to work at WCBA. In fact, it is one of the most sought-after university-related activities. The few students who are accepted to work at WCBA are always highly motivated because they value the opportunity to get hands-on media experience. In addition, those who are accepted also tend to be highly confident (sometimes naively so) of their own radio ability. Despite their eagerness, most of them lack a full understanding of the legal responsibilities of being on the air.

One of the biggest problems that confronts Ann every semester is how to train new students to follow the rules and procedures of WCBA when they are doing on-air announcing for news, sports, music, and other radio programs. It seems as if every semester numerous incidents arise in which an announcer violates in no small way the FCC rules for appropriate airtime communication. For example, rumor has it that one year a freshman student disc jockey on the evening shift announced that a new band was playing in town, the cover was five dollars, and everyone should go to hear the group. Making an announcement such as this is a clear violation of FCC rules—it is illegal.

Ann is frustrated with her predicament but cannot seem to figure out why it keeps occurring. She puts a lot of time and effort into helping new DJs, but they just do not seem to get the message that working at WCBA is a serious job and obeying the FCC rules is an absolute necessity. Ann is wondering if her leadership style is missing the mark.

Each semester, Ann gives the students a very complete handout on policies and procedures. In addition, she tries to get to know each of the new students personally. Because she wants everybody to be happy at WCBA, she tries very hard to build a relational climate at the station. Repeatedly, students say that Ann is the nicest adviser on campus. Because she recognizes the quality of her students, Ann lets them do mostly what they want at the station.

Questions

1. What's the problem at WCBA?
2. Using SLII as a basis, what would you advise Ann to do differently at the station?
3. Based on situational leadership, what creative schemes could she employ to reduce FCC infractions at WCBA?

———————————◆———————————

LEADERSHIP INSTRUMENT

Although different versions of instruments have been developed to measure situational leadership, nearly all of them are constructed similarly. As a rule, the questionnaires provide a series of 12 to 20 work-related situations and ask respondents to select their preferred style for each situation from four alternatives. The situations and styles are written so as to directly represent the leadership styles of the four quadrants in the model. Questionnaire responses are scored so as to give individuals information about their primary and secondary leadership style, their flexibility, and their leadership effectiveness.

The Brief Questionnaire provided in this section illustrates the way leadership style is measured in questionnaires of situational leadership. For each of the situations on the questionnaire, you have to identify the development level of the employees in the situation and then select one of the four response alternatives that indicate the style of leadership you would employ in that situation.

Expanded versions of the Brief Questionnaire provide respondents an overall profile of their leadership style. By analyzing the alternative choices a respondent makes on the questionnaire, a respondent's primary and secondary leadership styles can be determined. By analyzing the range of choices a respondent makes, leadership flexibility can be determined. Leadership effectiveness and diagnostic ability can be measured by analyzing the number of times the respondent made accurate assessments of a preferred leadership style.

In addition to these self-scored questionnaires, situational leadership also uses similar forms to tap the concurrent perceptions that bosses, associates, and followers have of an individual's leadership style. These questionnaires give an individual a wide range of feedback on his or her leadership style as well as the opportunity to compare his or her own view of leadership with the way others view him or her in a leadership role.

Situational Leadership:
A Brief Questionnaire

Instructions: Look at the four leadership situations below and indicate what the development level is in each situation, which leadership style each response represents, and which leadership style is needed in the situation—Action A, B, C, or D?

Situation 1

Because of budget restrictions imposed on your department, it is necessary to consolidate. You are thinking of asking a highly capable and experienced member of your department to take charge of the consolidation. This person has worked in all areas of your department and has the trust and respect of most of the staff. She is very willing to help with the consolidation.

    A. Assign the project to her and let her determine how to accomplish it.
    B. Assign the task to her, indicate to her precisely what must be done, and supervise her work closely.
    C. Assign the task to her and provide support and encouragement as needed.
    D. Assign the task to her and indicate to her precisely what needs to be done but make sure you incorporate her suggestions.

Development level _____ Action _____

Situation 2

You have recently been made a department head of the new regional office. In getting to know your departmental staff, you have noticed that one of your inexperienced employees is not following through on assigned tasks. She is enthusiastic about her new job and wants to get ahead in the organization.

    A. Discuss the lack of follow-through with her and explore the alternative ways this problem can be solved.
    B. Specify what she must do to complete the tasks but incorporate any suggestions she may have.
    C. Define the steps necessary to complete the assigned tasks and monitor her performance frequently.
    D. Let her know about the lack of follow-through and give her more time to improve her performance.

Development level _____ Action _____

Situation 3

Because of a new and very important unit project, for the past 3 months you have made sure that your staff members understood their responsibilities and expected level of performance, and you have supervised them closely. Due to some project setbacks recently, your staff has become somewhat discouraged. Their morale has dropped, and so has their performance.

  A. Continue to direct and closely supervise their performance.
  B. Give the group members more time to overcome the setbacks but occasionally check their progress.
  C. Continue to define group activities, but involve the group members more in decision making and incorporate their ideas.
  D. Participate in their problem-solving activities and encourage and support their efforts to overcome the project setbacks.

Development level _____   Action _____

Situation 4

As a director of the sales department, you have asked a member of your staff to take charge of a new sales campaign. You have worked with this person on other sales campaigns, and you know he has the job knowledge and experience to be successful at new assignments. However, he seems a little unsure about his ability to do the job.

  A. Assign the new sales campaign to him and let him function on his own.
  B. Set goals and objectives for this new assignment but consider his suggestions and involve him in decision making.
  C. Listen to his concerns but assure him he can do the job and support his efforts.
  D. Tell him exactly what the new campaign involves, what you expect of him, and supervise his performance closely.

Development level _____   Action _____

SOURCE: Adapted from *Game Plan for Leadership and the One Minute Manager* (Figure 5.20, Learning Activity, p. 5), by K. Blanchard, P. Zigarmi, and D. Zigarmi, 1992, Escondido, CA: Blanchard Training and Development (phone: 619-489-5005). Used with permission.

Scoring Interpretation

A brief discussion of the correct answers to the Brief Questionnaire will help to explain the nature of situational leadership questionnaires.

Situation 1 in the Brief Questionnaire describes a common problem faced by organizations during downsizing: having to consolidate. In this particular situation, the leader has identified an individual to direct the downsizing project who appears to be highly competent, experienced, and motivated. According to the SLII model, this individual is at developmental level 4, which would require a delegative approach. Of the four response alternatives, it is the (A) response, "Assign the project to her and let her determine how to accomplish it," that best represents *delegating* (S4)—low supportive and low directive leadership.

Situation 2 describes a problem familiar to leaders at all levels in nearly all organizations. It is the problem of lack of follow-through by an enthusiastic employee. In the given example, the described employee would fall in developmental level 1 because she lacks the experience to do the job even though she is highly motivated to succeed. The SLII approach prescribes *directing* (S1) leadership for this type of employee. She needs to be told when and how to do her specific job. After being given directions, her performance needs to be closely supervised. The correct response is (C), "Define the steps necessary to complete the assigned tasks and monitor her performance frequently."

Situation 3 describes a quite different circumstance. In this situation, the employees seem to have developed some experience and an understanding of what is required of them, but they have lost some of their motivation to complete the task. Their performance and commitment have stalled because of recent setbacks even though the leader has been directing them closely. According to SLII, the correct response for the leader is to shift to a more supportive *coaching* style (S2) of leadership. The action response that reflects coaching is (C), "Continue to define group activities, but involve the group members more in decision making and incorporate their ideas."

Situation 4 describes some of the concerns that arise for a director when attempting to identify the correct person to head up a new sales campaign. The person identified by the director for the position obviously has the skills necessary to do a good job with the new sales campaign, but he appears apprehensive about his own abilities. In this context, SLII suggests that the director should employ a *supportive* style (S3), which is consistent with leading employees who are competent but lacking a certain degree of confidence. A supportive style is represented by action response (C), "Listen to his concerns but assure him he can do the job and support his efforts."

Now select two employees. Diagnose their current development level on three different tasks and your style of leadership in each situation. Is there a match? If not, what specifically can you do for them as a leader to ensure that they have what they need to succeed?

SUMMARY

Situational leadership is a prescriptive approach to leadership that suggests how leaders can become effective in many different types of organizational settings involving a wide variety of organizational tasks. This approach provides a model that suggests to leaders how they should behave based on the demands of a particular situation.

Situational leadership classifies leadership into four styles: S1 is high directive-low supportive, S2 is high directive-high supportive, S3 is low directive-high supportive, and S4 is low directive-low supportive. The situational model (SLII) describes how each of the four leadership styles applies to subordinates who work at different levels of development, from D1 (low in competence and high in commitment) to D2 (moderately competent and low in commitment) to D3 (moderately competent but lacking commitment) to D4 (great deal of competence and a high degree of commitment).

Effective leadership occurs when the leader can accurately diagnose the development level of subordinates in a task situation and then exhibit the prescribed leadership style that matches that situation.

Leadership is measured in this approach through the use of questionnaires that ask individuals to assess a series of work-related situations. The questionnaires provide information about the leader's diagnostic ability, flexibility, and effectiveness. They are useful in helping leaders to learn about how they can change their leadership style to become more effective across different situations.

There are four major strengths to the situational approach. Foremost, it is an approach to leadership that is recognized by many as a standard for training leaders. Second, it is a practical approach that is easily understood and easily applied. Third, this approach sets forth a clear set of prescriptions for how leaders should act if they want to enhance their leadership effectiveness. Fourth, situational leadership recognizes and stresses that there is not one "best" style of leadership; instead, leaders need to be flexible and adapt their style to the requirements of the situation.

Criticisms of situational leadership suggest it also has limitations. Unlike many other leadership theories, this approach does not have a strong body of research findings to justify and support the theoretical underpinnings on which it stands. As a result, there is ambiguity regarding how the approach conceptualizes certain aspects of the leadership process. It is not clear in explaining how subordinates move from low development levels to high development levels, nor is it clear on how commitment changes over time for subordinates. Without the basic research findings, the validity of the basic prescriptions for matching leader styles to subordinates' development levels must be questioned. Also, the model does not address how demographic characteristics affect employees' preferences for leadership. Finally, in applying this approach, the model does not provide guidelines for how leaders use this approach in group settings as opposed to one-to-one contexts.

REFERENCES

Blanchard, K. H. (1985). *SLII: A situational approach to managing people.* Escondido, CA: Blanchard Training and Development.

Blanchard, K., Zigarmi, D., & Nelson, R. (1993). Situational leadership after 25 years: A retrospective. *Journal of Leadership Studies, 1*(1), 22-36.

Blanchard, K., Zigarmi, P., & Zigarmi, D. (1985). *Leadership and the one minute manager: Increasing effectiveness through situational leadership.* New York: William Morrow.

Blanchard, K., Zigarmi, P., & Zigarmi, D. (1992). *Game plan for leadership and the one minute manager.* Escondido, CA: Blanchard Training and Development.

Carew, P., Parisi-Carew, E., & Blanchard, K. H. (1990). *Group development and situational leadership II.* Escondido, CA: Blanchard Training and Development.

Fernandez, C. F., & Vecchio, R. P. (1997). Situational leadership theory revisited: A test of an across-jobs perspective. *Leadership Quarterly, 8*(1), 67-84.

Graeff, C. L. (1983). The situational leadership theory: A critical view. *Academy of Management Review, 8,* 285-291.

Graeff, C. L. (1997). Evolution of situational leadership theory: A critical review. *Leadership Quarterly, 8*(2), 153-170.

Hersey, P., & Blanchard, K. H. (1969a). Life-cycle theory of leadership. *Training and Development Journal, 23,* 26-34.

Hersey, P., & Blanchard, K. H. (1969b). *Management of organizational behavior: Utilizing human resources.* Englewood Cliffs, NJ: Prentice Hall.

Hersey, P., & Blanchard, K. H. (1977). *Management of organizational behavior: Utilizing human resources* (3rd ed.). Englewood Cliffs, NJ: Prentice Hall.

Hersey, P., & Blanchard, K. H. (1988). *Management of organizational behavior: Utilizing human resources* (5th ed.). Englewood Cliffs, NJ: Prentice Hall.

Hersey, P., & Blanchard, K. H. (1993). *Management of organizational behavior: Utilizing human resources* (6th ed.). Englewood Cliffs, NJ: Prentice Hall.

Reddin, W. J. (1967, April). The 3-D management style theory. *Training and Development Journal,* pp. 8-17.

Vecchio, R. P. (1987). Situational leadership theory: An examination of a prescriptive theory. *Journal of Applied Psychology, 72*(3), 444-451.

Vecchio, R. P., & Boatwright, K. J. (2002). Preferences for idealized style of supervision. *Leadership Quarterly, 13,* 327-342.

Vroom, V. H., & Yetton, P. W. (1973). *Leadership and decision-making.* Pittsburgh, PA: University of Pittsburgh Press.

Yukl, G. A. (1989). *Leadership in organizations* (2nd ed.). Englewood Cliffs, NJ: Prentice Hall.

Yukl, G. A. (1998). *Leadership in organizations* (4th ed.). Upper Saddle River, NJ: Prentice Hall.

Contingency Theory

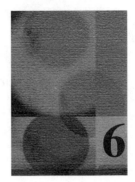

DESCRIPTION

Although several approaches to leadership could be called contingency theories, the most widely recognized is Fiedler's (1964, 1967; Fiedler & Garcia, 1987) contingency theory. Contingency theory is a *leader-match* theory (Fiedler & Chemers, 1974), which means it tries to match leaders to appropriate situations. It is called *contingency* because it suggests that a leader's effectiveness depends on how well the leader's style fits the context. To understand the performance of leaders, it is essential to understand the situations in which they lead. Effective leadership is *contingent* on matching a leader's style to the right setting.

Fiedler developed contingency theory by studying the styles of many different leaders who worked in different contexts, primarily military organizations. He assessed leaders' styles, the situations in which they worked, and whether or not they were effective. After analyzing the styles of hundreds of leaders who were both good and bad, Fiedler and his colleagues were able to make empirically grounded generalizations about which styles of leadership were best and which styles were worst for a given organizational context.

In short, contingency theory is concerned with *styles* and *situations*. It provides the framework for effectively matching the leader and the situation.

Leadership Styles

Within the framework of contingency theory, leadership styles are described as *task motivated* or *relationship motivated.* Task-motivated leaders are concerned primarily with reaching a goal, whereas relationship-motivated leaders are concerned with developing close interpersonal relations. To measure leader styles, Fiedler developed the Least Preferred Coworker (LPC) scale (see Leadership Instrument section). Leaders who score high on this scale are described as relationship motivated, and those who score low on the scale are identified as task motivated.

Situational Variables

Contingency theory suggests that situations can be characterized by assessing three factors: *leader-member relations, task structure,* and *position power* (see Figure 6.1). Leader-member relations refer to the group atmosphere and to the degree of confidence, loyalty, and attraction that followers feel for their leader. If group atmosphere is positive and subordinates trust, like, and get along with their leader, the leader-member relations are defined as good; on the other hand, if the atmosphere is unfriendly and friction exists within the group, the leader-member relations are defined as poor.

The second situational variable, task structure, refers to the degree to which the requirements of a task are clear and spelled out. Tasks that are completely structured tend to give more control to the leader, whereas vague and unclear tasks lessen the leader's control and influence. A task is considered structured when (a) the requirements of the task are clearly stated and known by the individuals required to perform them, (b) the path to accomplishing the task has few alternatives, (c) the completion of the task can be clearly demonstrated, and (d) only a limited number of correct solutions to the task exist. An example of a highly structured task would be cleaning the milkshake machine at McDonald's. The rules for doing it are clearly stated to the employees, there is only one way to do it, whether it has been done can be verified, and whether it has been done correctly can also be easily determined. An example of a highly unstructured task would be the task of running a fund-raiser for a local volunteer organization. Running a fund-raiser would not have any clear set of rules to follow, there would be many alternative ways of doing it, one could not verify the correctness of the way you did it, and no single best way exists to do the fund-raising.

Figure 6.1 *Contingency Model*

Leader-Member Relations	Good				Poor			
Task Structure	High Structure		Low Structure		High Structure		Low Structure	
Position Power	Strong Power	Weak Power	Strong Power	Weak Power	Strong Power	Weak Power	Strong Power	Weak Power
	1	2	3	4	5	6	7	8
Preferred Leadership Style	Low LPCs Middle LPCs				High LPCs			Low LPCs

SOURCE: Adapted from *A Theory of Leadership Effectiveness,* by F. E. Fiedler, 1967, New York: McGraw-Hill. Used by permission.

Position power, the third characteristic of situations, refers to the amount of authority a leader has to reward or to punish followers. It includes the legitimate power individuals acquire as a result of the position they hold in an organization. Position power is strong if an individual has the authority to hire and fire or give raises in rank or pay; it is weak if a leader does not have the right to do these things.

Together, these three situational factors determine the favorableness of various situations in organizations. Situations that are rated most favorable are those having good leader-follower relations, defined tasks, and strong leader position power. Situations that are rated least favorable have poor leader-follower relations, unstructured tasks, and weak leader position power. Situations that are rated moderately favorable fall in between these two extremes.

Based on research findings, contingency theory posits that certain styles will be effective in certain situations. Individuals who are task motivated (low LPC score) will be effective in both very favorable and in very unfavorable situations, that is, in situations that are going along very smoothly or when things are out of control. Individuals who are relationship motivated (high LPC score) will be effective in moderately favorable situations, that is, in situations in which there is some degree of certainty but things are neither completely under their control nor out of their control.

It is not entirely clear why leaders with high LPC scores are effective in moderately favorable situations or why leaders with low LPC scores are effective in both very favorable and very unfavorable situations. Fiedler's (1995) current interpretation of the theory adds a degree of clarity to this issue. He provides the following line of reasoning for why leaders who are working in the "wrong" (i.e., mismatched) situation are ineffective: (a) a leader whose LPC style does not match a particular situation experiences stress and anxiety; (b) under stress, the leader reverts to less mature ways of coping that were learned in early development; and (c) the leader's less mature coping style results in poor decision making, which results in negative work outcomes. Although various interpretations of contingency theory can be made, researchers are still unclear regarding the inner workings of the theory.

HOW DOES CONTINGENCY THEORY WORK?

By measuring a leader's LPC score and the three situational variables, one can predict whether or not a leader is going to be effective in a particular setting. The relationship between a leader's style and various types of situations is illustrated in Figure 6.1. The figure is best understood by interpreting the rows from top to bottom. For example, a situation that has good leader-member relations, a structured task, and strong position power would fall in Category 1 of preferred leadership style. Or a situation that has poor leader-member relations, a structured task, and weak position power would fall in Category 6 of leadership style. By assessing the three situational variables, any organizational context can be placed in one of the eight categories represented in Figure 6.1.

Once the nature of the situation is determined, the fit between the leader's style and the situation can be evaluated. The figure indicates that low LPCs (low LPC score) are effective in Categories 1, 2, 3, and 8, while high LPCs (high LPC score) are effective in Categories 4, 5, 6, and 7. Middle LPCs are effective in Categories 1, 2, and 3. If an individual's style matches the appropriate category in the model, the leader will be effective; if the individual's style does not match the category, that leader will not be effective.

It is important to point out that contingency theory stresses that leaders will not be effective in all situations. If your style is a good match for the situation in which you work, you will be good at the job; if your style does not match the situation, you will most likely fail.

STRENGTHS

Contingency theory has several major strengths. First, it is a theory that is supported by a great deal of empirical research (see Peters, Hartke, & Pohlman, 1985; Strube & Garcia, 1981). In an era in which popular newsstand accounts of "how to be a successful leader" abound, contingency theory offers an approach to leadership that has a long tradition. Many researchers have tested it and have found it to be a valid and reliable approach to explaining how effective leadership can be achieved. Contingency theory is grounded in research.

Second, contingency theory has broadened our understanding of leadership by forcing us to consider the impact of situations on leaders. Before contingency theory was developed, leadership theories focused on whether there was a single, best type of leadership (e.g., trait approach). Contingency theory, however, emphasized the importance of focusing on the relationship between the leader's style and the demands of various situations. In essence, contingency theory shifted the emphasis to leadership contexts, particularly the link between the leader and situations.

Third, contingency theory is predictive and therefore provides useful information regarding the type of leadership that will most likely be effective in certain contexts. From the data provided by the LPC scale and the descriptions of three aspects of a situation (i.e., leader-member relations, task structure, and position power), it is possible to determine the probability of success for a given individual in a given situation. This gives contingency theory predictive power that other leadership theories do not have.

Fourth, this theory is advantageous because it does not require that people be effective in all situations. So often leaders in organizations feel the need to be all things to all people, which may be asking too much of leaders. Contingency theory argues that leaders should not expect to be able to lead in every situation. Companies should try to place leaders in optimal situations, in situations that are ideal for their leadership style. When it is obvious that leaders are in the wrong situation, efforts should be made to change the work variables or move the leader to another context. Contingency theory matches the leader and the situation but does not demand that the leader fit every situation.

Fifth, contingency theory provides data on leaders' styles that could be useful to organizations in developing leadership profiles. The LPC score is one piece of information that could be used, along with other assessments in human resource planning, to develop profiles on individuals to determine how and where they would best serve an organization.

CRITICISMS

Although many studies underscore the validity of contingency theory, it has also received much criticism in the research literature. A brief discussion of these criticisms will help to clarify the overall value of contingency theory as a leadership theory.

First, contingency theory has been criticized because it fails to explain fully why individuals with certain leadership styles are more effective in some situations than in others. Fiedler (1993) calls this a "black box" problem because a level of mystery remains about why task-motivated leaders are good in extreme settings and relationship-motivated leaders are good in moderately favorable settings.

The answer provided by the theory for why individuals with low LPC scores are effective in extremes is that these individuals feel more certain in contexts where they have a lot of control and they feel comfortable strongly exerting themselves. On the other hand, high LPCs are not effective in extreme situations because when they have a lot of control they overreact; in situations in which they have little control, they tend to focus so much on relationships that they fail to do the task. In moderate situations, high LPCs are effective because they are allowed to focus on relationship issues, whereas low LPCs feel frustrated because of the lack of certainty. Because critics find these explanations somewhat inadequate, contingency theory is often challenged.

A second major criticism of this theory concerns the LPC scale. The LPC scale has been questioned because it does not seem valid on the surface, it does not correlate well with other standard leadership measures (Fiedler, 1993), and it is not easy to complete correctly.

The LPC scale measures a person's leadership style by asking the person to characterize another person's behavior. Because projection is involved in the measure, it is difficult for respondents to understand how their descriptions of another individual on the scale are a reflection of their own leadership style. It does not make sense on the surface to measure your style through your evaluations of another person's style.

Although it may not be adequate for many people, the answer to this criticism is that the LPC scale is a measure of an individual's motivational hierarchy. Those individuals who are highly task motivated see their least preferred coworker in a very negative light because that person gets in the way of their own accomplishment of a task. The primary need for these people is to get the job done, and only their secondary needs shift toward people issues. On the other hand, individuals who are relationship motivated see their least preferred coworker in more positive terms because their primary need motivation is to get along with people, and only their secondary needs revolve around tasks. In short, the LPC scale measures a respondent's style by assessing the degree to which the respondent sees another person getting in the way of his or her own goal accomplishment.

Although it takes only a few minutes to complete, the instructions on the LPC scale are not clear; they do not fully explain how the respondent is to select his or her least preferred coworker. Some respondents may get confused between an individual who is their least liked coworker and their least preferred coworker. Because their final LPC score is predicated on who they choose as a least preferred coworker, the lack of clear directions on who to choose as a least preferred coworker makes the LPC measure problematic.

Although Fiedler and his colleagues have research to back up the test-retest reliability of the LPC scale (Fiedler & Garcia, 1987), the scale remains suspect for many practitioners because it lacks face validity.

Another criticism of contingency theory is that it is cumbersome to use in real-world settings. It is cumbersome because it requires assessing the leader's style as well as three relatively complex situational variables (leader-member relations, task structure, and position power), each of which requires a different instrument. Administering a battery of questionnaires in ongoing organizations can be difficult because it breaks up the normal flow of organizational communication and operations.

A final criticism of contingency theory is that it fails to explain adequately what organizations should do when there is a mismatch between the leader and the situation in the workplace. Because it is a personality theory, contingency theory does not advocate teaching leaders how to adapt their styles to various situations as a means to improve leadership in an organization. Rather, this approach advocates that leaders engage in situational engineering, which means in essence changing situations to fit the leader. Although Fiedler and his colleagues argue that most situations can be changed in one respect or another to fit the leader's style, the prescriptions for how one engages in situational engineering are not clearly set forth in the theory.

In fact, situations are not always easily changed to match the leader's style. For example, if a leader's style does not match an unstructured, low-power situation, it may be impossible to make the task more structured and increase the position power to fit the leader's style. Similarly, progression up the management ladder in organizations may mean that a leader moves into a new situation in which her or his style does not fit. For example, a manager with a high LPC (relationship motivated) score might receive a promotion that places her in a context that has good leader-member relations, task structure, and position power, thus rendering her ineffective according to contingency theory. Certainly, it would be questionable for a company to change this situation that otherwise would be labeled nearly ideal in most ways. Overall, changing the situations can result in positive outcomes, but this does present significant workability problems for organizations.

APPLICATION

Contingency theory has many applications in the organizational world—it can be used to answer a host of questions about the leadership of individuals within various types of organizations. For example, it can be used to explain why an individual is ineffective in a particular position even though the person is a conscientious, loyal, and hard-working manager. Also, the theory can be used to predict whether an individual who has worked well in one position within an organization will be equally effective if moved into another quite different position within the same company. Furthermore, contingency theory can point to changes that upper management might like to make in a lower-level position in order to guarantee a good fit between an existing manager and a particular work context. These are just a few of the ways that this theory could be applied in organizational settings.

CASE STUDIES

The following three case studies (Cases 6.1, 6.2, and 6.3) provide leadership situations that can be analyzed and evaluated from the perspective of contingency theory. As you read the cases, try to diagnose them using the principles of contingency theory. It will be helpful to try to categorize each case using information provided in Figure 6.1. At the end of each case, there is a series of questions that will assist your analysis of the case.

CASE 6.1

No Control Over the Student Council

Tamara Popovich has been elected president of the student council at the local college she attends. She likes the other council members, and they seem to like her. Her first job as president of the council is to develop a new policy for student computer fees. Because this is the first year that computer fees are being assessed, there are no specific guidelines for what should be included in this policy. Because the council members are elected by the student body, Tamara has no control over how they work. She has no way of rewarding or punishing them. In a leadership course Tamara took, she filled out the LPC questionnaire and her score was 98.

Questions

1. How will Tamara do as president of the student council?
2. According to her LPC score, what are her primary needs?
3. How will these needs affect her ability to develop the new policy for computer fees?
4. How can Tamara change the situation to match her management style?

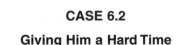

CASE 6.2

Giving Him a Hard Time

Bill Smith has been the high school band teacher for 15 years. Every year, he is in charge of planning and conducting a different type of concert for the holidays. This year, his plan is to present a special jazz program in conjunction with the senior choir. For some reason, the band and choir members have it in for Bill and are constantly giving him trouble. Band and choir are extracurricular activities in which students volunteer to participate. While taking a management class at a local university, Bill took the LPC scale and his score was 44.

Questions

According to Figure 6.1,

1. What category does this situation fall into?
2. Will Bill be successful in his efforts to run the holiday program?
3. Should the school administration make any changes regarding Bill's position?

CASE 6.3

What's the Best Leader Match?

Universal Drugs is a family-owned pharmaceutical company that manufactures generic drugs such as aspirin and vitamin pills. The owners of the company have expressed a strong interest in making the management of the company, which traditionally has been very authoritarian, more teamwork oriented.

To design and implement the new management structure, the owners have decided to create a new position. The person in this position would report directly to the owners and have complete freedom to conduct performance reviews of all managers directly involved in the new system.

Two employees from within the company have applied for the new position.

Mrs. Lee has been with Universal for 15 years and has been voted by her peers most outstanding manager three different times. She is friendly, honest, and extremely conscientious about reaching short-term and long-term goals. When given the LPC scale by the personnel department, Mrs. Lee received a score of 52.

Mr. Washington came to Universal 5 years ago with an advanced degree in organizational development. He is presently director of training, where all of his subordinates say he is the most caring manager they have ever had. While at Universal, Mr. Washington has built a reputation for being a real people person. Reflecting his reputation is his score on the LPC scale, an 89.

Questions

According to contingency theory,

1. Which of the two applicants should the new owner choose to head up the new management structure? Why?
2. Could the owner define the new position, according to contingency theory, in such a way that it would qualify one of the applicants better than the other?
3. Will Universal Drugs benefit by using contingency theory in its decision making regarding its new management structure?

————————————◆————————————

LEADERSHIP INSTRUMENT

The LPC scale is used in contingency theory to measure a person's leadership style. For example, it measures your style by having you describe a coworker with whom you had difficulty completing a job. This does not need to be a coworker you disliked a great deal, but rather someone with whom you least like to work. After you have selected this individual, the LPC instrument asks you to describe your coworker on 18 sets of adjectives.

Low LPCs are task motivated. They are individuals whose primary needs are to accomplish tasks and whose secondary needs are focused on getting along with people. In a work setting, they are concerned with achieving success on assigned tasks, even if at the cost of having poor interpersonal relationships with coworkers. Low LPCs gain self-esteem through achieving their goals. They attend to interpersonal relationships, but only after they first have directed themselves toward the tasks of the group.

Middle LPCs are socio-independent leaders. In the context of work, they are self-directed and not overly concerned with the task or with how others view them. They are more removed from the situation and act more independent than low or high LPCs.

High LPCs are motivated by relationships. These individuals derive their major satisfaction in an organization from interpersonal relationships. A high LPC sees positive qualities even in the coworker she or he least prefers, even though the high LPC does not work well with that person. In an organizational setting, the high LPC attends to tasks, but only after she or he is certain that the relationships between people are in good shape.

Least Preferred Coworker (LPC) Measure

Instructions: Think of the person with whom you can work least well. He or she may be someone you work with now or someone you knew in the past. He or she does not have to be the person you like the least but should be the person with whom you had the most difficulty in getting a job done. Describe this person as he or she appears to you.

Scoring

Pleasant									Unpleasant	____
	8	7	6	5	4	3	2	1		
Friendly									Unfriendly	____
	8	7	6	5	4	3	2	1		
Rejecting									Accepting	____
	1	2	3	4	5	6	7	8		
Tense									Relaxed	____
	1	2	3	4	5	6	7	8		
Distant									Close	____
	1	2	3	4	5	6	7	8		
Cold									Warm	____
	1	2	3	4	5	6	7	8		
Supportive									Hostile	____
	8	7	6	5	4	3	2	1		
Boring									Interesting	____
	1	2	3	4	5	6	7	8		
Quarrelsome									Harmonious	____
	1	2	3	4	5	6	7	8		
Gloomy									Cheerful	____
	1	2	3	4	5	6	7	8		
Open									Closed	____
	8	7	6	5	4	3	2	1		
Backbiting									Loyal	____
	1	2	3	4	5	6	7	8		
Untrustworthy									Trustworthy	____
	1	2	3	4	5	6	7	8		
Considerate									Inconsiderate	____
	8	7	6	5	4	3	2	1		
Nasty									Nice	____
	1	2	3	4	5	6	7	8		
Agreeable									Disagreeable	____
	8	7	6	5	4	3	2	1		
Insincere									Sincere	____
	1	2	3	4	5	6	7	8		
Kind									Unkind	____
	8	7	6	5	4	3	2	1		
									Total	____

SOURCE: Adapted from *Improving Leadership Effectiveness: The Leader Match Concept* (2nd ed.), by F. E. Fiedler and M. M. Chemers, 1984, New York: John Wiley. Copyright 1984. Reprinted by permission of John Wiley & Sons, Inc.

Scoring Interpretation

Your final LPC score is determined by adding up the numbers you circled on all of the 18 scales.

If your score is 57 or below, you are a low LPC, which suggests that you are task motivated. If your score is within the range of 58 to 63, you are a middle LPC, which means you are independent. Individuals who score 64 or above are called high LPCs, and they are thought to be more relationship motivated.

Because the LPC is a personality measure, the score you get on the LPC scale is believed to be quite stable over time and not easily changed. Low LPCs tend to remain low, moderate LPCs tend to remain moderate, and high LPCs tend to remain high. As was pointed out earlier in the chapter, research shows that the test-retest reliability of the LPC is very strong (Fiedler & Garcia, 1987).

◆

SUMMARY

Contingency theory represents a shift in leadership research from focusing on only the leader to looking at the leader in conjunction with the situation in which the leader works. It is a leader-match theory that emphasizes the importance of matching a leader's style with the demands of a situation.

To measure leadership style, a personality-like measure called the Least Preferred Coworker (LPC) scale is used. It delineates individuals who are highly task motivated (low LPCs), those who are socio-independent (middle LPCs), and those who are relationship motivated (high LPCs).

To measure situations, three variables are assessed: leader-member relations, task structure, and position power. Taken together, these variables point to the style of leadership that has the best chance of being successful. In general, contingency theory suggests that low LPCs are effective in extremes and that high LPCs are effective in moderately favorable situations.

The strengths of contingency theory include that it is backed by a considerable amount of research, it is the first leadership theory to emphasize the impact of situations on leaders, it is predictive of leadership effectiveness, it allows leaders not to be effective in all situations, and it can provide useful leadership profile data.

On the negative side, contingency theory can be criticized because it has not adequately explained the link between styles and situations, and it relies heavily on the LPC scale, which has been questioned for its face validity and workability. Contingency theory is not easily used in ongoing organizations. Finally, it does not fully explain how organizations can use the results of this theory in situational engineering. Regardless of these criticisms, contingency theory has made a substantial contribution to our understanding of the leadership process.

REFERENCES

Fiedler, F. E. (1964). A contingency model of leadership effectiveness. In L. Berkowitz (Ed.), *Advances in experimental social psychology* (Vol. 1, pp. 149-190). New York: Academic Press.

Fiedler, F. E. (1967). *A theory of leadership effectiveness.* New York: McGraw-Hill.

Fiedler, F. E. (1993). The leadership situation and the black box in contingency theories. In M. M. Chemers & R. Ayman (Eds.), *Leadership, theory, and research: Perspectives and directions* (pp. 1-28). New York: Academic Press.

Fiedler, F. E. (1995). Reflections by an accidental theorist. *Leadership Quarterly, 6*(4), 453-461.

Fiedler, F. E., & Chemers, M. M. (1974). *Leadership and effective management.* Glenview, IL: Scott, Foresman.

Fiedler, F. E., & Chemers, M. M. (1984). *Improving leadership effectiveness: The leader match concept* (2nd ed.). New York: John Wiley.

Fiedler, F. E., & Garcia, J. E. (1987). *New approaches to leadership: Cognitive resources and organizational performance.* New York: John Wiley.

Peters, L. H., Hartke, D. D., & Pohlman, J. T. (1985). Fiedler's contingency theory of leadership: An application of the meta-analysis procedures of Schmidt and Hunter. *Psychological Bulletin, 97,* 274-285.

Strube, M. J., & Garcia, J. E. (1981). A meta-analytic investigation of Fiedler's contingency model of leadership effectiveness. *Psychological Bulletin, 90,* 307-321.

Path-Goal Theory

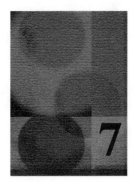

DESCRIPTION

Path-goal theory is about how leaders motivate subordinates to accomplish designated goals. Drawing heavily from research on what motivates employees, path-goal theory first appeared in the leadership literature in the early 1970s in the works of Evans (1970), House (1971), House and Dessler (1974), and House and Mitchell (1974). The stated goal of this leadership theory is to enhance employee performance and employee satisfaction by focusing on employee motivation.

In contrast to the situational approach, which suggests that a leader must adapt to the development level of subordinates (see Chapter 5), and unlike contingency theory, which emphasizes the match between the leader's style and specific situational variables (see Chapter 6), path-goal theory emphasizes the relationship between the leader's style and the characteristics of the subordinates and the work setting. The underlying assumption of path-goal theory is derived from expectancy theory, which suggests that subordinates will be motivated if they think they are capable of performing their work, if they believe their efforts will result in a certain outcome, and if they believe that the payoffs for doing their work are worthwhile.

For the leader, the challenge is to use a leadership style that best meets subordinates' motivational needs. This is done by choosing behaviors that complement or supplement what is missing in the work setting. Leaders try

Figure 7.1 *The Basic Idea Behind Path-Goal Theory*

to enhance subordinates' goal attainment by providing information or rewards in the work environment (Indvik, 1986); leaders provide subordinates with the elements they think their subordinates need to reach their goals.

According to House and Mitchell (1974), leadership generates motivation when it increases the number and kinds of payoffs that subordinates receive from their work. Leadership also motivates when it makes the path to the goal clear and easy to travel through coaching and direction, when it removes obstacles and roadblocks to attaining the goal, and when it makes the work itself more personally satisfying (see Figure 7.1).

In brief, path-goal theory is designed to explain how leaders can help subordinates along the path to their goals by selecting specific behaviors that are best suited to subordinates' needs and to the situation in which subordinates are working. By choosing the appropriate style, leaders increase subordinates' expectations for success and satisfaction.

Conceptually, path-goal theory is relatively complex; it is therefore useful to break it down into smaller units so that we can better understand the complexities of this approach.

Figure 7.2 illustrates the different components of path-goal theory, including leader behaviors, subordinate characteristics, task characteristics, and

Figure 7.2 Major Components of *Path-Goal Theory*

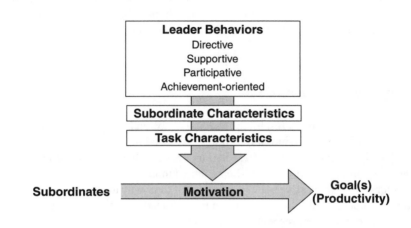

motivation. Path-goal theory suggests that each type of leader behavior has a different kind of impact on subordinates' motivation. Whether or not a particular leader behavior is motivating to subordinates is contingent on the subordinates' characteristics and the characteristics of the task.

LEADER BEHAVIORS

Although many different leadership behaviors could have been selected to be a part of path-goal theory, this approach has so far examined *directive, supportive, participative,* and *achievement-oriented* leadership behaviors (House & Mitchell, 1974, p. 83). Path-goal theory is explicitly left open to the inclusion of other variables.

Directive Leadership

Directive leadership is similar to the "initiating structure" concept described in the Ohio State studies (Halpin & Winer, 1957) and the "telling" style described in situational leadership. It characterizes a leader who gives subordinates instructions about their task, including what is expected of them, how it is to be done, and the time line for when it should be completed. A directive leader sets clear standards of performance and makes the rules and regulations clear to subordinates.

Supportive Leadership

Supportive leadership resembles the consideration behavior construct that was identified by the Ohio State studies discussed in Chapter 4. Supportive leadership refers to being friendly and approachable as a leader and includes attending to the well-being and human needs of subordinates. Leaders using supportive behaviors go out of their way to make work pleasant for subordinates. In addition, supportive leaders treat subordinates as equals and give them respect for their status.

Participative Leadership

Participative leadership refers to leaders who invite subordinates to share in the decision making. A participative leader consults with subordinates, obtains their ideas and opinions, and integrates their suggestions into the decisions regarding how the group or organization will proceed.

Achievement-Oriented Leadership

Achievement-oriented leadership is characterized by a leader who challenges subordinates to perform work at the highest level possible. This leader establishes a high standard of excellence for subordinates and seeks continuous improvement. In addition to expecting a lot from subordinates, achievement-oriented leaders show a high degree of confidence that subordinates are capable of establishing and accomplishing challenging goals.

House and Mitchell (1974) suggested that leaders may exhibit any or all of these four styles with various subordinates and in different situations. Path-goal theory is not a trait approach that locks leaders into only one kind of leadership; leaders should adapt their styles to the situation or to the motivational needs of their subordinates. For example, if subordinates need participative leadership at one point in a task and directive leadership at another, the leader can change her or his style as needed. Different situations may call for different types of leadership behavior. Furthermore, there may be instances when it is appropriate for a leader to use a blend of leadership styles that incorporates more than one style at the same time.

In addition to leader behaviors, Figure 7.2 illustrates two other major components of path-goal theory: subordinate characteristics and task characteristics. Each of these two sets of characteristics influences the way leaders' behaviors affect subordinate motivation. In other words, the impact of leadership is *contingent* on the characteristics of both subordinates and their task.

SUBORDINATE CHARACTERISTICS

Subordinate characteristics determine how a leader's behavior will be interpreted by subordinates in a given work context. Researchers have focused on subordinates' needs for affiliation, preferences for structure, desires for control, and self-perceived level of task ability. These characteristics, as well as many others, determine the degree to which subordinates find the behavior of a leader an immediate source of satisfaction or instrumental to some future satisfaction.

Path-goal theory predicts that subordinates who have strong needs for affiliation prefer supportive leadership because friendly and concerned leadership is a source of satisfaction. For subordinates who are dogmatic and authoritarian and have to work in uncertain situations, path-goal theory suggests directive leadership because that provides psychological structure and task clarity. Directive leadership helps these subordinates by clarifying the path to the goal and making it less ambiguous. The authoritarian type of individual feels more comfortable when the leader provides a greater sense of certainty in the work setting.

Subordinates' desires for control have received special attention in path-goal research through studies of a personality construct locus of control that can be subdivided into internal and external dimensions. Subordinates with internal locus of control believe that they are in charge of the things that occur in their life, while individuals with external locus of control believe that chance, fate, or outside forces are the determinants of life events. Path-goal theory suggests that for subordinates with internal locus of control, participative leadership is most satisfying because it allows subordinates to feel in charge of their work and to be an integral part of the decision-making process. For subordinates with external locus of control, the path-goal theory suggests that directive leadership is best because it parallels subordinates' feelings that outside forces control their circumstances.

Another way that leadership affects subordinates' motivation is the subordinates' perception of their own ability to perform a specific task. As subordinates' perception of their own abilities and competence goes up, the need for directive leadership goes down. In effect, directive leadership becomes redundant and perhaps excessively controlling in situations where subordinates feel competent to complete their own work.

TASK CHARACTERISTICS

In addition to subordinate characteristics, *task characteristics* also have a major impact on the way a leader's behavior influences the motivation of subordinates (see Figure 7.2). Task characteristics include the design of the subordinate's task, the formal authority system of the organization, and the primary work group of subordinates. Collectively, these characteristics in and of themselves can provide motivation for subordinates. When a situation provides a clearly structured task, strong group norms, and an established authority system, then subordinates will find the paths to desired goals apparent and will not have a need for a leader to clarify goals or to coach subordinates in how to reach these goals. Subordinates will feel as if they can accomplish their work and that their work is of value. Leadership in these types of contexts could be seen as unnecessary, unempathic, and excessively controlling.

In some situations, however, the task characteristics may call for leadership involvement. Tasks that are unclear and ambiguous call for leadership input that provides structure. Also, tasks that are highly repetitive require leadership that gives support in order to maintain subordinates' motivation. In work settings where the formal authority system is weak, leadership becomes a tool that helps subordinates by making the rules and work requirements clear. In contexts where the group norms are weak or nonsupportive, leadership assists in building cohesiveness and role responsibility.

A special focus of path-goal theory is on helping subordinates to overcome obstacles. Obstacles could be just about anything in the work setting that gets in the way of subordinates. Specifically, obstacles create excessive uncertainties, frustrations, or threats for subordinates. In these settings, path-goal theory suggests that it is the leader's responsibility to help subordinates by removing these obstacles or helping them around them. Assisting subordinates around these obstacles will increase subordinates' expectations to complete the task and increase their sense of job satisfaction.

In 1996, House published a reformulated path-goal theory that extends his original work to include eight classes of leadership behaviors. Besides the four leadership behaviors discussed previously in this chapter, (a) directive, (b) supportive, (c) participative, and (d) achievement-oriented behavior, the new theory adds (e) work facilitation, (f) group-oriented decision process, (g) work-group representation and networking, and (h) value-based leader behavior. The essence of the new theory is the same as the original: To be effective, leaders need to help subordinates by giving them what is missing in their environment and by helping them compensate for deficiencies in their abilities.

HOW DOES PATH-GOAL THEORY WORK?

Path-goal theory is an approach to leadership that is theoretically complex but also pragmatic. In theory, it provides a set of assumptions about how various leadership styles will interact with characteristics of subordinates and the work setting to affect the motivation of subordinates. In practice, the theory provides direction about how leaders can help subordinates to accomplish their work in a satisfactory manner. Table 7.1 illustrates how leader behaviors are related to subordinate and task characteristics in path-goal theory.

Theoretically, the path-goal approach suggests that leaders need to choose a leadership style that best fits the needs of subordinates and the work they are doing. The theory predicts that a directive style of leadership is best in situations in which subordinates are dogmatic and authoritarian, the task demands are ambiguous, and the organizational rules and procedures are unclear. In these situations, directive leadership complements the work by providing guidance and psychological structure for subordinates (House & Mitchell, 1974, p. 90).

For work that is structured, unsatisfying, or frustrating, path-goal theory suggests that leaders should use a supportive style. The supportive style provides what is missing by giving nurturance to subordinates when

Table 7.1 *Path-Goal Theory: How it Works*

LEADER BEHAVIOR	GROUP MEMBERS	TASK CHARACTERISTICS
DIRECTIVE LEADERSHIP *"Provides guidance and psychological structure"*	Dogmatic Authoritarian	Ambiguous Unclear rules Complex
SUPPORTIVE LEADERSHIP *"Provides nurturance"*	Unsatisfied Need affiliation Need human touch	Repetitive Unchallenging Mundane and mechanical
PARTICIPATIVE *"Provides involvement"*	Autonomous Need for control Need for clarity	Ambiguous Unclear Unstructured
ACHIEVEMENT ORIENTED *"Provides challenges"*	High expectations Need to excel	Ambiguous Challenging Complex

they are engaged in tasks that are repetitive and unchallenging. Supportive leadership offers a sense of "human touch" for subordinates engaged in mundane mechanized activity.

Participative leadership is considered best when a task is ambiguous because participation gives greater clarity to how certain paths lead to certain goals—it helps subordinates to learn what leads to what (House & Mitchell, 1974, p. 92). In addition, participative leadership has a positive impact when subordinates are autonomous and have a strong need for control, because this kind of subordinate responds favorably to being involved in decision making and in the structuring of work.

Furthermore, path-goal theory predicts that achievement-oriented leadership is most effective in settings in which subordinates are required to perform ambiguous tasks. In settings such as these, leaders who challenge and set high standards for subordinates raise subordinates' confidence that they have the ability to reach their goals. In effect, achievement-oriented leadership helps subordinates feel that their efforts will result in effective performance. In settings where the task is more structured and less ambiguous, however, achievement-oriented leadership appears to be unrelated to subordinates' expectations about their work efforts.

Pragmatically, path-goal theory is straightforward. An effective leader has to attend to the needs of subordinates. The leader should help subordinates to define their goals and the paths they wish to take in reaching those goals. When obstacles arise, the leader needs to help subordinates confront them. This may mean helping the subordinate around the obstacle or it may mean removing the obstacle. The leader's job is to help subordinates reach their goals by directing, guiding, and coaching them along the way.

STRENGTHS

Path-goal theory is an approach to leadership that has several positive features. First, path-goal theory provides a useful theoretical framework for understanding how various leadership behaviors affect the satisfaction of subordinates and their work performance. It was one of the first theories to specify four conceptually distinct varieties of leadership (e.g., directive, supportive, participative, and achievement oriented), expanding the focus of prior research, which dealt exclusively with task- and relationship-oriented behaviors (Jermier, 1996). The path-goal approach was also one of the first situational/contingency theories of leadership to explain how task and subordinate characteristics affect the impact of leadership on subordinate performance. The framework provided in path-goal theory informs leaders about how to choose an appropriate leadership style based on the various demands of the task and the type of subordinates being asked to do the task.

A second positive feature of path-goal theory is that it attempts to integrate the motivation principles of expectancy theory into a theory of leadership. This makes path-goal theory unique because no other leadership approach deals directly with motivation in this way. Path-goal theory forces us continually to ask questions such as these about subordinate motivation: How can I motivate subordinates to feel that they have the ability to do the work? How can I help them feel that if they successfully do their work, they will be rewarded? What can I do to improve the payoffs that subordinates expect from their work? Path-goal theory is designed to keep these kinds of questions, which address issues of motivation, at the forefront of the leader's mind.

A third strength, and perhaps its greatest, is that path-goal theory provides a model that in certain ways is very practical. The representation of the model (see Figure 7.1) underscores and highlights the important ways leaders help subordinates. It shouts out, in essence, for leaders to clarify the paths to the goals and remove or help subordinates around the obstacles to the goals. In its simplest form, the theory reminds leaders that the over-arching purpose of leadership is to guide and coach subordinates as they move along the path to achieve a goal.

CRITICISMS

Although path-goal theory has various strengths, it also has several identi-fiable weaknesses. First, path-goal theory is so complex and incorporates so many different aspects of leadership that interpreting the meaning of the theory can be confusing. For example, path-goal theory makes predictions about which of four different leadership styles is appropriate for tasks with different degrees of structure, for goals with different levels of clarity, for workers at different levels of ability, and for organizations with different degrees of formal authority. To say the least, it is a daunting task to incor-porate all of these factors simultaneously into one's selection of a preferred leadership style. Because the scope of path-goal theory is so broad and encompasses so many different interrelated sets of assumptions, it is diffi-cult to use this theory fully in trying to improve the leadership process in a given organizational context.

A second limitation of path-goal theory is that it has received only partial support from the many empirical research studies that have been conducted to test its validity (House & Mitchell, 1974; Indvik, 1986; Schriesheim & Kerr, 1977; Schriesheim & Schriesheim, 1980; Stinson & Johnson, 1975; Wofford & Liska, 1993). For example, some research sup-ports the prediction that leader directiveness is positively related to worker satisfaction when tasks are ambiguous, but other research has failed to confirm this relationship. Furthermore, not all aspects of the theory have been given equal attention. There has been a great deal of research designed to study directive and supportive leadership and only a limited number of studies that address participative and achievement leadership. The claims of path-goal theory remain tentative because the research find-ings to date do not provide a full and consistent picture of the basic assumptions and corollaries of path-goal theory (Evans, 1996; Jermier, 1996; Schriesheim & Neider, 1996).

Another criticism of path-goal theory is that it fails to explain adequately the relationship between leadership behavior and worker motivation. Path-goal theory is unique because it incorporates the tenets of expectancy theory; however, it must be criticized because it does not go far enough in explicating how leadership is related to these tenets. The principles of expectancy theory suggest that subordinates will be motivated if they feel competent and trust that their efforts will get results, but path-goal theory does not describe how a leader could employ various styles directly to assist subordinates to feel competent or assured of success. For example, path-goal theory does not explain how directive leadership during ambiguous tasks increases subordinate motivation. Similarly, it does not explain how supportive leadership during tedious work relates to subordinate motivation. The result is that the practitioner is left with an inadequate understanding of how her or his leadership will affect subordinates' expectations about their work.

A final criticism that can be made of path-goal theory concerns a practical outcome of the theory. Path-goal theory suggests that it is important for leaders to provide coaching, guidance, and direction for subordinates; to help subordinates to define and clarify goals; and to help subordinates around obstacles as they attempt to reach their goals. In effect, this approach treats leadership as a one-way event—the leader affects the subordinate. The potential difficulty in this type of "helping" leadership is that subordinates may easily become dependent on the leader to accomplish their work. Path-goal theory places a great deal of responsibility on leaders and much less on subordinates. Over time, this kind of leadership could be counterproductive because it promotes dependency and fails to recognize the full abilities of subordinates.

APPLICATION

Path-goal theory is not an approach to leadership for which many management training programs have been developed. Nor will you find many seminars with titles such as "Improving Your Path-Goal Leadership" or "Assessing Your Skills in Path-Goal Leadership." Nevertheless, path-goal theory does offer significant insights that can be applied in ongoing settings to improve one's leadership.

Path-goal theory provides a set of general recommendations based on the characteristics of subordinates and tasks for how leaders should act in various situations if they want to be effective. It informs us about when to be directive, supportive, participative, or achievement oriented. For instance, the theory suggests that leaders should be directive when tasks are complex, and when tasks are dull the leader should give support. Similarly, it suggests that leaders be participative when subordinates need control, and that leaders should be achievement oriented when subordinates have needs to excel. In a general way, path-goal theory offers leaders a road map that gives directions about ways to improve subordinate satisfaction and performance.

The principles of path-goal theory can be employed by leaders at all levels within the organization as well as for all types of tasks. To apply path-goal theory, a leader must carefully assess his or her subordinates and their tasks and then choose an appropriate leadership style to match those characteristics. If subordinates are feeling insecure about doing a task, the leader needs to adopt a style that builds subordinate confidence. For example, in a university setting where a junior faculty member feels apprehensive about his or her teaching and research, a department chair should give supportive leadership. By giving care and support, the chair helps the junior faculty member gain a sense of confidence about his or her ability to perform the work (Bess & Goldman, 2001). If subordinates are uncertain if their efforts will result in reaching their goals, the leader needs to prove to them that their efforts will be rewarded. As discussed earlier in the chapter, path-goal theory is useful because it continually reminds leaders that their central purpose as a leader is to help subordinates define their goals and then to help subordinates reach their goals in the most efficient manner.

CASE STUDIES

The following cases provide descriptions of various situations in which a leader is attempting to apply path-goal theory. Two of the cases, Cases 7.1 and 7.2, are from traditional business contexts; the third, Case 7.3, is from an informal social organization. As you read the cases, try to apply the principles of path-goal theory to determine the degree to which you think the leaders in the cases have done a good job of using this theory.

CASE 7.1

Three Shifts, Three Supervisors

Brako is a small manufacturing company that produces parts for the automobile industry. The company has several patents on parts that fit in the brake assembly of nearly all domestic and foreign cars. Each year, the company produces 3 million parts that it ships to assembly plants throughout the world. To produce the parts, Brako runs three shifts with about 40 workers on each shift.

The supervisors for the three shifts (Art, Tom, and Carol) are experienced employees, each of whom has been with the company for more than 20 years. The supervisors appear satisfied with their work and have reported no major difficulty in supervising employees at Brako.

Art supervises the first shift. Employees describe him as being a very hands-on type of leader. He gets very involved in the day-to-day operations of the facility. Workers joke that Art knows to the milligram the amount of raw materials the company has on hand at any given time. Art can frequently be found walking through the plant and reminding people of the correct procedures to follow in doing their work. Even for those working on the production line, Art always has some directions and reminders.

Workers on the first shift have relatively few negative comments to make about Art's leadership. However, they are negative about many other aspects of their work. Most of the work on this shift is very straightforward and repetitive and as a result is monotonous. The rules for working on the production line or in the packaging area are all clearly spelled out and require no independent decision making on the part of workers. Workers simply need to show up and go through the motions. On lunch breaks, workers are often heard complaining about how bored they are doing the same old thing over and over. Workers do not criticize Art, but they do not think he really understands their situation.

Tom supervises the second shift. He really enjoys working at Brako and wants all the workers on the afternoon shift to enjoy their work as well. Tom is a people-oriented supervisor whom workers describe as very genuine and caring. Hardly a day goes by that Tom does not post a message about someone's birthday or someone's personal accomplishment. Tom works hard at creating comradery, including sponsoring a company softball team, taking people out to lunch, and having people over to his house for social events.

Despite Tom's personableness, absenteeism and turnover are highest on the second shift. The second shift is responsible for setting up the machines and equipment when changes are made from making one part to making another. In addition, the second shift is responsible for the complex computer programs that monitor the machines. Workers on the second shift take a lot of heat from others at Brako for not doing a good job. Workers on the second shift feel pressure because it is not always easy to figure out how to do their tasks. Each setup is different and requires different procedures. Although the computer is extremely helpful when it is calibrated appropriately to the task, it can be extremely problematic when the software it uses is off the mark. Workers have complained to Tom and upper management many times about the difficulty of their jobs.

Carol supervises the third shift. Her style is different from that of the others at Brako. Carol routinely has meetings, which she labels troubleshooting sessions, for the purpose of identifying problems workers may be experiencing. Any time there is a glitch on the production line, Carol wants to know about it so she can help workers find a solution. If workers cannot do a particular job, she shows them how. For those who are uncertain of their competencies, Carol gives reassurance. Carol tries to spend time with each worker and help the workers focus on their personal goals. In addition, she stresses company goals and the rewards that are available if workers are able to make the grade.

Individuals on the third shift like to work for Carol. They find she is good at helping them do their job. They say she has a wonderful knack for making everything fall into place. When there are problems, she addresses them. When workers feel down, she builds them up. Carol was described by one worker as an interesting mixture of part parent, part coach, and part manufacturing expert. Upper management at Brako is pleased with Carol's leadership, but they have experienced problems repeatedly when workers from Carol's shift have been rotated to other shifts at Brako.

Questions

Based on the principles of path-goal theory,

1. Describe why Art and Tom appear to be less effective than Carol.
2. How does the leadership of each of the three supervisors affect the motivation of their respective subordinates?
3. If you were consulting with Brako about leadership, what changes and recommendations would you make regarding the supervision of Art, Tom, and Carol?

CASE 7.2

Direction for Some, Support for Others

Daniel Shivitz is the manager of a small business called The Copy Center, which is located near a large university. The Copy Center employs about 18 people, most of whom work part-time while going to school full-time. The store caters to the university community by specializing in coursepacks, but it also provides desktop publishing and standard copying services. It has three large, state-of-the-art copy machines and several computer work stations.

There are two other national chain copy stores in the immediate vicinity of The Copy Center, yet this store does more business than both of the other stores combined. A major factor contributing to the success of this store is Daniel Shivitz's leadership style.

One of the things that stands out about Daniel is the way he works with his part-time staff. Most of them are students, who have to schedule their work hours around their class schedules, and Daniel has a reputation of being really helpful with working out schedule conflicts. No conflict is too small for Daniel, who is always willing to juggle schedules to meet the needs of everyone. Students talk about how much they feel included and like the spirit at The Copy Center. It is as if Daniel makes the store like a second family for them.

Work at The Copy Center divides itself into primarily two areas: duplicating services and desktop publishing. In both areas, Daniel Shivitz's leadership is effective.

Duplicating is a rather straightforward operation that simply requires taking a customer's originals and making copies of them. Because this job is tedious, Daniel goes out of his way to help the staff make it tolerable. He promotes a friendly work atmosphere by doing such things as letting the staff wear casual attire, letting them choose their own tapes for background music, and letting them be a bit wild on the job. Daniel spends a lot of time each day conversing informally with each employee; he also welcomes staff talking with each other. Daniel has a knack for making each worker feel significant even when the work is insignificant. He promotes comradery among his staff, and he is not afraid to become involved in their activities.

The desktop publishing area is more complex than duplicating. It involves creating business forms, advertising pieces, and résumés for customers. Working in desktop publishing requires skills in writing, editing, design, and layout. It is challenging work because it is not always easy to satisfy these customers' needs. Most of the employees in this area are full-time workers.

Through the years, Daniel Shivitz has found that employees who work best in desktop publishing are a unique type of individual, very different from those who work in duplicating. They are usually quite independent, self-assured, and self-motivated. In supervising them, Daniel gives them a lot of space, is available when they need help, but otherwise leaves them alone.

Daniel likes the role of being the resource person for these employees. For example, if an employee is having difficulty on a customer's project, he willingly joins the employee in troubleshooting the problem. Similarly, if one of the staff is having problems with a software program, Daniel is quick to offer his technical expertise. Because the employees in desktop publishing are self-directed, Daniel spends far less time with them than with those who work in duplicating.

Overall, Daniel feels successful with his leadership at The Copy Center. Profits for the store continue to grow each year, and its reputation for quality service is widespread.

Questions

According to path-goal theory,

1. Why is Daniel an effective leader?
2. How does his leadership style affect the motivation of employees at The Copy Center?
3. How do characteristics of the task and the subordinates influence Daniel's leadership?
4. One of the principles of path-goal theory is to make the end goal valuable to workers. What could Daniel do to improve subordinate motivation in this area?

CASE 7.3

Marathon Runners at Different Levels

David Abruzzo is the newly elected president of the Metrocity Striders Track Club (MSTC). As president of the track club, one of his duties is to serve as the coach for runners who hope to complete the New York City

Marathon. Because David has run many marathons and ultramarathons successfully, he feels quite comfortable assuming the role and responsibilities of acting as coach for the marathon runners.

The training period for runners intending to run New York is 16 weeks. During the first couple of weeks of training, David was pleased with the progress of the runners and had little difficulty in his role as coach. However, when the runners reached week eight, the halfway mark, some things began to occur that raised some questions in David's mind regarding how best to help his runners. The issues of concern for runners seemed quite different from those that David had expected to hear from runners in a marathon training program. All in all, the runners and their concerns could be divided into three different groups.

One group of runners, most of whom had never run a marathon, peppered the coach with all kinds of questions. They were very concerned about how to do the marathon and whether they had the ability to complete such a challenging event successfully. They asked questions about how far to run in training, what to eat, how much to drink, and what kind of shoes to wear. One runner wanted to know what to eat the night before the marathon, and another wanted to know if it was likely that he would pass out when he crossed the finish line. For David the questions were never-ending and rather basic in nature.

Another set of individuals seemed most concerned about the effects of training on their running. For example, they wanted to know precisely how their per-week running mileage related to their possible marathon finishing time. Would running long practice runs help them through the wall at the 20-mile mark in the marathon? Would carbo-loading improve their overall performance during the marathon? Would taking a rest day during training actually help their overall conditioning? Basically, all the runners in this group seemed to want assurances from David that they were training in the right way for New York.

A third group was made up of seasoned runners, most of whom had run several marathons and many of whom had finished in the top 10 of their respective age divisions. Regardless of their experience, these runners still seemed to be having troubles. They complained of feeling flat and acted a bit moody and down about training. Even though they had confidence in their ability to compete and finish well, they lacked excitement about running in the New York event. The occasional questions they raised usually concerned such things as whether their overall training strategy was appropriate or whether their training would help them in other races besides the New York City Marathon.

Questions

Based on the principles described in path-goal theory,

1. What kind of leadership should David exhibit with each of the three running groups?
2. What is it that David has to do to help the runners accomplish their goals?
3. Are there obstacles that David can remove or help runners to confront?
4. In general, how can David motivate each of the three groups?

LEADERSHIP INSTRUMENT

Because the path-goal theory was developed as a complex set of theoretical assumptions to direct researchers in developing new leadership theory, it has used many different instruments to measure the leadership process. The Path-Goal Leadership Questionnaire illustrates one of the questionnaires that has been useful in measuring and learning about important aspects of path-goal leadership (Indvik, 1985, 1988).

This questionnaire provides information for respondents about four different leadership styles: directive, supportive, participative, and achievement oriented. The way respondents score on each of the different styles provides them with information on their strong and weak styles, as well as the relative importance they place on each of the styles.

To understand the path-goal questionnaire better, it may be useful to analyze a hypothetical set of scores. For example, hypothesize that your scores on the questionnaire were 29 for directive, which is high; 22 for supportive, which is low; 21 for participative, which is average; and 25 for achievement, which is high. These scores suggest that you are a leader who is typically more directive and achievement oriented than most other leaders, less supportive than other leaders, and quite similar to other leaders in the degree to which you act participatively.

According to the principles of path-goal theory, if your scores matched these hypothetical scores, you would be effective in situations where the tasks and procedures are unclear and your subordinates have a need for certainty. You would be less effective in work settings that are structured and unchallenging. In addition, you would be moderately effective in ambiguous situations with subordinates who want control. Last, you would do very well in uncertain situations where you could set high standards, challenge subordinates to meet these standards, and help them feel confident in their abilities.

In addition to the Path-Goal Leadership Questionnaire, leadership researchers have commonly used multiple instruments to study path-goal theory, including measures of task structure, locus of control, employee expectancies, employee satisfaction, and others. Although the primary use of these instruments has been for theory building, many of the instruments offer valuable information related to practical leadership issues.

———————————◆———————————

Path-Goal Leadership Questionnaire

Instructions: This questionnaire contains questions about different styles of path-goal leadership. Indicate how often each statement is true of your own behavior.

Key: 1 = Never   2 = Hardly ever   3 = Seldom   4 = Occasionally   5 = Often
        6 = Usually   7 = Always

_____   1. I let subordinates know what is expected of them.
_____   2. I maintain a friendly working relationship with subordinates.
_____   3. I consult with subordinates when facing a problem.
_____   4. I listen receptively to subordinates' ideas and suggestions.
_____   5. I inform subordinates about what needs to be done and how it needs to be done.
_____   6. I let subordinates know that I expect them to perform at their highest level.
_____   7. I act without consulting my subordinates.
_____   8. I do little things to make it pleasant to be a member of the group.
_____   9. I ask subordinates to follow standard rules and regulations.
_____   10. I set goals for subordinates' performance that are quite challenging.
_____   11. I say things that hurt subordinates' personal feelings.
_____   12. I ask for suggestions from subordinates concerning how to carry out assignments.
_____   13. I encourage continual improvement in subordinates' performance.
_____   14. I explain the level of performance that is expected of subordinates.
_____   15. I help subordinates overcome problems that stop them from carrying out their tasks.
_____   16. I show that I have doubts about subordinates' ability to meet most objectives.
_____   17. I ask subordinates for suggestions on what assignments should be made.
_____   18. I give vague explanations of what is expected of subordinates on the job.
_____   19. I consistently set challenging goals for subordinates to attain.
_____   20. I behave in a manner that is thoughtful of subordinates' personal needs.

SOURCE: Adapted from *A Path-Goal Theory Investigation of Superior Subordinate Relationships,* by J. Indvik, unpublished doctoral dissertation, University of Wisconsin–Madison, 1985, and Indvik (1988). Based on the work of House and Dessler (1974) and House (1976) cited in Fulk and Wendler (1982). Used by permission.

Scoring

1. Reverse the scores for items 7, 11, 16, and 18.
2. Directive style: Sum of scores on items 1, 5, 9, 14, and 18.
3. Supportive style: Sum of scores on items 2, 8, 11, 15, and 20.
4. Participative style: Sum of scores on items 3, 4, 7, 12, and 17.
5. Achievement-oriented style: Sum of scores on items 6, 10, 13, 16, and 19.

Scoring Interpretation

- Directive style: A common score is 23; scores above 28 are considered high and scores below 18 are considered low.
- Supportive style: A common score is 28; scores above 33 are considered high and scores below 23 are considered low.
- Participative style: A common score is 21; scores above 26 are considered high and scores below 16 are considered low.
- Achievement-oriented style: A common score is 19; scores above 24 are considered high and scores below 14 are considered low.

The scores you received on the path-goal questionnaire provide information about which style of leadership you use most often and which you use less frequently. In addition, these scores can be used to assess your use of each style relative to your use of the other styles.

SUMMARY

Path-goal theory was developed to explain how leaders motivate subordinates to be productive and satisfied with their work. It is a contingency approach to leadership because effectiveness depends on the fit between the leader's behavior and the characteristics of subordinates and the task.

The basic principles of path-goal theory are derived from expectancy theory, which suggests that employees will be motivated if they feel competent, if they think their efforts will be rewarded, and if they find the payoff for their work is valuable. A leader can help subordinates by selecting a style of leadership (directive, supportive, participative, or achievement oriented) that provides what is missing for subordinates in a particular work setting. In simple terms, it is the leader's responsibility to help subordinates to reach their goals by directing, guiding, and coaching them along the way.

Path-goal theory offers a large set of predictions for how a leader's style interacts with subordinates' needs and the nature of the task. Among other things, it predicts that directive leadership is effective with ambiguous tasks, that supportive leadership is effective for repetitive tasks, that participative leadership is effective when tasks are unclear and subordinates are autonomous, and that achievement-oriented leadership is effective for challenging tasks.

Path-goal theory has three major strengths. First, it provides a theoretical framework that is useful for understanding how directive, supportive, participative, and achievement-oriented styles of leadership affect the productivity and satisfaction of subordinates. Second, path-goal theory is unique in that it integrates the motivation principles of expectancy theory into a theory of leadership. Third, it provides a practical model that underscores the important ways that leaders help subordinates.

On the negative side, four criticisms can be leveled at path-goal theory. Foremost, the scope of path-goal theory encompasses so many interrelated sets of assumptions that it is hard to use this theory in a given organizational setting. Second, research findings to date do not support a full and consistent picture of the claims of the theory. Furthermore, path-goal theory does not show in a clear way how leader behaviors directly affect subordinate motivation levels. Last, path-goal theory is very leader oriented and fails to recognize the transactional nature of leadership. It does not promote subordinate involvement in the leadership process.

REFERENCES

Bess, J. L., & Goldman, P. (2001). Leadership ambiguity in universities and K-12 schools and the limits of contemporary leadership theory. *Leadership Quarterly, 12,* 419-450.

Evans, M. G. (1970). The effects of supervisory behavior on the path-goal relationship. *Organizational Behavior and Human Performance, 5,* 277-298.

Evans, M. G. (1996). R. J. House's "A path-goal theory of leader effectiveness." *Leadership Quarterly, 7*(3), 305-309.

Fulk, J., & Wendler, E. R. (1982). Dimensionality of leader-subordinate interactions: A path-goal investigation. *Organizational Behavior and Human Performance, 30,* 241-264.

Halpin, A. W., & Winer, B. J. (1957). A factorial study of the leader behavior descriptions. In R. M. Stogdill & A. E. Coons (Eds.), *Leader behavior: Its description and measurement.* Columbus: Ohio State University, Bureau of Business Research.

House, R. J. (1971). A path-goal theory of leader effectiveness. *Administrative Science Quarterly, 16,* 321-328.

House, R. J. (1996). Path-goal theory of leadership: Lessons, legacy, and a reformulated theory. *Leadership Quarterly, 7*(3), 323-352.

House, R. J., & Dessler, G. (1974). The path-goal theory of leadership: Some post hoc and a priori tests. In J. Hunt & L. Larson (Eds.), *Contingency approaches in leadership* (pp. 29-55). Carbondale: Southern Illinois University Press.

House, R. J., & Mitchell, R. R. (1974). Path-goal theory of leadership. *Journal of Contemporary Business, 3,* 81-97.

Indvik, J. (1985). *A path-goal theory investigation of superior subordinate relationships.* Unpublished doctoral dissertation, University of Wisconsin–Madison.

Indvik, J. (1986). Path-goal theory of leadership: A meta-analysis. In *Proceedings of the Academy of Management meeting* (pp. 189-192). Briarcliff Manor, NY: Academy of Management.

Indvik, J. (1988). *A more complete testing of path-goal theory.* Paper presented at the Academy of Management, Anaheim, CA.

Jermier, J. M. (1996). The path-goal theory of leadership: A subtextual analysis. *Leadership Quarterly, 7*(3), 311-316.

Schriesheim, C. A., & Kerr, S. (1977). Theories and measures of leadership: A critical appraisal. In J. G. Hunt & L. L. Larson (Eds.), *Leadership: The cutting edge* (pp. 9-45). Carbondale: Southern Illinois University Press.

Schriesheim, C. A., & Neider, L. L. (1996). Path-goal leadership theory: The long and winding road. *Leadership Quarterly, 7*(3), 317-321.

Schriesheim, J. R., & Schriesheim, C. A. (1980). A test of the path-goal theory of leadership and some suggested directions for future research. *Personnel Psychology, 33,* 349-370.

Stinson, J. E., & Johnson, R. W. (1975). The path-goal theory of leadership: A partial test and suggested refinement. *Academy of Management Journal, 18,* 242-252.

Wofford, J. C., & Liska, L. Z. (1993). Path-goal theories of leadership: A meta-analysis. *Journal of Management, 19*(4), 857-876.

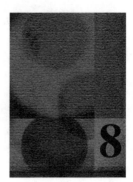

Leader-Member Exchange Theory

DESCRIPTION

Most of the leadership theories discussed thus far in the book have emphasized leadership from the point of view of the leader (e.g., trait approach, skills approach, and style approach) or the follower and the context (e.g., situational leadership, contingency theory, and path-goal theory). Leader-member exchange (LMX) theory takes still another approach and conceptualizes leadership as a process that is centered on the *interactions* between leaders and followers. As Figure 8.1 illustrates, LMX theory makes the *dyadic relationship* between leaders and followers the focal point of the leadership process.

LMX theory was first described 28 years ago in the works of Dansereau, Graen, and Haga (1975), Graen and Cashman (1975), and Graen (1976). Since it first appeared it has undergone several revisions, and it continues to be of interest to researchers who study the leadership process.

Prior to LMX theory, researchers treated leadership as something leaders did toward all of their followers. This assumption implied that leaders treated followers in a collective way, as a group, using an average leadership style. LMX theory challenged this assumption and directed researchers' attention to the differences that might exist between the leader and each of her or his followers.

Figure 8.1 *Dimensions of Leadership*

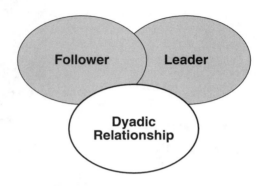

SOURCE: Adapted from "Relationship-Based Approach to Leadership: Development of Leader-Member Exchange (LMX) Theory of Leadership Over 25 Years: Applying a Multi-Level, Multi-Domain Perspective," by G. B. Graen and M. Uhl-Bien, 1995, *Leadership Quarterly, 6*(2), 219-247.

EARLY STUDIES

In the first studies of exchange theory, which was then called vertical dyad linkage (VDL) theory, researchers focused on the nature of the *vertical linkages* leaders formed with each of their followers (see Figure 8.2). A leader's relationship to the work unit as a whole was viewed as a series of vertical dyads (see Figure 8.3). In assessing the characteristics of these vertical dyads, researchers found two general types of linkages (or relationships): those that were based on expanded and negotiated role responsibilities (extra-roles), which were called the *in-group,* and those that were based on the formal employment contract (defined roles), which were called the *out-group* (see Figure 8.4).

Within an organizational work unit, subordinates become a part of the in-group or the out-group based on how well they work with the leader and how well the leader works with them. Personality and other personal characteristics are related to this process (Dansereau et al., 1975). In addition, becoming part of one group or the other is based on how subordinates involve themselves in expanding their role responsibilities with the leader (Graen, 1976). Subordinates who are interested in negotiating with the

Figure 8.2 *The Vertical Dyad*

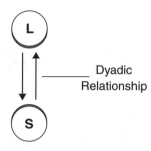

NOTE: The leader (L) forms an individualized working relationship with each of his or her subordinates (S). The exchanges (both content and process) between the leader and subordinate define their dyadic relationship.

leader what they are willing to do for the group can become a part of the in-group. These negotiations involve exchanges in which subordinates do certain activities that go beyond their formal job descriptions, and the leader, in turn, does more for these subordinates. If subordinates are not interested in taking on new and different job responsibilities, they become a part of the out-group.

Figure 8.3 *Vertical Dyads*

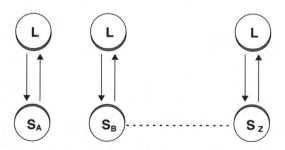

NOTE: The leader (L) forms special relationships with all of his or her subordinates (S). Each of these relationships is special and has its own unique characteristics.

Figure 8.4 *In-Groups and Out-Groups*

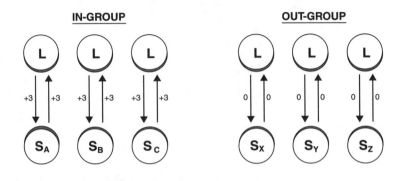

NOTE: A leader (L) and his or her subordinate (S) form unique relationships. Relationships within the in-group are marked by mutual trust, respect, liking, and reciprocal influence. Relationships within the out-group are marked by formal communication based on job descriptions. Plus 3 is a high-quality relationship and zero is a stranger.

Subordinates in the in-group receive more information, influence, confidence, and concern from their leaders than do out-group subordinates (Dansereau et al., 1975). In addition, they are more dependable, more highly involved, and more communicative than out-group subordinates (Dansereau et al., 1975). Whereas in-group members do extra things for the leader and the leader does the same for them, subordinates in the out-group are less compatible with the leader and usually just come to work, do their job, and go home.

LATER STUDIES

After the first set of studies, there was a shift in the focus of LMX theory. Whereas the initial studies of this theory primarily addressed the nature of the differences between in-groups and out-groups, a subsequent line of research addressed how LMX theory was related to organizational effectiveness. Specifically, these studies focused on how the quality of leader-member exchanges was related to positive outcomes for leaders, followers, groups, and the organization in general (Graen & Uhl-Bien, 1995). Researchers found that high-quality leader-member exchanges produced less employee turnover, more positive performance evaluations, higher frequency of promotions, greater organizational commitment, more desirable work assignments, better job attitudes, more attention and support from the leader, greater participation, and faster career progress over 25 years (Graen & Uhl-Bien, 1995; Liden, Wayne, & Stilwell, 1993).

In essence, the above findings clearly illustrate that organizations stand to gain much from having leaders who can create good working relationships. When leaders and followers have good exchanges, they feel better, accomplish more, and the organization prospers.

LEADERSHIP MAKING

The findings from the later studies were the impetus for the most current research on LMX theory, which focuses on how exchanges between leaders and subordinates can be used for "leadership making" (Graen & Uhl-Bien, 1991). Leadership making is a prescriptive approach to leadership that emphasizes that a leader should develop high-quality exchanges with all of her or his subordinates, rather than just a few. It attempts to make every subordinate feel as if he or she is a part of the in-group and, by so doing, avoids the inequities and negative implications of being in an out-group. In general, leadership making promotes building partnerships in which the leader tries to build effective dyads with all employees in the work unit (Graen & Uhl-Bien, 1995). In addition, leadership making suggests that leaders can create networks of partnerships throughout the organization, which will benefit the organization's goals as well as their own career progress.

Graen and Uhl-Bien (1991) suggested that leadership making develops progressively over time in three phases: (a) the stranger phase, (b) the acquaintance phase, and (c) the mature partnership phase (see Table 8.1). During Phase 1, the stranger phase, the interactions within the leader-subordinate dyad are generally rule bound, relying heavily on contractual relationships. Leaders and subordinates relate to each other within prescribed organizational roles. They have lower-quality exchanges, similar to those of out-group members that we discussed earlier in the chapter. The subordinate complies with the formal leader, who has hierarchical status for the purpose of achieving the economic rewards the leader controls. The motives of the subordinate during the stranger phase are directed toward self-interest rather than the good of the group (Graen & Uhl-Bien, 1995).

Table 8.1 *Phases in Leadership Making*

	Phase 1 STRANGER	Phase 2 ACQUAINTANCE	Phase 3 PARTNER
Roles	Scripted	Tested	Negotiated
Influences	One way	Mixed	Reciprocal
Exchanges	Low quality	Medium quality	High quality
Interests	Self	Self / other	Group
		Time →	

SOURCE: Adapted from the Life Cycles of Leadership Making in "Relationship-Based Approach to Leadership: Development of Leader-Member Exchange (LMX) Theory of Leadership Over 25 Years: Applying a Multi-Level, Multi-Domain Perspective," by G. B. Graen and M. Uhl-Bien, 1995, *Leadership Quarterly, 6*(2), 231.

Phase 2, the acquaintance phase, begins with an "offer" by the leader or the subordinate for improved career-oriented social exchanges, which involve sharing more resources and personal or work-related information. It is a testing period for both the leader and the subordinate to assess whether the subordinate is interested in taking on more roles and responsibilities and to assess whether the leader is willing to provide new challenges for subordinates. During this time, dyads shift away from interactions that are strictly governed by job descriptions and defined roles and move toward new ways of relating. As measured by LMX theory, it could be said that the quality of their exchanges has improved. Successful dyads in the acquaintance phase begin to develop greater trust and respect for each other. They also tend to focus less on their own self-interests and more on the purposes and goals of the group.

Phase 3, mature partnership, is marked by high-quality leader-member exchanges. Individuals who have progressed to this stage in their relationships experience a high degree of mutual trust, respect, and obligation toward each other. They have tested their relationship and found that they can depend on each other. In mature partnerships, there is a high degree of reciprocity between leaders and subordinates; each affects and is affected by the other. For example, in a study of 75 bank managers and 58 engineering managers, Schriesheim, Castro, Zhou, and Yammarino (2001) found that good leader-member relations were more egalitarian and that influence and control were more evenly balanced between the supervisor and the subordinate. In addition, during Phase 3, members may depend on each other for favors and special assistance. Leaders, for example, may rely on subordinates to do extra assignments, and subordinates may rely on leaders for needed support or encouragement. The point is that leaders and subordinates are tied together in productive ways that go well beyond a traditional hierarchically defined work relationship. They have developed an extremely effective way of relating that produces positive outcomes for both themselves and the organization. In effect, partnerships are transformational in that they assist leaders and followers in moving beyond their own self-interests to accomplish the greater good of the team and organization (see Chapter 9).

To evaluate leader-member exchanges, researchers have typically used a brief questionnaire that asks leaders and followers to report on the effectiveness of their working relationships. The questionnaire assesses the degree to which respondents express respect, trust, and obligation in their exchanges with others. At the end of this chapter, a version of the LMX questionnaire is provided for you to take for the purpose of analyzing some of your own leader-member relationships.

HOW DOES LMX THEORY WORK?

LMX theory works in two ways: It describes leadership and it prescribes leadership. In both instances, the central concept is the dyadic relationship that a leader forms with each of her or his subordinates. Descriptively, LMX theory suggests it is important to recognize the existence of in-groups and out-groups within a group or organization.

The differences in how goals are accomplished using in-groups as compared with out-groups are substantial. Working with an in-group allows a leader to accomplish more work in a more effective manner than working without one. In-group members are willing to do more than is required in their job description and look for innovative ways to advance the group's goals. In response to their extra effort and devotion, leaders give them more responsibilities and more opportunities. Leaders also give in-group members more of their time and support.

Out-group members act quite differently from in-group members. Rather than trying to do extra work, out-group members operate strictly within their prescribed organizational roles. They do what is required of them, but nothing more. Leaders treat out-group members fairly and according to the formal contract, but they do not give them special attention. For their efforts, out-group members receive the standard benefits as described by the job description.

Prescriptively, LMX theory is best understood within the leadership-making model of Graen and Uhl-Bien (1991). The authors advocated that leaders should create a special relationship with all subordinates, similar to those relationships described as in-group relationships. Leaders should offer each subordinate the opportunity to take on new roles and responsibilities. Furthermore, leaders should nurture high-quality exchanges with their subordinates. Rather than focusing on the differences between in-group and out-group members, the leadership-making model suggests that leaders should look for ways to build trust and respect with all of their subordinates, thus making the entire work unit an in-group. In addition, leaders should look beyond their own work unit and create quality partnerships with individuals throughout the organization.

Whether descriptive or prescriptive, LMX theory works by focusing our attention on the special, unique relationship that leaders can create with others. When these relationships are of high quality, the goals of the leader, the followers, and the organization are all advanced.

STRENGTHS

LMX theory makes several positive contributions to our understanding of the leadership process. First, it is a strong descriptive theory. Intuitively, it makes sense to describe work units in terms of those who contribute more and those who contribute less or the bare minimum to the organization. Anyone who has ever worked in an organization has felt the presence of in-groups and out-groups. Despite the potential harm of out-groups, we all know that leaders have special relationships with certain people who do more and get more. We may not like this because it seems unfair, but it is a reality and the LMX theory has accurately described this situation. LMX theory validates our experience of how people within organizations relate to each other and the leader. Some contribute more and receive more; others contribute less and get less.

Second, LMX theory is unique because it is the only leadership approach that makes the concept of the dyadic relationship the centerpiece of the leadership process. Other approaches emphasize the characteristics of leaders, followers, contexts, or a combination of these, but none of them addresses the specific relationships between the leader and each subordinate. LMX theory underscores that effective leadership is contingent on effective leader-member exchanges.

Third, LMX theory is noteworthy because it directs our attention to the importance of communication in leadership. The high-quality exchanges advocated in LMX theory are inextricably bound to effective communication. Communication is the vehicle through which leaders and subordinates create, nurture, and sustain useful exchanges. Effective leadership occurs when the communication of leaders and subordinates is characterized by mutual trust, respect, and commitment.

Fourth, there is a large body of research that substantiates how the practice of LMX theory is related to positive organizational outcomes. In a review of this research, Graen and Uhl-Bien (1995) point out that it is related to performance, organizational commitment, job climate, innovation, organizational citizenship behavior, empowerment, procedural and distributive justice, career progress, and many other important organizational variables. By linking the use of LMX theory to real outcomes, researchers have been able to validate the theory and increase its practical value.

CRITICISMS

The most obvious criticism that can be made of LMX theory is that on the surface it runs counter to the basic human value of fairness. Throughout our lives, beginning when we were very young, we have been taught to try to get along with everyone and to treat everyone equally. We have been taught that it is wrong to form in-groups or cliques because they are harmful to those who cannot be a part of them. Because LMX theory divides the work unit into two groups and one group receives special attention, it gives the appearance of discrimination against the out-group.

Our culture is replete with examples of people of different genders, ages, cultures, and abilities who have been discriminated against. Although LMX theory was not designed to do so, it supports the development of privileged groups in the workplace. In so doing, it appears unfair and discriminatory. Furthermore, as reported by McClane (1991), the existence of in-groups and out-groups may have undesirable effects on the group as a whole.

Whether LMX theory actually creates inequalities is questionable (cf. Harter & Evanecky, 2002; Scandura, 1999). If a leader does not intentionally keep out-group members "out," and if they are free to become members of the in-group, then LMX theory may not create inequalities. However, the theory does not elaborate on strategies for how one gains access to the in-group if one chooses.

Furthermore, LMX theory does not address other fairness issues, such as subordinates' perceptions of the fairness of pay increases and promotion opportunities (distributive justice), subordinates' perceptions of the fairness of decision-making rules (procedural justice), or subordinates' perceptions of the fairness in how issues are communicated within the organization (interactional justice) (Scandura, 1999). There is a need for further research on how these types of fairness issues affect the development and maintenance of LMX relationships.

A second criticism of LMX theory is that the basic ideas of the theory are not fully developed. For example, it fails to explain fully the way high-quality leader-member exchanges are created. In the early studies, it was implied that they were formed because a leader found certain subordinates more compatible in regard to personality, interpersonal skills, or job competencies, but these studies never described the relative importance of these factors or how this process worked (Yukl, 1994). In more recent research, it is suggested that leaders should work to create high-quality exchanges with all subordinates, but the guidelines for how this is done are not clearly spelled out. For example, the model on leadership making highlights the importance of role making, incremental influence, and type of reciprocity (see Figure 8.5), but it does not explain how these concepts function to build mature partnerships. Similarly, the model strongly promotes building trust, respect, and obligation in leader-subordinate relationships, but it does not describe the means through which these factors are developed in relationships.

Based on a review and examination of 147 studies of leader-member exchange, Schriesheim, Castro, and Cogliser (1999) concluded that improved theorization about leader-member exchange and its basic process is needed. Although many studies have been conducted on leader-member exchange, these studies have not resulted in a clear refined set of definitions, concepts, and propositions about the theory.

Third, there have been questions raised regarding the measurement of leader-member exchanges in LMX theory (Graen & Uhl-Bien, 1995; Schriesheim et al., 1999; Schriesheim et al., 2001). For example, no empirical studies have used dyadic measures to analyze the LMX process (Schriesheim et al., 2001). In addition, leader-member exchanges have been measured with different versions of leader-member exchange scales and with different levels of analysis so the results were not always directly comparable. Furthermore, the measurement scales lack content validity (Schriesheim et al., 2001). This means the scales may not actually be measuring what they were intended to measure. Finally, there have been questions regarding whether the standard scale used to measure exchanges is unidimensional or multidimensional (Graen & Uhl-Bien, 1995).

APPLICATION

Although LMX theory has not been packaged in a way to be used in standard management training and development programs, it offers many insights that managers could use to improve their own leadership behavior. Foremost, LMX theory directs managers to assess their leadership from a relationship perspective. This assessment will sensitize managers to how in-groups and out-groups develop within their own work unit. In addition, LMX theory suggests ways that managers can improve their work unit by building strong leader-member exchanges with all of their subordinates.

The ideas set forth in LMX theory can be used by managers at all levels within an organization. For example, LMX theory could be used to explain the way chief executive officers (CEOs) develop special relationships with select individuals in upper management to develop new strategic and tactical corporate goals. So, too, it could be used to explain how line managers in a plant use a select few workers to accomplish the production quotas of their work unit. The point is that the ideas presented in LMX theory have application throughout organizations.

In addition, the ideas of LMX theory can be used to explain how individuals create leadership networks throughout an organization to help them accomplish work more effectively (Graen & Scandura, 1987). A person with a network of high-quality partnerships can call on many people to help solve problems and advance the goals of the organization.

LMX theory can also be applied in different types of organizations. It applies in volunteer settings as well as traditional business, education, and government settings. Imagine a community leader who heads up a volunteer program to assist the elderly. To run the program effectively, the leader depends on a few of the volunteers who are more dependable and committed than the rest of the volunteers. This process of working closely with a small cadre of trusted volunteers is explained by the principles of LMX theory. Similarly, a manager of a traditional business setting might use certain individuals to achieve a major change in the company's policies and procedures. The way the manager goes about this process is explicated in LMX theory.

In summary, LMX theory tells us to be aware of how we relate to our subordinates. It tells us to be sensitive to whether some subordinates receive special attention and some subordinates do not. In addition, it tells us to be fair to all employees and allow each of them to become as much involved in the work of the unit as they want to be. LMX theory tells us to be respectful and to build trusting relationships with all of our subordinates, recognizing that each employee is unique and wants to relate to us in a special way.

CASE STUDIES

In the following section, three case studies (Cases 8.1, 8.2, and 8.3) are presented to clarify how LMX theory can be applied to various group settings. The first case is about the creative director at an advertising agency, the second is about a production manager at a mortgage company, and the third describes the leadership of the manager of a district office of the Social Security Administration. Following each of the case studies, there are questions that will help you to analyze the case, using the ideas from LMX theory.

CASE 8.1

His Team Gets the Best Assignments

Carly Peters directs the creative department of the advertising agency of Mills, Smith, & Peters. The agency has about 100 employees, 20 of whom work for Carly in the creative department. Typically, the agency maintains 10 major accounts as well as a number of smaller accounts. It has a reputation for being one of the best advertising and public relations agencies in the country.

In the creative department, there are four major account teams. Each is led by an associate creative director, who reports directly to Carly. In addition, each team has a copywriter, an art director, and a production artist. At Mills, Smith, & Peters, the account teams are headed up by Jack, Terri, Julie, and Sarah.

Jack and his team get along really well with Carly, and they have done excellent work for their clients at the agency. Of all the teams, Jack's team is the most creative and talented, and the most willing to go the extra mile for Carly. As a result, when Carly has to showcase accounts to upper management, she often uses the work of Jack's team. Jack and his team members are comfortable confiding with Carly and she with them. Carly is not afraid to allocate extra resources to Jack's team or to give them free rein on their accounts because they always come through for her.

Terri's team also performs well for the agency, but Terri is unhappy with how her team is treated by Carly. She feels that Carly is not fair because she favors Jack's team. For example, Terri's team was counseled out of pursuing an ad campaign because the campaign was too risky, whereas Jack's group was praised for developing a very provocative campaign. Terri feels that Jack's team is Carly's pet—they get the best assignments, accounts, and budgets. Terri finds it hard to hold back the animosity she feels toward Carly.

Like Terri, Julie is also concerned that her team is not in the inner circle, close to Carly. She has noticed repeatedly that Carly favors the other teams. For example, whenever additional people are assigned to team projects, it is always the other teams who get the best writers and art directors. Julie is mystified as to why Carly doesn't notice her team or try to help it with its work. She feels Carly undervalues her team because Julie knows the quality of her team's work is indisputable.

Although Sarah agrees with some of Terri's and Julie's observations about Carly, she does not feel any antagonism about Carly's leadership. Sarah has worked for the agency for nearly 10 years, and nothing seems to bother her. Her account teams have never been "earth-shaking," but they have never been problematic either. Sarah views her team and its work more like a "nuts and bolts" operation in which the team is given an assignment and carries it out. Being in Carly's inner circle would require putting in extra time in the evening or on weekends, and would create more headaches for Sarah. Hence, Sarah is happy with her role as it is, and she has little interest in trying to change the way the department works.

Questions

Based on the principles of LMX theory,

1. What observations would you make about Carly's leadership at Mills, Smith, & Peters?
2. Is there an in-group and out-group and, if so, who are they?
3. In what way is Carly's relationship with the four groups productive or counter-productive to the overall goals of the agency?
4. Do you think Carly should change her approach toward the associate directors? If so, what should she do differently?

CASE 8.2

Working Hard at Being Fair

City Mortgage is a medium-sized mortgage company that employs about 25 people. Jenny Hernandez, who has been with the company for 10 years, is the production manager who oversees its day-to-day operations. Reporting to Jenny are loan originators (salespeople), closing officers, mortgage underwriters, and processing and shipping personnel. Jenny is proud of the company and feels as if she has contributed substantially to its steady growth and expansion.

The climate at City Mortgage is very positive. People like to come to work because the office environment is comfortable. They respect each other at the company and show tolerance for those who are different from themselves.

Whereas at many mortgage companies it is common for resentments to build between individuals who earn different incomes, this is not the case at City Mortgage.

Jenny Hernandez's leadership has been instrumental in shaping the success of City Mortgage. Her philosophy stresses listening to employees and then determining how they can best contribute to the mission of the company. She makes a point of helping each individual explore her or his own talents and challenges each one to try new things.

At the annual holiday party, Jenny devised an interesting event that symbolizes her leadership style. She bought a large piece of colorful glass and had it cut into 25 pieces and handed out one piece to each person. Then she asked each employee to come forward with the piece of glass and briefly state what he or she liked about City Mortgage and how he or she felt he or she had contributed to the company in the past year. After the statements were made, the pieces of glass were formed into a cut glass window that hangs in the front lobby of the office. The glass is a reminder of how each individual contributes his or her uniqueness to the overall purpose of the company.

Another characteristic of Jenny's style is her fairness. She does not want to give anyone the impression that certain people have the "inside track," and she goes to great lengths to prevent this from happening. For example, she avoids social lunches because she thinks they foster the perception of favoritism. Similarly, even though her best friend is one of the loan originators, she is seldom seen talking with her, and if she is, it is always about business matters.

Ms. Hernandez also applies her fairness principle to how information is shared in the office. She does not want anyone to feel as if they are "out of the loop," so she tries very hard to keep everyone informed on all the matters that could affect them. Much of this she does through her open-door office policy. Jenny does not have a special group of employees with whom she confides her concerns; rather, she shares openly with each of them.

Jenny is very committed to her work at City Mortgage. She works long hours and carries a beeper on the weekend. At this point in her career, her only concern is that she could be burning out.

Questions

Based on the LMX model, which was presented in Figure 8.5,

1. How would you describe Jenny Hernandez's leadership?
2. How do you think the employees at City Mortgage respond to Jenny?
3. If you were asked to follow in the footsteps of Ms. Hernandez, do you think you could or would want to manage City Mortgage with a similar style?

CASE 8.3

Taking On Additional Responsibilities

Jim Madison is manager of a district office for the Social Security Administration. The office serves a community of 200,000 people and has a staff of 30 employees, most of whom work as claims representatives. The primary work of the office is to provide the public with information about social security benefits, and to process retirement, survivor, disability, and Medicare claims.

Mr. Madison has been the manager of the office for 6 years, and during that time has made a considerable number of improvements in the overall operations of the office. People in the community have a favorable view of the office and have few complaints about the services it provides. On the annual survey of community service organizations, the district office receives consistently high marks for overall effectiveness and customer satisfaction.

Almost all of the employees who work for Jim have been employed at the district office for 6 years or more; one employee has been there for 22 years. Although Jim takes pride in knowing all of them personally, he calls on a few of them more frequently to help him accomplish his goals.

When it comes to training staff members about new laws affecting claims procedures, Mr. Madison relies heavily on two particular claims representatives, Shirley and Patti, both of whom are very knowledgeable and competent. Shirley and Patti view the additional training responsibilities as a challenge. This helps Jim because he does not need to do the job himself nor supervise them closely because they are highly respected people within the office and they have a history of being mature and conscientious about their work. Shirley and Patti like the additional responsibilities because it gives them greater recognition as well as increased benefits from receiving positive job appraisals.

To showcase the office's services to the community, Mr. Madison calls on two other employees, Ted and Jana. Ted and Jana serve as field representatives for the office and give presentations to community organizations about the nature of social security and how it serves the citizens of the district. In addition, they speak on local radio stations, answering call-in questions about the various complexities of social security benefits.

Although many of the claims people in the office could act as field representatives, Mr. Madison typically calls on Ted and Jana because of their willingness to take on the public relations challenge and because of their special capabilities in this area. This is advantageous for Jim for two reasons: First, these individuals do an outstanding job in representing the office to the public, and second, Jim is a reticent person and he finds it quite threatening to be in the public's eye. Ted and Jana like to take on this additional role because it gives them added prestige and greater freedom. Being a field representative has its perks because field staff can actually function as their own bosses when they are not in the office—they can set their own schedules and come and go as they please.

A third area in which Mr. Madison calls on a few representatives for added effort is in helping him supervise the slower claims representatives who seem to be continually behind in writing up the case reports of their clients. When even a few staff members get behind with their work, it affects the entire office operation. To ameliorate this problem, Jim calls on Glenda and Annie, who are both highly talented, to help the slower staff complete their case reports. Although it means taking on more work themselves, Glenda and Annie do it to be kind and to help the office run more smoothly. Other than personal satisfaction, no additional benefits accrue to these individuals for taking on the additional responsibilities.

Overall, the people who work under Mr. Madison's leadership are satisfied with his supervision. There are some who feel that he caters too much to a few special representatives, but most of the staff think Jim is fair and impartial. Even though he depends more on these few, Jim tries very hard to attend to the wants and needs of his entire staff.

Questions

From an LMX theory point of view,

1. How would you describe Jim Madison's leadership at the district social security office?
2. Can you identify an in-group and an out-group?
3. Do you think the trust and respect Jim places in some of his staff is productive or counterproductive? Why?

◆

LEADERSHIP INSTRUMENT

Many different questionnaires have been used by researchers to study LMX theory. All of them have been designed to measure the quality of the working relationship between leaders and followers. We have selected to include in this chapter the LMX 7, a seven-item questionnaire that provides a reliable and valid measure of the quality of leader-member exchanges (Graen & Uhl-Bien, 1995).

The LMX 7 is designed to measure three dimensions of leader-member relationships: respect, trust, and obligation. It assesses the degree to which leaders and followers have mutual respect for each other's capabilities, feel a deepening sense of reciprocal trust, and have a strong sense of obligation to one another. Taken together, these dimensions are the ingredients necessary to create strong partnerships.

By completing the LMX 7, you can gain a fuller understanding of how LMX theory works. The score you obtain on the questionnaire is reflective of the quality of your leader-member relationship(s), and it indicates the degree to which your relationships are characteristic of partnerships, as described in the LMX model.

You can complete the questionnaire both as a leader and as a subordinate. In the leader role, you can complete the questionnaire multiple times, making an assessment of the quality of the relationships you have with each one of your subordinates. In the subordinate role, you would complete the questionnaire based on the leader(s) to whom you report.

Although the LMX 7 is most commonly used by researchers to explore theoretical questions, it can also be used to analyze your own leadership. The scores you obtain on the LMX 7 can be interpreted using the following guidelines: very high = 30-35, high = 25-29, moderate = 20-24, low = 15-19, and very low = 7-14. Scores in the upper ranges are indicative of stronger, higher-quality leader-member exchanges (e.g., in-group members), whereas scores in the lower ranges are indicative of exchanges of lesser quality (e.g., out-group members).

LMX 7 Questionnaire

Instructions: This questionnaire contains items that ask you to describe your relationship with either your leader or one of your subordinates. For each of the items, indicate the degree to which you think the item is true for you by circling one of the responses that appear below the item.

1. Do you know where you stand with your leader (follower) . . . do you usually know how satisfied your leader (follower) is with what you do?

Rarely	Occasionally	Sometimes	Fairly often	Very often
1	2	3	4	5

2. How well does your leader (follower) understand your job problems and needs?

Not a bit	A little	A fair amount	Quite a bit	A great deal
1	2	3	4	5

3. How well does your leader (follower) recognize your potential?

Not at all	A little	Moderately	Mostly	Fully
1	2	3	4	5

4. Regardless of how much formal authority he or she has built into his or her position, what are the chances that your leader (follower) would use his or her power to help you solve problems in your work?

None	Small	Moderate	High	Very high
1	2	3	4	5

5. Again, regardless of the amount of formal authority your leader (follower) has, what are the chances that he or she would "bail you out" at his or her expense?

None	Small	Moderate	High	Very high
1	2	3	4	5

6. I have enough confidence in my leader (follower) that I would defend and justify his or her decision if he or she were not present to do so.

Strongly disagree	Disagree	Neutral	Agree	Strongly agree
1	2	3	4	5

7. How would you characterize your working relationship with your leader (follower)?

Extremely ineffective	Worse than average	Average	Better than average	Extremely effective
1	2	3	4	5

SOURCE: Reprinted from "Relationship-Based Approach to Leadership: Development of Leader-Member Exchange (LMX) Theory of Leadership Over 25 Years: Applying a Multi-Level, Multi-Domain Perspective," by G. B. Graen and M. Uhl-Bien, 1995, *Leadership Quarterly, 6*(2), 219-247. Copyright © 1995. Reprinted with permission from Elsevier Science.

SUMMARY

Since it first appeared 28 years ago, under the title "vertical dyad linkage theory," LMX theory has been and continues to be a much-studied approach to leadership. LMX theory addresses leadership as a process centered on the interactions between leaders and followers. It makes the leader-member relationship the pivotal concept in the leadership process.

In the early studies of LMX theory, a leader's relationship to the overall work unit was viewed as a series of vertical dyads, categorized as being of two different types. Leader-member dyads based on expanded role relationships were called the leader's in-group, and those based on formal job descriptions were called the out-group. It is believed that subordinates become in-group members based on how well they get along with the leader and whether they are willing to expand their role responsibilities. Subordinates who maintain only formal hierarchical relationships with their leader become out-group members. While in-group members receive extra influence, opportunities, and rewards, out-group members receive standard job benefits.

Subsequent studies of LMX theory were directed toward how leader-member exchanges affected organizational performance. Researchers found that high-quality exchanges between leaders and followers produced multiple positive outcomes (e.g., less employee turnover, greater organizational commitment, and more promotions). In general, researchers determined that good leader-member exchanges resulted in followers feeling better, accomplishing more, and helping the organization prosper.

The most recent emphasis in LMX research has been on leadership making, which emphasizes that leaders should try to develop high-quality exchanges with all of their subordinates. Leadership making develops over time and includes a stranger phase, acquaintance phase, and partner phase. By taking on and fulfilling new role responsibilities, followers move through these three phases to develop mature partnerships with their leaders. These partnerships, which are marked by a high degree of mutual trust, respect, and obligation toward one another, have positive payoffs for the individuals themselves and they also help the organization run more effectively.

There are several positive features to LMX theory. First, LMX theory is a strong descriptive approach that explains how leaders use some subordinates (in-group members) more than others (out-group members) to accomplish organizational goals effectively. Second, LMX theory is unique in that, unlike other approaches, it makes the leader-member relationship the focal point of the leadership process. Related to this focus, LMX theory is noteworthy because it directs our attention to the importance of effective communication in leader-member relationships. Last, LMX theory is supported by a multitude of studies that link high-quality leader-member exchanges to positive organizational outcomes.

There are also negative features in LMX theory. Foremost, LMX theory runs counter to our principles of fairness and justice in the workplace by suggesting that some members of the work unit receive special attention and others do not. The perceived inequalities created by the use of in-groups can have a devastating impact on the feelings, attitudes, and behavior of out-group members. Second, LMX theory emphasizes the importance of leader-member exchanges, but fails to explain the intricacies of how one goes about creating high-quality exchanges. Although the model promotes building trust, respect, and commitment in relationships, it does not fully explicate how this takes place. Finally, there are questions regarding whether the measurement procedures used in LMX research are adequate to fully capture the complexities of the leader-member exchange process.

REFERENCES

Dansereau, F., Graen, G. G., & Haga, W. (1975). A vertical dyad linkage approach to leadership in formal organizations. *Organizational Behavior and Human Performance, 13,* 46-78.

Graen, G. B. (1976). Role-making processes within complex organizations. In M. D. Dunnette (Ed.), *Handbook of industrial and organizational psychology* (pp. 1202-1245). Chicago: Rand McNally.

Graen, G. B., & Cashman, J. (1975). A role-making model of leadership in formal organizations: A developmental approach. In J. G. Hunt & L. L. Larson (Eds.), *Leadership frontiers* (pp. 143-166). Kent, OH: Kent State University Press.

Graen, G. B., & Scandura, T. A. (1987). Toward a psychology of dyadic organizing. In B. Staw & L. L. Cumming (Eds.), *Research in organizational behavior* (Vol. 9, pp. 175-208). Greenwich, CT: JAI.

Graen, G. B., & Uhl-Bien, M. (1991). The transformation of professionals into self-managing and partially self-designing contributions: Toward a theory of leader-making. *Journal of Management Systems, 3*(3), 33-48.

Graen, G. B., & Uhl-Bien, M. (1995). Relationship-based approach to leadership: Development of leader-member exchange (LMX) theory of leadership over

25 years: Applying a multi-level, multi-domain perspective. *Leadership Quarterly, 6*(2), 219-247.

Harter, N., & Evanecky, D. (2002). Fairness in leader-member exchange theory: Do we all belong on the inside? *Leadership Review, 2*(2), 1-7.

Liden, R. C., Wayne, S. J., & Stilwell, D. (1993). A longitudinal study on the early development of leader-member exchange. *Journal of Applied Psychology, 78,* 662-674.

McClane, W. E. (1991). Implications of member role differentiation: Analysis of a key concept in the LMX model of leadership. *Group & Organization Studies, 16*(1), 102-113.

Scandura, T. A. (1999). Rethinking leader-member exchange: An organizational justice perspective. *Leadership Quarterly, 10*(1), 25-40.

Schriesheim, C. A., Castro, S. L., & Cogliser, C. C. (1999). Leader-member exchange (LMX) research: A comprehensive review of theory, measurement, and data-analytic practices. *Leadership Quarterly, 10,* 63-113.

Schriesheim, C. A., Castro, S. L., Zhou, X., & Yammarino, F. J. (2001). The folly of theorizing "A" but testing "B": A selective level-of-analysis review of the field and a detailed leader-member exchange illustration. *Leadership Quarterly, 12,* 515-551.

Yukl, G. (1994). *Leadership in organizations* (3rd ed.). Englewood Cliffs, NJ: Prentice Hall.

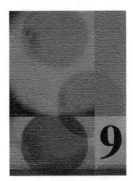

Transformational Leadership

DESCRIPTION

One of the current approaches to leadership that has been the focus of much research since the early 1980s is the transformational approach. In fact, it has grown in popularity since the first edition of this book was published. Transformational leadership is part of the "New Leadership" paradigm (Bryman, 1992), which gives more attention to the charismatic and affective elements of leadership. In a content analysis of articles published in the *Leadership Quarterly,* Lowe and Gardner (2001) found that one third of the research was about transformational/charismatic leadership. Clearly, many scholars are studying transformational leadership, and it occupies a central place in leadership research.

As its name implies, transformational leadership is a process that changes and transforms individuals. It is concerned with emotions, values, ethics, standards, and long-term goals, and includes assessing followers' motives, satisfying their needs, and treating them as full human beings. Transformational leadership involves an exceptional form of influence that moves followers to accomplish more than what is usually expected of them. It is a process that often incorporates charismatic and visionary leadership.

An encompassing approach, transformational leadership can be used to describe a wide range of leadership, from very specific attempts to influence followers on a one-to-one level to very broad attempts to influence whole organizations and even entire cultures. Although the transformational leader plays a pivotal role in precipitating change, followers and leaders are inextricably bound together in the transformation process.

TRANSFORMATIONAL LEADERSHIP DEFINED

The term *transformational leadership* was first coined by Downton (1973); however, its emergence as an important approach to leadership began with a classic work by the political sociologist James MacGregor Burns titled *Leadership* (1978). In his work, Burns attempted to link the roles of leadership and followership. He wrote of leaders as those individuals who tap the motives of followers in order to better reach the goals of leaders and followers (p. 18). For Burns, leadership is quite different from wielding power because it is inseparable from followers' needs.

Burns distinguished between two types of leadership: *transactional* and *transformational*. Transactional leadership refers to the bulk of leadership models, which focus on the exchanges that occur between leaders and their followers. Politicians who win votes by promising no new taxes are demonstrating transactional leadership. Similarly, managers who offer promotions to employees who surpass their goals are exhibiting transactional leadership. In the classroom, teachers are being transactional when they give students a grade for work completed. The exchange dimension of transactional leadership is very common and can be observed at many levels throughout all types of organizations.

In contrast to transactional leadership, transformational leadership refers to the process whereby an individual engages with others and creates a connection that raises the level of motivation and morality in both the leader and the follower. This type of leader is attentive to the needs and motives of followers and tries to help followers reach their fullest potential. Burns points to Mohandas Gandhi as a classic example of transformational leadership. Gandhi raised the hopes and demands of millions of his people and in the process was changed himself.

A more recent example of transformational leadership can be observed in the life of Ryan White. Ryan White raised the American people's awareness about AIDS and in the process became a spokesperson for increasing government support of AIDS research. In Canada, Terry Fox is an example of a transformational leader. At 18, Terry was diagnosed with bone cancer and had to have his right leg amputated 6 inches above the knee. Moved by the suffering of other patients, Terry decided to run across Canada to raise money for cancer research. He called his journey the "Marathon of Hope." Although he passed away, his legacy remains strong, and to date, more than $300 million has been raised in Terry's name. In the organizational world, an example of transformational leadership would be a manager who attempts to change his or her company's corporate values to reflect a more human standard of fairness and justice. In the process, both the manager and followers may emerge with a stronger and higher set of moral values.

TRANSFORMATIONAL LEADERSHIP AND CHARISMA

At about the same time Burns's book was published, House (1976) published a theory of charismatic leadership. Since its publication, charismatic leadership has received a great deal of attention by researchers (e.g., Conger, 1999; Hunt & Conger, 1999). It is often described in ways that make it similar to, if not synonymous with, transformational leadership.

The concept "charisma" was first used to describe a special gift that select individuals possess that gives them the capacity to do extraordinary things. Weber (1947) provided the most well-known definition of charisma as a special personality characteristic that gives a person superhuman or exceptional powers and is reserved for a few, is of divine origin, and results in the person being treated as a leader. Despite Weber's emphasis on charisma as a personality characteristic, he also recognized the important role played by followers in validating charisma in these leaders (Bryman, 1992; House, 1976).

In his theory of charismatic leadership, House suggested that charismatic leaders act in unique ways that have specific charismatic effects on their followers (see Table 9.1). For House, the personal characteristics of a charismatic leader include being dominant, having a strong desire to influence others, being self-confident, and having a strong sense of one's own moral values.

In addition to displaying certain personality characteristics, charismatic leaders also demonstrate specific types of behaviors. First, they are strong role models for the beliefs and values they want their followers to adopt. For example, Gandhi advocated nonviolence and was an exemplary role model of civil disobedience. Second, charismatic leaders appear competent to

Table 9.1 *Personality Characteristics, Behaviors, and Effects on Followers of Charismatic Leadership*

Personality Characteristics	Behaviors	Effects on Followers
Dominant	Sets strong role model	Trust in leader's ideology
Desire to influence	Shows competence	Belief similarity between leader and follower
Confident	Articulates goals	Unquestioning acceptance
Strong values	Communicates high expectations	Affection toward leader
	Expresses confidence	Obedience
	Arouses motives	Identification with leader
		Emotional involvement
		Heightened goals
		Increased confidence

followers. Third, they articulate ideological goals that have moral overtones. Martin Luther King Jr.'s famous "I Have a Dream" speech is an example of this type of charismatic behavior.

Fourth, charismatic leaders communicate high expectations for followers, and they exhibit confidence in followers' abilities to meet these expectations. The impact of this behavior is to increase followers' sense of competence and self-efficacy (Avolio & Gibbons, 1988), which in turn increases their performance. Fifth, charismatic leaders arouse task-relevant motives in followers that may include affiliation, power, or esteem. For example, John F. Kennedy appealed to the human values of the American people when he stated, "Ask not what your country can do for you; ask what you can do for your country."

According to House's charismatic theory, there are several effects that are the direct result of charismatic leadership. They include follower trust in the leader's ideology, similarity between the followers' beliefs and the leader's beliefs, unquestioning acceptance of the leader, expression of warmth toward the leader, follower obedience, identification with the leader, emotional involvement in the leader's goals, heightened goals for followers, and follower confidence in goal achievement. Consistent with Weber, House contends that these charismatic effects are more likely to occur in contexts in which followers feel distress, because in stressful situations followers look to leaders to deliver them from their difficulties.

House's charismatic theory has been extended and revised through the years (see Conger, 1999; Conger & Kanungo, 1998). One major revision to the theory was made by Shamir, House, and Arthur (1993). They postulated that charismatic leadership transforms followers' self-concepts and tries to link the identity of followers to the collective identity of the organization. Charismatic leaders forge this link by emphasizing the intrinsic rewards of work and de-emphasizing the extrinsic rewards. The hope is that followers will view work as an expression of themselves. Throughout the process, leaders express high expectations for followers and help them gain a sense of confidence and self-efficacy. In summary, charismatic leadership works because it ties followers and their self-concepts to the organizational identity.

A MODEL OF TRANSFORMATIONAL LEADERSHIP

In the mid-1980s, Bass (1985) provided a more expanded and refined version of transformational leadership that was based on, but not fully consistent with, the prior works of Burns (1978) and House (1976). In his approach, Bass extended Burns's work by giving more attention to followers' rather than leaders' needs, by suggesting that transformational leadership could apply to situations in which the outcomes were not positive, and by describing transactional and transformational leadership as a single continuum (see Figure 9.1) rather than mutually independent continua (Yammarino, 1993). Bass extended House's work by giving more attention to the emotional elements and origins of charisma and by suggesting that charisma is a necessary but not sufficient condition for transformational leadership (Yammarino, 1993).

Bass (1985) argues that transformational leadership motivates followers to do more than the expected by doing the following: (a) raising followers' levels of consciousness about the importance and value of specified and idealized goals, (b) getting followers to transcend their own self-interest for the sake of the team or organization, and (c) moving followers to address higher-level needs (p. 20). An elaboration of the dynamics of the transformation process is provided in his "model of transformational and transactional

Figure 9.1 *Leadership Continuum From Transformational to
Laissez-Faire Leadership*

Transformational	Transactional	Laissez-faire
Leadership	Leadership	Leadership

leadership" (Bass, 1985, 1990; Bass & Avolio, 1993, 1994). Additional clarification of the model is provided by Avolio in his book *Full Leadership Development: Building the Vital Forces in Organizations* (1999).

As can be seen in Table 9.2, the model of transformational and transactional leadership incorporates seven different factors. These factors are also illustrated in the full range of leadership model, which is provided in Figure 9.2. A discussion of each of these seven factors will help to clarify Bass's model. This discussion will be divided into three parts: transformational factors (4), transactional factors (2), and the nonleadership/nontransactional factor (1).

Transformational Leadership Factors

Transformational leadership is concerned with the performance of followers and also with developing followers to their fullest potential (Avolio, 1999; Bass & Avolio, 1990a). Individuals who exhibit transformational leadership often have a strong set of internal values and ideals, and they are effective at motivating followers to act in ways that support the greater good rather than their own self-interests (Kuhnert, 1994).

Idealized Influence

Factor 1 is called *charisma* or *idealized influence*. It describes leaders who act as strong role models for followers; followers identify with these leaders and want very much to emulate them. These leaders usually have very high standards of moral and ethical conduct and can be counted on to

Table 9.2 *Leadership Factors*

TRANSFORMATIONAL LEADERSHIP	TRANSACTIONAL LEADERSHIP	LAISSEZ-FAIRE LEADERSHIP
Factor 1 Idealized Influence Charisma	**Factor 5** Contingent Reward Constructive Transactions	**Factor 7** Laissez-faire Nontransactional
Factor 2 Inspirational Motivation	**Factor 6** Management-by-Exception, Active and Passive Corrective Transactions	
Factor 3 Intellectual Stimulation		
Factor 4 Individualized Consideration		

do the right thing. They are deeply respected by followers, who usually place a great deal of trust in them. They provide followers with a vision and a sense of mission.

In essence, the charisma factor describes individuals who are special and who make others want to follow the vision they put forward. A person whose leadership exemplifies the charisma factor is Nelson Mandela, the first nonwhite president of South Africa. Mandela is viewed as a leader with high moral standards and a vision for South Africa that resulted in monumental change in how the people of South Africa would be governed. His charismatic qualities and the people's response to them transformed an entire nation.

Inspirational Motivation

Factor 2 is labeled *inspiration* or *inspirational motivation*. This factor is descriptive of leaders who communicate high expectations to followers, inspiring them through motivation to become committed to and a part of the

Figure 9.2 *Full Range of Leadership Model*

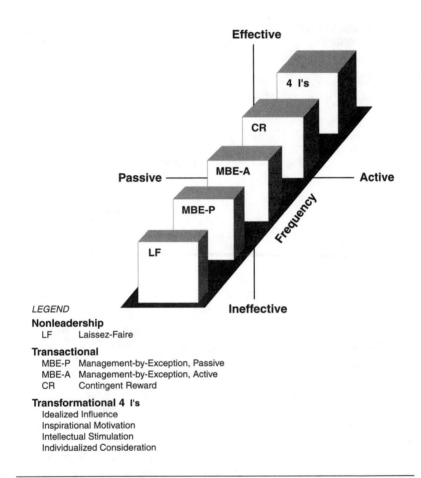

LEGEND
Nonleadership
    LF   Laissez-Faire

Transactional
    MBE-P   Management-by-Exception, Passive
    MBE-A   Management-by-Exception, Active
    CR   Contingent Reward

Transformational 4 I's
    Idealized Influence
    Inspirational Motivation
    Intellectual Stimulation
    Individualized Consideration

SOURCE: From *Improving Organizational Effectiveness Through Transformational Leadership*, by B. M. Bass and B. J. Avolio, 1994, Thousand Oaks, CA: Sage. Used with permission of the author.

shared vision in the organization. In practice, leaders use symbols and emotional appeals to focus group members' efforts to achieve more than they would in their own self-interest. Team spirit is enhanced by this type of leadership. An example of this factor would be a sales manager who motivates his or her sales force to excel in their work through encouraging words and pep talks that clearly communicate the integral role they play in the future growth of the company.

Intellectual Stimulation

Factor 3 refers to *intellectual stimulation*. It includes leadership that stimulates followers to be creative and innovative, and to challenge their own beliefs and values as well as those of the leader and the organization. This type of leadership supports followers as they try new approaches and develop innovative ways of dealing with organizational issues. It promotes followers' thinking things out on their own and engaging in careful problem solving. An example of this type of leadership is a plant manager who promotes workers' individual efforts to develop unique ways to solve problems that have caused slowdowns in production.

Individualized Consideration

Factor 4 of the transformational factors is called *individualized consideration*. This factor is representative of leaders who provide a supportive climate in which they listen carefully to the individual needs of followers. Leaders act as coaches and advisers while trying to assist individuals in becoming fully actualized. These leaders may use delegation as a means to help followers grow through personal challenges. An example of this type of leadership is a manager who spends time treating each employee in a caring and unique way. For some employees, the leader may give strong affiliation; for others, the leader may give specific directives with a high degree of structure.

In essence, transformational leadership produces greater effects than transactional leadership (see Figure 9.3). While transactional leadership results in expected outcomes, transformational leadership results in performance that goes well beyond what is expected. In a meta-analysis of 39 studies in the transformational literature, for example, Lowe, Kroeck, and Sivasubramaniam (1996) found that individuals who exhibited transformational leadership were perceived to be more effective leaders with better work outcomes than were individuals who exhibited only transactional leadership. These findings were true for higher- and lower-level leaders as well as for leaders in public and private settings. Transformational leadership moves followers to accomplish more than what is usually expected of them. They become motivated to transcend their own self-interests for the good of the group or organization (Bass & Avolio, 1990a).

Figure 9.3 *The Additive Effect of Transformational Leadership*

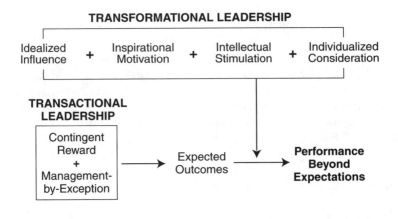

SOURCE: Adapted from "The Implications of Transactional and Transformational
Leadership for Individual, Team, and Organizational Development," by B. M. Bass and
B. J. Avolio, 1990a, *Research in Organizational Change and Development, 4,* 231-272.

Transactional Leadership Factors

Transactional leadership diverges from transformational leadership in that the transactional leader does not individualize the needs of subordinates nor focus on their personal development. Transactional leaders exchange things of value with subordinates to advance their own as well as their subordinates' agenda (Kuhnert, 1994). Transactional leaders are influential because it is in the best interest of subordinates to do what the leader wants (Kuhnert & Lewis, 1987).

Contingent Reward

Factor 5, labeled *contingent reward,* is the first of two transactional leadership factors (see Figure 9.2). It refers to an exchange process between leaders and followers in which effort by followers is exchanged for specified rewards. With this kind of leadership, the leader tries to obtain agreement from followers on what needs to be done and what the payoffs will be for the people doing it. An example of this type of transaction is a parent who negotiates with a child how much television she or he can watch after practicing on the piano. Another example often occurs in the academic setting—a dean negotiates with a college professor about the number and quality of publications he or she needs in order to receive tenure and promotion.

Management-by-Exception

Factor 6 is labeled in the model as *management-by-exception* and refers to leadership that involves corrective criticism, negative feedback, and negative reinforcement. Management-by-exception takes two forms: active and passive. A leader using the active form of management-by-exception watches followers closely for mistakes or rule violations and then takes corrective action. An example of active management-by-exception can be illustrated in the leadership of a sales supervisor who daily monitors how employees approach customers; she quickly corrects those salespeople who are slow to approach customers in the prescribed manner. A leader using the passive form intervenes only after standards have not been met or problems have arisen. An example of passive management-by-exception is illustrated in the leadership of a supervisor who gives an employee a poor performance evaluation without ever talking with the employee about her or his prior work performance. In essence, both the active and passive management types use more negative reinforcement patterns than the positive reinforcement pattern described in Factor 5 under contingent reward.

Nonleadership Factor

In the model, the nonleadership factor diverges further from transactional leadership and represents behaviors that are nontransactional.

Laissez-Faire

Factor 7 describes leadership that falls at the far right side of the transactional-transformational leadership continuum (see Figure 9.1). This factor represents the absence of leadership. As the French phrase implies, the *laissez-faire* leader takes a "hands-off—let-things-ride" approach. This leader abdicates responsibility, delays decisions, gives no feedback, and makes little effort to help followers satisfy their needs. There is no exchange with followers or any attempt to help them grow. An example of a laissez-faire leader is the president of a small manufacturing firm who calls no meetings with plant supervisors, has no long-range plan for her or his company, and makes little contact with employees within the organization.

OTHER TRANSFORMATIONAL PERSPECTIVES

In addition to Bass's (1985, 1990; Bass & Avolio, 1994) work, two other lines of research have contributed in unique ways to our understanding of the nature of transformational leadership. They are the research of Bennis and Nanus (1985) and the work of Tichy and DeVanna (1986, 1990). The methods used by these researchers to collect data were quite similar. They simply identified a number of chief executive officers (CEOs) or leaders at large corporations and then interviewed them, using a relatively unstructured, open-ended question-and-answer format.

Bennis and Nanus

Bennis and Nanus (1985) asked 90 leaders basic questions such as: What are your strengths and weaknesses? What past events most influenced your leadership approach? What were the critical points in your career? From the answers leaders provided to these questions, Bennis and Nanus identified four common strategies used by leaders in transforming organizations.

First, transforming leaders had a clear *vision* of the future state of their organizations. It was an image of an attractive, realistic, and believable future (Bennis & Nanus, 1985, p. 89). The vision was usually simple, understandable, beneficial, and energy creating. The compelling nature of the vision touched the experiences of followers and pulled them into supporting the organization. When an organization has a clear vision, it is easier for individuals within the organization to learn how they fit in with the overall direction of the organization and even the society in general. It empowers them because they feel they are a significant dimension of a worthwhile enterprise (pp. 90-91). Bennis and Nanus found that to be successful, the vision needed to grow out of the needs of the entire organization and be claimed by those within it. Although leaders play a large role in articulating the vision, the emergence of the vision originates from both the leaders and the followers within the organization.

Second, transforming leaders were *social architects* for their organizations. This means they created a shape or form for the shared meanings individuals maintained within their organizations. These leaders communicated a direction that transformed their organization's values and norms. In many cases, these leaders were able to mobilize people to accept a new group identity or a new philosophy for their organizations.

Third, transforming leaders created *trust* in their organizations by making their own positions clearly known and then standing by them. Trust has to do with being predictable or reliable, even in situations that are uncertain. For organizations, leaders built trust by articulating a direction and then consistently implementing the direction even though the vision may have involved a high degree of uncertainty. Bennis and Nanus (1985) found that when leaders established trust in an organization it gave the organization a sense of integrity analogous to a healthy identity (p. 48).

Fourth, transforming leaders used *creative deployment of self through positive self-regard*. Leaders knew their strengths and weaknesses, and they emphasized their strengths rather than dwelling on their weaknesses. Based on an awareness of their own competence, effective leaders were able to immerse themselves in their tasks and the overarching goals of their organizations. They were able to fuse a sense of self with the work at hand. Bennis and Nanus also found that positive self-regard in leaders had a reciprocal impact on followers, creating in them feelings of confidence and high expectations. In addition, leaders in the study were committed to learning and relearning, so in their organizations there was consistent emphasis on education.

Tichy and DeVanna

Similar to Bennis and Nanus, Tichy and DeVanna (1986, 1990) studied the transformational leadership of 12 CEOs at mostly large corporations. Tichy and DeVanna were interested in how organizations change—how they are transformed. In particular, they were concerned with how leaders carried out the change process.

Tichy and DeVanna wanted to find out how leaders worked under the challenging conditions brought about by rapid technological change, social and cultural changes, increased competition, and increased interdependence with economies of other nations. The data from their interviews suggested that leaders manage change in organizations through a three-act process.

Act 1 of this transformation process involves *recognizing the need for change*. There is a tendency for organizations and individuals within organizations to be comfortable with the status quo and to resist change. People want to sustain the present system. As a result, the need for change may go unrecognized. Transformational leaders are change agents. They have the responsibility of pointing out to the organization how change in the environment could positively or negatively affect how the organization operates.

Tichy and DeVanna suggested several techniques that can assist organizations in increasing their openness to change. First, encourage dissent and allow people to disagree. Next, encourage objective assessment of how well the organization is meeting its goals. Third, encourage members of the organization to visit other organizations within and outside the organization to obtain alternative viewpoints of how other organizations work and solve problems. Last, encourage organizations to assess their performance based on a wide range of economic and noneconomic indicators relative to other companies on these same indicators.

Act 2 in the change process requires the *creation of a vision*. The vision acts as a conceptual road map for where the organization is headed in the future and what it will look like (Tichy & DeVanna, 1990, p. 128). For Tichy and DeVanna, a vision is constructed not by a single leader but as a result of bringing together the differing viewpoints within an organization. A central aspect of creating a vision is developing a mission statement that describes the vision and the values implied by it.

Act 3 in transforming organizations involves *institutionalizing changes*. To do this, leaders need to break down old structures and establish new ones. They need to find appropriate followers to implement new ideas. The breaking down of old structures may require that the leader create new coalitions of employees who will be compatible with the new vision. In the process, individuals will need to be helped to find new roles in the organization as different structures are designed so as to enhance the new directions for the organization.

HOW DOES THE
TRANSFORMATIONAL APPROACH WORK?

The transformational approach to leadership is a broad-based perspective that encompasses many facets and dimensions of the leadership process. In general, it describes how leaders can initiate, develop, and carry out significant changes in organizations. Although not definitive, the steps followed by transformational leaders usually take the following form.

Transformational leaders set out to empower followers and nurture them in change. They attempt to raise the consciousness in individuals and to get them to transcend their own self-interests for the sake of others.

To create change, transformational leaders become strong role models for their followers. They have a highly developed set of moral values and a self-determined sense of identity (Avolio & Gibbons, 1988). They are confident, competent, and articulate, and they express strong ideals. They listen to followers and are not intolerant of opposing viewpoints. A spirit of cooperation often develops between these leaders and their followers. Followers want to emulate transformational leaders because they learn to trust them and believe in the ideas for which they stand.

It is common for transformational leaders to create a vision. The vision emerges from the collective interests of various individuals and units within an organization. The vision is a focal point for transformational leadership. It gives the leader and the organization a conceptual map for where the organization is headed; it gives meaning and clarifies the organization's identity. Furthermore, the vision gives followers a sense of identity within the organization and also a sense of self-efficacy (Shamir et al., 1993).

Transformational leaders also act as change agents who initiate and implement new directions within organizations. They listen to opposing viewpoints within the organization as well as threats to the organization that may arise from outside the organization. Sometimes leaders generate instability themselves through nurturing the expression of discordant viewpoints or issues. Out of the uncertainty, transformational leaders create change.

The transformational approach also requires that leaders become social architects. This means they make clear the emerging values and norms of the organization. They involve themselves in the culture of the organization and help shape its meaning. People need to know their roles and understand how they are contributors to the greater purposes of the organization. Transformational leaders are "out front" in interpreting and shaping for organizations the shared meanings that exist within them.

STRENGTHS

In its present stage of development, the transformational approach has several strengths. First, transformational leadership has been widely researched from many different perspectives, including a series of qualitative studies of prominent leaders and CEOs in large, well-known organizations, and has also been the focal point for a large body of leadership research since its introduction in the 1970s. For example, a recent content analysis of all the articles published in the *Leadership Quarterly* over the past decade showed that 34% of the articles were about transformational/ charismatic leadership (Lowe & Gardner, 2001). In addition, there have been well over 200 theses, dissertations, and research projects conducted using this approach.

Second, transformational leadership has intuitive appeal. The transformational perspective describes how the leader is out front advocating change for others, and this concept is consistent with society's popular notion of what leadership means. People are attracted to transformational leadership because it makes sense to them. It is appealing that a leader will provide a vision for the future.

Third, transformational leadership treats leadership as a process that occurs between followers and leaders. Because this process incorporates both the followers' and the leader's needs, leadership is not the sole responsibility of a leader but rather emerges from the interplay between leaders and followers. The needs of others are central to the transformational leader. As a result, followers gain a more prominent position in the leadership process because the attributions of followers are instrumental in the evolving transformational process (Bryman, 1992, p. 176).

Fourth, the transformational approach provides a broader view of leadership that augments other leadership models. Many leadership models focus primarily on how leaders exchange rewards for achieved goals—the transactional process. The transformational approach provides an expanded picture of leadership that includes not only the exchange of rewards but also leaders' attention to the needs and growth of followers (Avolio, 1999; Bass, 1985).

Fifth, transformational leadership places a strong emphasis on followers' needs, values, and morals. Burns (1978) suggested that transformational leadership involves attempts by leaders to move individuals to higher standards of moral responsibility. It includes motivating followers to transcend their own self-interests for the good of the team, organization, or community (Howell & Avolio, 1992; Shamir et al., 1993). Transformational leadership is fundamentally "morally uplifting" (Avolio, 1999). This emphasis sets the transformational approach apart from all other approaches to leadership because it suggests that leadership has a moral dimension. By emphasizing this aspect, the coercive uses of power by individuals such as Hitler, Jim Jones, and David Koresch can be disregarded as models of leadership.

Finally, there is substantial evidence that transformational leadership is an effective form of leadership (Yukl, 1999). In a critique of transformational and charismatic leadership, Yukl reported that in studies that used the Multifactor Leadership Questionnaire (MLQ) to appraise leaders, transformational leadership was positively related to subordinate satisfaction, motivation, and performance. Furthermore, in studies that used interviews and observations, transformational leadership was shown to be effective in a variety of different situations.

CRITICISMS

Transformational leadership also has several weaknesses. One criticism is that it lacks conceptual clarity. Because it covers such a wide range, including creating a vision, motivating, being a change agent, building trust, giving nurturance, and acting as a social architect, to name a few, it is difficult to define exactly the parameters of transformational leadership. Specifically, research by Tracey and Hinkin (1998) has shown substantial overlap between each of the Four I's (idealized influence, inspirational motivation, intellectual stimulation, and individualized consideration), suggesting that the dimensions are not clearly delimited. There is a need to theoretically distinguish between these factors (Yukl, 1999). Furthermore, the parameters of transformational leadership often overlap with other similar conceptualizations of leadership. Bryman (1992), for example, points out that transformational and charismatic leadership are often treated synonymously even though in some models of leadership (e.g., Bass, 1985) charisma is only one component of transformational leadership.

Another criticism revolves around how transformational leadership is measured. For the past 15 years, many leadership studies have been conducted using some form of the MLQ. However, the validity of the MLQ has not been fully established (cf. Bycio, Hackett, & Allen, 1995; Tepper & Percy, 1994). In some versions of the MLQ, the four factors of transformational leadership (idealized influence, inspirational motivation, intellectual stimulation, and individualized consideration) correlate highly with each other, which means they are not distinct factors (Tejeda, Scandura, & Pillai, 2001). In addition, some of the transformational factors correlate with the transactional and laissez-faire factors, which means they are not unique to the transformational model (Tejeda et al., 2001).

These findings raise questions about the MLQ and about the clarity of the transformational leadership model. More attention needs to be given to the substance of the MLQ and how it is used in research. Although there are questions and concerns regarding the MLQ, a new, improved 27-item version of the MLQ has been developed that has promise in validating the legitimacy of the theory (Tejeda et al., 2001).

A third criticism some have made is that transformational leadership treats leadership as a personality trait or personal predisposition rather than a behavior in which people can be instructed (Bryman, 1992, pp. 100-102). If it is a trait, training people in this approach becomes more problematic because it is difficult to teach people how to change their traits. Even though many scholars, including Weber, House, and Bass, emphasize that transformational leadership is concerned with leader behaviors, such as how leaders involve themselves with followers, there is an inclination to see this approach from a trait perspective. Perhaps this problem is exacerbated because the word *transformational* creates images of one person being the most active component in the leadership process. For example, even though "creating a vision" involves follower input, there is a tendency to see transformational leaders as visionaries. There is also a tendency to see transformational leaders as individuals who have special qualities that *transform* others. These images accentuate a trait characterization of transformational leadership.

A fourth criticism some have made is that transformational leadership is elitist and antidemocratic (Avolio, 1999; Bass & Avolio, 1993). Transformational leaders often play a direct role in creating changes, establishing a vision, and advocating new directions. This gives the strong impression that the leader is acting independently of followers or putting himself or herself above the followers' needs. Although this criticism of elitism has been refuted by Bass and Avolio (1993) and Avolio (1999), who contend that transformational leaders can be directive and participative as well as democratic and authoritarian, the substance of the criticism raises valid questions about transformational leadership.

Related to this criticism, some have argued that transformational leadership suffers from a "heroic leadership" bias (Yukl, 1999). Transformational leadership stresses that it is the *leader* who moves *followers* to do exceptional things. By focusing primarily on the leader, researchers have failed to give attention to shared leadership or reciprocal influence. Followers can influence leaders just as leaders can influence followers. More attention needs to be directed toward how leaders can encourage followers to challenge the leader's vision and share in the leadership process.

Another criticism is that transformational leadership is based primarily on qualitative data collected from leaders who were very visible serving in positions that were at the top of their organizations (Bryman, 1992). As

Bryman points out (p. 157), the data apply to leadership *of* organizations but not necessarily leadership *in* organizations. For example, can transformational leadership be applied equally to plant managers and CEOs? Can supervisors and department heads learn about leadership from a model that was constructed from interviews with senior corporate leaders? Bass and his associates have begun to report findings from quantitative studies of leaders at all levels that substantiate the assumptions of transformational leadership. But until more data are available, the questions remain of how transformational leadership applies to lower-level leaders.

A final criticism of transformational leadership is that it has the potential to be abused. Transformational leadership is concerned with changing people's values and moving them to a new vision. But who is to determine if the new directions are good and more affirming? Who decides that a new vision is a better vision? If the values to which the leader is moving his or her followers are not better, and if the set of human values is not more redeeming, then the leadership must be challenged. However, the dynamics of how followers challenge leaders or respond to their visions is not fully understood.

There is a need to understand how transformational leaders affect followers psychologically and how leaders respond to followers' reactions. In fact, Burns argues that understanding this area (i.e., charisma and follower worship) is one of the central problems in leadership studies today (Bailey & Axelrod, 2001). The charismatic nature of transformational leadership presents significant risks for organizations because it can be used for destructive purposes (Conger, 1999; Howell & Avolio, 1992). History is full of examples of charismatic individuals who used coercive power to lead people to evil ends. For this reason, transformational leadership puts a burden on individuals and organizations to be aware of how they are being influenced and in what directions they are being asked to go.

APPLICATION

Rather than being a model that tells leaders what to do, transformational leadership provides a broad set of generalizations of what is typical of leaders who are transforming or who work in transforming contexts. Unlike other leadership approaches, such as contingency theory and situational leadership, transformational leadership does not provide a clearly defined set of assumptions about how leaders should act in a particular situation to be successful. Rather, it provides a general way of thinking about leadership that emphasizes ideals, inspiration, innovations, and individual concerns. Transformational leadership requires that leaders be aware of how their own behavior relates to the needs of their subordinates and the changing dynamics within their organizations.

Bass and Avolio (1990a) suggested that transformational leadership can be taught to individuals at all levels within an organization and that it can positively affect a firm's performance. It can be used in recruitment, selection and promotion, and training and development. It can also be used in improving team development, decision-making groups, quality initiatives, and reorganizations (Bass & Avolio, 1994).

Programs designed to develop transformational leadership usually require that individuals or their associates take the MLQ (Bass & Avolio, 1990b) or a similar questionnaire to determine the leader's particular strengths and weaknesses in transformational leadership. Taking the MLQ assists leaders in pinpointing areas in which they could improve their leadership. For example, leaders might learn that it would be beneficial if they were more confident in expressing their goals, or that they needed to spend more time nurturing followers, or that they needed to be more tolerant of opposing viewpoints within the organization. The MLQ is the springboard to helping leaders improve a whole series of their leadership attributes.

One particular aspect of transformational leadership that has been given special emphasis in training programs is the process of building a vision. For example, it has become quite common for training programs to have leaders write elaborate statements that describe their own 5-year career plans as well as their perceptions of the future directions for their organizations. Working with leaders on vision statements is one way to help them enhance their transformational leadership behavior. Another important aspect of training is teaching leaders to exhibit greater individual consideration and intellectual stimulation toward their followers. Lowe et al. (1996) found that this is particularly valuable for lower-level leaders in organizations.

Overall, transformational leadership provides leaders with information about a full range of their behaviors, from nontransactional to transactional to transformational. In the next section, we provide some actual leadership examples to which an application can be made of the principles of transformational leadership.

CASE STUDIES

In the following section, three brief case studies (Cases 9.1, 9.2, and 9.3) from very different contexts are provided. Each case describes a situation in which transformational leadership is present to some degree. The questions at the end of each case point to some of the unique issues surrounding the use of transformational leadership in ongoing organizations.

CASE 9.1

The Vision Failed

High Tech Engineering (HTE) is a 50-year-old family-owned manufacturing company with 250 employees that produces small parts for the aircraft industry. The president of HTE is Mr. Barelli, who came to the company from a smaller business with strong credentials as a leader in advanced aircraft technology. Prior to Mr. B, the only president of HTE was the founder and owner of the company. The organizational structure at HTE was very traditional, and it was supported by a very rich organizational culture.

As the new president, Mr. B sincerely wanted to transform HTE. He wanted to prove that new technologies and advanced management techniques could make HTE one of the best manufacturing companies in the country. To that end, Mr. B created a vision statement that was displayed throughout the company. The two-page statement, which had a strong democratic tone, described the overall purposes, directions, and values of the company.

During the first 3 years of Mr. B's tenure as president, several major reorganizations took place at the company. These were designed by Mr. B and a select few of his senior managers. The intention of each reorganization was to implement advanced organizational structures to bolster the declared HTE vision.

Yet the major outcome of each of the changes was to dilute the leadership and create a feeling of instability among the employees. Most of the changes were made from the top down, with little input from lower or middle management. Some of the changes gave employees more control in circumstances where they needed less, whereas other changes limited employee input in contexts where employees should have been given more input. There were some situations in which individual workers reported to three different bosses, and other situations where one manager had far too many workers to oversee. Rather than feeling comfortable in their various roles within HTE, employees began to feel uncertain about their responsibilities and how they contributed to stated goals of the company. The overall effect of the reorganizations was a precipitous drop in worker morale and production.

In the midst of all the changes, the vision that Mr. B had for the company became lost. The instability that employees felt made it difficult for them to support the company's vision. People at HTE complained that although mission statements were displayed throughout the company, no one understood in which direction they were going.

To the employees at HTE, Mr. B was an enigma. HTE was an American company that produced U.S. products, but Mr. B drove a foreign car. Mr. B claimed to be democratic in his style of leadership, but he was arbitrary in how he treated people; he acted in a nondirective style toward some people and he showed arbitrary control toward others. He wanted to be seen as a hands-on manager, but he delegated operational control of the company to others while he focused on external customer relations and board of directors matters.

At times Mr. B appeared to be insensitive to employees' concerns. He wanted HTE to be an environment in which everyone could feel empowered, but he often failed to listen closely to what employees were saying. He seldom engaged in open, two-way communication. HTE had a long, rich history with many unique stories, but the employees felt that Mr. B either misunderstood or did not care about that history.

Four years after arriving at HTE, Mr. B stepped down as president after his operations officer ran the company into a large debt and cash flow crisis. His dream of building HTE into a world-class manufacturing company was never realized.

Questions

1. If you were consulting with the board of directors at HTE, what would you advise them regarding Mr. B's leadership from a transformational perspective?
2. Did Mr. B have a clear vision for HTE, and was he able to implement it?
3. How effective was Mr. B as a change agent and a social architect for HTE?
4. What would you tell Mr. B to do differently if he had the chance to return as president of HTE?

CASE 9.2

Students Dig It

Every year, Dr. Cook, a college professor, leads a group of 25 college students to the Middle East on an archaeological dig that usually lasts about 8 weeks. The participants, who come from big and small colleges throughout the country, usually have little knowledge or background in what takes place during an excavation. Dr. Cook enjoys leading these expeditions because he likes teaching students about archaeology and because the outcomes of the digs actually advance his own scholarly work.

While planning for his annual summer excavation, Dr. Cook told the following story:

This summer will be interesting because I have 10 people returning from last year. Last year was quite a dig. During the first couple of weeks everything was very disjointed. Team members seemed lost, unmotivated, and tired. In fact, there was one time early on when it seemed as if nearly half the students were either physically ill or mentally exhausted. Students seemed lost and uncertain about the meaning of the entire project.

For example, it is our tradition to get up every morning at 4:30 a.m. to depart for the excavation site at 5:00 a.m. However, during the first weeks of the dig, few people were ever ready at 5, even after several reminders.

Every year it takes some time for people to learn where they fit with each other and with the purposes of the dig. The students all come from such different backgrounds. Some are from small, private, religious schools, and others are from large state universities. Each comes with a different agenda, with different skills, and with different work habits. One person may be a good photographer, another a good drawer, and another a good surveyor. It is my job to complete the excavation with the resources available to us.

At the end of Week 2, I called a meeting to assess how things were going. We talked about a lot of things including personal things, how our work was progressing, and what we needed to change. The students seemed to appreciate the chance to talk at this meeting. Each of them described their special circumstances and their hopes for the summer.

I told the students several stories about past digs; some were humorous and others highlighted accomplishments. I shared my particular interests in this project and how I thought we as a group could accomplish the work that needed to be done at this important historical site. In particular, I stressed two points: (a) that they shared the responsibility for the successful outcome of the venture and (b) that they had independent authority to design, schedule, and carry out the details of their respective assignments, with the director and other senior staff available at all times as advisers and resource persons. In regard to the departure time issue, I told the participants that the standard departure time on digs was 5:00 a.m.

Well, shortly after our meeting I observed a real shift in the group attitude and atmosphere. People seemed to become more involved in the work, there was less sickness, and there was more camradery. All assignments were completed without constant prodding and in a spirit of mutual support. Each morning at 5:00 a.m. everyone was ready to go.

I find that each year my groups are different. It's almost as if each of them has a unique personality. Perhaps that is why I find it so challenging. I try to listen to the students and utilize their particular strengths. It really is quite amazing how these students can develop in 8 weeks. They really become good at archaeology and they accomplish a great deal.

This coming year will again be different because of the 10 returning "veterans."

Questions

1. How is this an example of transformational leadership?
2. Where are Dr. Cook's strengths on the full range of leadership model (see Figure 9.3)?
3. What is the vision Dr. Cook has for the archaeology excavations?

CASE 9.3

Her Vision Was a Model Research Center

Ms. Adams began as a researcher at a large pharmaceutical company. After several years of observing the way clinical drug studies were conducted, she realized that there was a need and opportunity for a research center not connected with a specific pharmaceutical company. In collaboration with other researchers, she launched a new company that was the first of its kind in the country. Within 5 years, Ms. Adams became president and CEO of the Independent Center for Clinical Research (ICCR). Under Ms. Adams's leadership, ICCR grew over a 10-year period to become a company with revenues of $6 million and profits of $1 million. ICCR employed 100 full-time employees, most of whom were women.

Ms. Adams wants ICCR to continue its pattern of formidable growth. Her vision for the company is to make it a model research center that will blend credible science with efficient and cost-effective clinical trials. To that end, the company, which is situated in a large urban setting, maintains strong links to academia, industry, and the community.

Ms. Adams and her style have a great deal to do with the success of ICCR. She is a free thinker who is always open to new ideas, opportunities, and approaches. She is a positive person who enjoys the nuances of life, and she is not afraid to take risks. Her optimistic approach has had a significant influence on the company's achievements and its organizational climate. People employed at ICCR claim they have never worked at a place that is so progressive and so positive in how it treats its employees and customers. The women employees at ICCR feel particularly strongly about Ms. Adams's leadership, and many of them use Ms. Adams as a role model. It is not by accident that the majority (85%) of the people who work at ICCR are women. Her support for women's concerns is evident in the type of drug studies the company selects to conduct and in her service to national committees on women's health and research issues. Within ICCR, Ms. Adams has designed an on-site day care program, flex-time scheduling for mothers with young children, and a benefits package that gives full health coverage to part-time employees. At a time when most companies are searching for ways to include more women in decision making, ICCR has women in established leadership positions at all levels.

Although Ms. Adams has been extremely effective at ICCR, the success of the company has resulted in many changes that have affected Ms. Adams's leadership at the company.

Rapid growth of ICCR has required that Ms. Adams spend a great deal of time traveling throughout the country. Due to her excessive travel, Ms. Adams has begun to feel distant from the day-to-day operations of ICCR. She has begun to feel as if she is losing her handle on what makes the company "tick." For example, although she used to give weekly pep talks to supervisors, she finds that she now gives two formal presentations a year. Ms. Adams also complains of feeling estranged from employees at the company. At a recent directors meeting she expressed frustration that people no longer called her by her first name and others did not even know who she was.

Growth at ICCR has also demanded that more planning and decision making be delegated to department heads. This has been problematic for Ms. Adams, particularly in the area of strategic planning. Ms. Adams finds the department heads are beginning to shift the focus of ICCR in a direction that contradicts her ideal model of what the company should be and what it is best at doing. Ms. Adams built the company on the idea that ICCR would be a strong blend of credible science and cost-effective clinical trials, and she does not want to give up that model. The directors, on the other hand, would like to see ICCR become similar to a standard pharmaceutical company dedicated primarily to the research and development of new drugs.

Questions

1. What is it about Ms. Adams's leadership that clearly suggests that she is engaged in transformational leadership?
2. In what ways has the growth of ICCR had an impact on the leadership of Ms. Adams?
3. Given the problems Ms. Adams is confronting as a result of the growth of the company, what should she do to reestablish herself as a transformational leader at ICCR?

———————————◆———————————

LEADERSHIP INSTRUMENT

The most widely used measure of transformational leadership is the MLQ. An earlier version of the MLQ was originally developed by Bass (1985), based on a series of interviews he and his associates conducted with 70 senior executives in South Africa. These executives were asked to recall leaders within their experiences who had raised their awareness to broader goals, moved them to higher motives, or inspired them to put others' interests ahead of their own. The executives were then asked to describe how these leaders behaved—what they did to effect change. From these descriptions and from numerous other interviews with both junior and senior executives, Bass constructed the questions that make up the MLQ. Since it was first designed, the MLQ has gone through many revisions, and it continues to be refined to strengthen its reliability and validity (Bass & Avolio, 1993).

The MLQ is made up of questions that measure followers' perceptions of a leader's behavior for each of the seven factors in the transformational and transactional leadership model (see Figure 9.2), and it also has items that measure extra effort, effectiveness, and satisfaction.

Based on a summary analysis of a series of studies that used the MLQ to predict how transformational leadership relates to outcomes such as effectiveness, Bryman (1992) and Bass and Avolio (1994) have suggested that the charisma and motivation factors on the MLQ are the most likely to be related to positive effects. Individualized consideration, intellectual stimulation, and contingent reward are the next most important factors. Management-by-exception in its passive form has been found to be somewhat related to outcomes, and in its active form it has been found to be negatively related to outcomes. Generally, laissez-faire leadership has been found to be negatively related to outcomes such as effectiveness and satisfaction in organizations.

Bass and Avolio (1992) have developed an abbreviated version of the MLQ, called the MLQ-6S. We present it in this section so that you can assess your own transformational, transactional, and nontransactional leadership style. At the end of the questionnaire, we provide information you can use to interpret your scores.

As you assess your own scores, you may wish to divide the seven factors into three groups. The first group would be your scores on Factors 1 through 4, which represent items that directly assess the degree to which your leadership is transformational. Higher scores on these factors indicate more frequently displayed transformational leadership. The second group would be your totals for Factors 5 and 6. These factors represent the transactional dimensions of your leadership. Higher scores on these factors suggest you tend to use reward systems and/or corrective structures in your leadership style. The last factor, laissez-faire leadership, assesses the degree to which you employ hands-off leadership, or nonleadership. On this factor, higher scores indicate that you tend to provide little structure or guidance to subordinates.

As you can see, the MLQ-6S covers a number of dimensions of leadership, or what Bass and Avolio (1994) have called a full range of leadership styles. This questionnaire should give you a clearer picture of your own style as well as the complexity of transformational leadership itself.

◆

Multifactor Leadership
Questionnaire (MLQ) Form 6S

Instructions: This questionnaire provides a description of your leadership style. Twenty-one descriptive statements are listed below. Judge how frequently each statement fits you. The word *others* may mean your followers, clients, or group members.

Key: 0 = Not at all   1 = Once in a while   2 = Sometimes   3 = Fairly often
        4 = Frequently, if not always

1. I make others feel good to be around me.	1 2 3 4
2. I express with a few simple words what we could and should do.	1 2 3 4
3. I enable others to think about old problems in new ways.	1 2 3 4
4. I help others develop themselves.	1 2 3 4
5. I tell others what to do if they want to be rewarded for their work.	1 2 3 4
6. I am satisfied when others meet agreed-upon standards.	1 2 3 4
7. I am content to let others continue working in the same wayas always.	1 2 3 4
8. Others have complete faith in me.	1 2 3 4
9. I provide appealing images about what we can do.	1 2 3 4
10. I provide others with new ways of looking at puzzling things.	1 2 3 4
11. I let others know how I think they are doing.	1 2 3 4
12. I provide recognition/rewards when others reach their goals.	1 2 3 4
13. As long as things are working, I do not try to change anything.	1 2 3 4
14. Whatever others want to do is OK with me.	1 2 3 4
15. Others are proud to be associated with me.	1 2 3 4
16. I help others find meaning in their work.	1 2 3 4
17. I get others to rethink ideas that they had never questioned before.	1 2 3 4
18. I give personal attention to others who seem rejected.	1 2 3 4
19. I call attention to what others can get for what they accomplish.	1 2 3 4
20. I tell others the standards they have to know to carry out their work.	1 2 3 4
21. I ask no more of others than what is absolutely essential.	1 2 3 4

SOURCE: Copyright © 1992 B. M. Bass and B. J. Avolio. Adapted with permission. MLQ forms can be obtained from Mind Garden, Inc., 1690 Woodside Rd., Suite 202, Redwood City, CA 94061, USA; (650) 261-3500.

Scoring

The MLQ-6S measures your leadership on seven factors related to transformational leadership. Your score for each factor is determined by summing three specified items on the questionnaire. For example, to determine your score for Factor 1, *Idealized influence,* sum your responses for items 1, 8, and 15. Complete this procedure for all seven factors.

	Total	
Idealized influence (items 1, 8, and 15)	_____	Factor 1
Inspirational motivation (items 2, 9, and 16)	_____	Factor 2
Intellectual stimulation (items 3, 10, and 17)	_____	Factor 3
Individualized consideration (items 4, 11, and 18)	_____	Factor 4
Contingent reward (items 5, 12, and 19)	_____	Factor 5
Management-by-exception (items 6, 13, and 20)	_____	Factor 6
Laissez-faire leadership (items 7, 14, and 21)	_____	Factor 7

Score range: high = 9-12, moderate = 5-8, low = 0-4

Scoring Interpretation

Factor 1. *Idealized influence* indicates whether you hold subordinates' trust, maintain their faith and respect, show dedication to them, appeal to their hopes and dreams, and act as their role model.

Factor 2. *Inspirational motivation* measures the degree to which you provide a vision, use appropriate symbols and images to help others focus on their work, and try to make others feel their work is significant.

Factor 3. *Intellectual stimulation* shows the degree to which you encourage others to be creative in looking at old problems in new ways, create an environment that is tolerant of seemingly extreme positions, and nurture people to question their own values and beliefs and those of the organization.

Factor 4. *Individualized consideration* indicates the degree to which you show interest in others' well-being, assign projects individually, and pay attention to those who seem less involved in the group.

Factor 5. *Contingent reward* shows the degree to which you tell others what to do in order to be rewarded, emphasize what you expect from them, and recognize their accomplishments.

Factor 6. *Management-by-exception* assesses whether you tell others the job requirements, are content with standard performance, and are a believer in "if it ain't broke, don't fix it."

Factor 7. *Laissez-faire* measures whether you require little of others, are content to let things ride, and let others do their own thing.

◆

SUMMARY

One of the newest and most encompassing approaches to leadership, transformational leadership is concerned with the process of how certain leaders
are able to inspire followers to accomplish great things. This approach
stresses that leaders need to understand and adapt to the needs and motives
of followers. Transformational leaders are recognized as change agents
who are good role models, who can create and articulate a clear vision for
an organization, who empower followers to achieve at higher standards,
who act in ways that make others want to trust them, and who give meaning to organizational life.

Transformational leadership emerged from and is rooted in the writings of
scholars such as Burns (1978), Bass (1985), Bennis and Nanus (1985), and
Tichy and DeVanna (1986).

Transformational leadership can be assessed through use of the
Multifactor Leadership Questionnaire (MLQ), which measures a leader's
behavior in seven areas: idealized influence (charisma), inspirational motivation, intellectual stimulation, individualized consideration, contingent
reward, management-by-exception, and laissez-faire behavior. High scores
on individualized consideration and motivation factors are most indicative
of strong transformational leadership.

There are several positive features of the transformational approach,
including that it is a current model that has received a lot of attention by
researchers, it has strong intuitive appeal, it emphasizes the importance of
followers in the leadership process, it goes beyond traditional transactional
models and broadens leadership to include the growth of followers, and it
places strong emphasis on morals and values.

Balancing off the positive features of transformational leadership are
several weaknesses. These include that the approach lacks conceptual
clarity; it is based on the MLQ, which has produced inconsistent results; it
creates a framework that implies that transformational leadership has a trait-
like quality; it is sometimes seen as elitist and undemocratic; it is derived
from and supported by data that focus heavily on senior-level leaders, it
suffers from a "heroic leadership" bias; and it has the potential to be used
counterproductively in negative ways by leaders. Despite the weaknesses,
transformational leadership appears to be a valuable and widely used
approach.

REFERENCES

Avolio, B. J. (1999). *Full leadership development: Building the vital forces in organizations.* Thousand Oaks, CA: Sage.

Avolio, B. J., & Gibbons, T. C. (1988). Developing transformational leaders: A life span approach. In J. A. Conger, R. N. Kanungo, & Associates (Eds.), *Charismatic leadership: The elusive factor in organizational effectiveness* (pp. 276-308). San Francisco: Jossey-Bass.

Bailey, J., & Axelrod, R. H. (2001). Leadership lessons from Mount Rushmore: An interview with James MacGregor Burns. *Leadership Quarterly, 12,* 113-127.

Bass, B. M. (1985). *Leadership and performance beyond expectations.* New York: Free Press.

Bass, B. M. (1990). From transactional to transformational leadership: Learning to share the vision. *Organizational Dynamics, 18,* 19-31.

Bass, B. M., & Avolio, B. J. (1990a). The implications of transactional and transformational leadership for individual, team, and organizational development. *Research in Organizational Change and Development, 4,* 231-272.

Bass, B. M., & Avolio, B. J. (1990b). *Multifactor Leadership Questionnaire.* Palo Alto, CA: Consulting Psychologists Press.

Bass, B. M., & Avolio, B. J. (1992). *Multifactor Leadership Questionnaire—Short form 6S.* Binghamton, NY: Center for Leadership Studies.

Bass, B. M., & Avolio, B. J. (1993). Transformational leadership: A response to critiques. In M. M. Chemers & R. Ayman (Eds.), *Leadership theory and research: Perspectives and directions* (pp. 49-80). San Diego, CA: Academic Press.

Bass, B. M., & Avolio, B. J. (1994). *Improving organizational effectiveness through transformational leadership.* Thousand Oaks, CA: Sage.

Bennis, W. G., & Nanus, B. (1985). *Leaders: The strategies for taking charge.* New York: Harper & Row.

Bryman, A. (1992). *Charisma and leadership in organizations.* London: Sage.

Burns, J. M. (1978). *Leadership.* New York: Harper & Row.

Bycio, P., Hackett, R. D., & Allen, J. S. (1995). Further assessments of the Bass (1985) conceptualization of transactional and transformational leadership. *Journal of Applied Psychology, 80,* 468-478.

Conger, J. A. (1999). Charismatic and transformational leadership in organizations: An insider's perspective on these developing streams of research. *Leadership Quarterly, 10*(2), 145-179.

Conger, J. A., & Kanungo, R. N. (1998). *Charismatic leadership in organizations.* Thousand Oaks, CA: Sage.

Downton, J. V. (1973). *Rebel leadership: Commitment and charisma in a revolutionary process.* New York: Free Press.

House, R. J. (1976). A 1976 theory of charismatic leadership. In J. G. Hunt & L. L. Larson (Eds.), *Leadership: The cutting edge* (pp. 189-207). Carbondale: Southern Illinois University Press.

Howell, J. M., & Avolio, B. J. (1992). The ethics of charismatic leadership: Submission or liberation? *Academy of Management Executive, 6*(2), 43-54.

Hunt, J. G., & Conger, J. A. (1999). From where we sit: An assessment of transformational and charismatic leadership research. *Leadership Quarterly, 10*(3), 335-343.

Kuhnert, K. W. (1994). Transforming leadership: Developing people through delegation. In B. M. Bass & B. J. Avolio (Eds.), *Improving organizational effectiveness through transformational leadership* (pp. 10-25). Thousand Oaks, CA: Sage.

Kuhnert, K. W., & Lewis, P. (1987). Transactional and transformational leadership: A constructive/developmental analysis. *Academy of Management Review, 12*(4), 648-657.

Lowe, K. B., & Gardner, W. L. (2001). Ten years of the *Leadership Quarterly:* Contributions and challenges for the future. *Leadership Quarterly, 11*(4), 459-514.

Lowe, K. B., Kroeck, K. G., & Sivasubramaniam, N. (1996). Effectiveness correlates of transformational and transactional leadership: A meta-analytic review of the MLQ literature. *Leadership Quarterly, 7*(3), 385-425.

Shamir, B., House, R. J., & Arthur, M. B. (1993). The motivational effects of charismatic leadership: A self-concept based theory. *Organization Science, 4*(4), 577-594.

Tejeda, M. J., Scandura, T. A., & Pillai, R. (2001). The MLQ revisited: Psychometric properties and recommendations. *Leadership Quarterly, 12,* 31-52.

Tepper, B. J., & Percy, P. M. (1994). Structural validity of the Multifactor Leadership Questionnaire. *Educational and Psychological Measurement, 54,* 734-744.

Tichy, N. M., & DeVanna, M. A. (1986). *The transformational leader.* New York: John Wiley.

Tichy, N. M., & DeVanna, M. A. (1990). *The transformational leader* (2nd ed.). New York: John Wiley.

Tracey, J. B., & Hinkin, T. R. (1998). Transformational leadership or effective managerial practices? *Group & Organization Management, 23*(3), 220-236.

Weber, M. (1947). *The theory of social and economic organizations* (T. Parsons, Trans.). New York: Free Press.

Yammarino, F. J. (1993). Transforming leadership studies: Bernard Bass' leadership and performance beyond expectations. *Leadership Quarterly, 4*(3), 379-382.

Yukl, G. A. (1999). An evaluation of conceptual weaknesses in transformational and charismatic leadership theories. *Leadership Quarterly, 10*(2), 285-305.

Team Leadership

Susan E. Kogler Hill

DESCRIPTION

Leadership in organizational groups or work teams has become one of the most popular and rapidly growing areas of leadership theory and research. Teams are organizational groups composed of members who are interdependent, who share common goals, and who must coordinate their activities to accomplish these goals. Examples of such groups might include project management teams, task forces, work units, standing committees, quality teams, and improvement teams. Popular bookstores have an ever-increasing collection of books on teams and effective teamwork, and college courses in communication, business, and education are proliferating on these topics as well.

In a comprehensive review of the historical roots of team research, Porter and Beyerlein (2000) provide a clear explanation of the long and diverse study of human groups. Porter and Beyerlein indicate that the study of groups actually began in the 1920s and 1930s with the focus of the human relations movement on collaborative efforts at work as opposed to the individual efforts previously advocated by the scientific management theorists. In the 1940s the focus shifted to the study of group dynamics and the development of social science theory. In the 1950s the focus moved to sensitivity training and T-groups and the role of leadership in these groups. In the 1960s and 1970s the era of organizational development focused on developing team and leadership effectiveness through interventions in ongoing work teams. In the 1980s competition from Japan and others encouraged the focus on quality teams, benchmarking, and continuous improvement. In the 1990s the focus on organizational teams, while still focusing on quality, shifted to a global perspective focusing on organizational strategies to maintain a competitive advantage. Organizations have faster response capability due to the flatter organizational structure that relies on teams and new technology to enable communication across time and geographical distance (Porter & Beyerlein, 2000, pp. 3-19). Mankin, Cohen, and Bikson (1996) refer to this new organization as "team-based, technology-enabled" (p. 217). Today's organization presents new and challenging questions for team researchers as they study virtual teams within organizations that seem to have no boundaries.

Organizations today are facing rapidly changing conditions with new technology, new structure, global economic competition, and increasing diversity, among other changes. The organizational team structure is one way an organization can respond quickly and adapt to these constant and rapid changes in workplace conditions. For the near future, teams seem to be ensconced firmly in organizational design, and it is important to understand what is needed for teams to be effective.

Researchers are attempting to determine the factors that lead to successful implementation of these teams with current research focusing on the practical problems of work teams and how to make them more effective (Ilgen, Major, Hollenbeck, & Sego, 1993). Research on the effectiveness of organizational teams has suggested that the use of teams has led to greater productivity, more effective use of resources, better decisions and problem solving, better-quality products and services, and increased innovation and creativity (Parker, 1990). The failures of teams have also been very dramatic and visible, however, making the need for information about and understanding of team effectiveness and team leadership essential for today's organizations.

Understanding the team leadership process is very complex and presents a significant challenge to researchers (Ilgen et al., 1993). In fact, current scholars argue that effective team leadership might be the primary ingredient of team success. "Indeed, we would argue that effective leadership processes represent perhaps the most critical factor in the success of organizational teams" (Zaccaro, Rittman, & Marks, 2001, p. 452). Ineffective leadership is frequently seen as a major obstacle to team effectiveness. "More specifically, work team management or supervision is often identified as a primary reason why self-managing teams fail to properly develop and yield improvements in productivity, quality, and quality of life for American workers" (Stewart & Manz, 1995, p. 748).

The new team-based structure of organizations has encouraged research into the entire process of team leadership, whether it be performed by members of the group in self-managed teams or performed by an individual formal leader of the team. It is essential to understand the role of leadership within these teams to ensure team success and to avoid team failure. The practical necessity of understanding the nature of organizational teams and the leadership within them are forcing theory and research into new directions that offer great promise for understanding team leadership. Not only do we have to understand the functions leaders must perform, but we also need to understand the complexity involved in performing these functions. In addition, of course, we need to know how the performance of these complex functions relates to actual real-life team performance.

A FUNCTIONAL MODEL OF TEAM LEADERSHIP

Most early scholars studying groups agreed on two critical functions of leadership: (a) to help the group accomplish its task (task function) and (b) to keep the group maintained and functioning (maintenance function). Scholars studying intact work teams have also referred to these same two functions as *team performance* and *team development.* Team performance refers to the leadership functions of task, and team development refers to leadership functions of relational maintenance. Superior team leadership should constantly be focused on both functions (Kinlaw, 1998). Task or team performance functions include, for example, getting the job done, making decisions, solving problems, adapting to changes, making plans, and achieving goals. Maintenance or team development functions include, for example, developing a positive climate, solving interpersonal problems, satisfying members' needs, and developing cohesion. Both functions are interrelated. If the team is well maintained and developed, then the members will be able to work effectively together and get their job done. Similarly, if the team is productive and successful, it will be easier to maintain a positive climate and good relations. Conversely, failing teams take this failure out on each other in the team, and teams in which members do not like each other do not seem to accomplish very much.

The current focus of researchers is on "teams" as opposed to "groups." Early researchers created artificially constructed temporary groups to study group dynamics. Now researchers are focused on real-life organizational work teams. This shift not only focuses on the ongoing nature of such teams but also focuses on the effect of the environment or context in which such teams function. A real-life group exists within a larger organizational context. In addition to dealing with and balancing the ongoing task and relational needs of the team, the leader also has to help the group to adapt to the external environment. Effective team leaders need to learn to analyze and balance the internal and external demands of the group and react appropriately by changing or remaining consistent (Barge, 1996).

McGrath (as cited in Hackman & Walton, 1986) formulated a model to demonstrate the critical leadership functions of group effectiveness, which takes into account the analysis of the situation both internally and externally and whether or not this analysis indicates that the leader should take an immediate action or not. The model looks at two dimensions of leadership behavior: (a) *monitoring versus taking action* and (b) focusing on *internal group issues versus external group issues*. As a leader, we can diagnose, analyze, or forecast problems (monitoring) or we can take immediate action to solve a problem that we observe (taking action). As a leader, we can also focus on the problems within the group (internal) or problems outside the group (external). These two dimensions result in the four types of group leadership functions shown in Figure 10.1.

The first two quadrants focus on the internal operations of the team. In the first quadrant, the leader is diagnosing group problems, and in the second quadrant the leader is acting to repair or remedy the observed problems. The third and fourth quadrants focus on the external operations of the team. In the third quadrant, the leader is scanning the environment to determine any external changes that will affect the group. In the fourth quadrant, the leader acts to prevent any negative changes in the environment from hurting the team.

It is important to note that these critical functions need not exclusively be carried out by the leader. Experienced members in a mature team might well take on and share these "leadership" behaviors themselves. As long as the team's critical needs have been met, then the leadership behavior,

Figure 10.1 *McGrath's Critical Leadership Functions*

	MONITOR	**EXECUTIVE ACTION**
INTERNAL	Diagnosing Group Deficiencies 1	Taking Remedial Action 2
EXTERNAL	Forecasting Environmental Changes 3	Preventing Deleterious Changes 4

SOURCE: McGrath's critical leadership functions as cited in Hackman and Walton (1986, p. 76).

whether enacted by the leader or team members, has been effective. The key assertion of the functional perspective is that the leader is to do whatever is necessary to take care of unmet needs of the group. If the group members are taking care of most of the needs, then the leader has to do very little.

The functional perspective was designed to be practical and to answer the question, What functions does a leader have to perform to help a group be more effective? The leader possesses special responsibility for functioning in a manner that will help the group achieve effectiveness. Within this perspective, leadership behavior would be seen as team-based problem solving in which the leader attempts to achieve team goals by analyzing the internal and external situation and then selecting and implementing the appropriate behaviors to ensure team effectiveness (Fleishman et al., 1991). In addition to leaders diagnosing internal and external problems, Zaccaro et al. (2001) indicate that leaders must use discretion about which problems need intervention and need to make choices about which solutions are the most appropriate. The appropriate solution varies by circumstance and focuses on what needs to be done to make the team more effective. Effective leaders have the ability to determine what leadership interventions are needed (if any) to solve team problems.

DIMENSIONS OF LEADERSHIP ON TEAMS

In determining the appropriate functions of leadership at any particular point in time, it becomes readily apparent that team leadership is a very complex process. Fisher (1985) metaphorically describes the leader as the "medium" or the one who processes and acts on information. Barge (1996) sees leadership as "mediation" and "coordination." The ability to monitor the situation (objection mediation) and the ability to take action (action mediation) are both necessary for effective leadership. A good leader helps the group to develop an organizing framework or a set of procedures. This structure helps the leader, as well as other group members, interpret the information inside as well as outside of the group, make judgments, and take actions for the good of the group. Effective team performance begins with the leader's *mental model* of the situation.

> This mental model reflects not only the components of the problem con-
> fronting the team, but also the environmental and organizational contingen-
> cies that define the larger context of team action. Here, the leader develops a
> model of what the team problem is and what solutions are possible in this
> context, given particular environmental and organizational constraints and
> resources. (Zaccaro et al., 2001, p. 462)

To respond appropriately to the problem envisioned in the mental model, a good leader needs to be behaviorally flexible and have a wide repertoire of actions or skills to meet the diverse needs of the team (Barge, 1996). When the leader's behavior matches the complexity in the situation, then the leader is behaving with "requisite variety," or the required set of behaviors necessary to meet the group's needs (Drecksel, 1991). Effective team leaders can both construct accurate mental models of the team's problems by observing team functioning and take appropriate requisite action to solve these problems.

Monitoring

To develop an accurate mental model of team functioning, leaders need to monitor both the internal and external environments of the team to continually gather information, reduce equivocality, provide structure, and over-come barriers. Fleishman et al. (1991) have described two phases in this initial process: information search and structuring. A leader must first seek out information to understand the current state of the team's functioning (information search), and then this information must be analyzed, organized, and interpreted so that the leader can decide how to act (information structuring). In addition to scanning the team and observing internal and external activities, leaders can also help their information search process by obtaining feedback from team members, engaging in networking with others outside the team, conducting team assessment surveys, and evaluating group outcomes. Once information on the team is gathered, the leader needs to structure or interpret this information so that plans of action can be made. Leaders can interpret information gathered more effectively if they are aware of the dynamics of teams and leadership and how these dynamics relate to team effectiveness.

All members of the group can engage in monitoring (information search and structuring) and collectively help the group adapt to changing conditions. In fast-paced rapidly changing situations, the team leader and members might have to work in concert to assess the situation accurately. The official leader of the team might be so busy processing information externally from the environment that his or her ability to process information internal to the team might be low. The team members can help the leader in such a situation stay on top of all of the problems and issues. Together they can form an accurate team mental model of the team's effectiveness.

Action Taking

In addition to the mediation involved with gathering and interpreting information, there is also mediation involved with taking the right action based on this information. "Action mediation is at the heart of leadership because it involves selecting from among competing courses of action and helping the group create a system of organizing that allows it to make quality decisions" (Barge, 1996, p. 324). The first skill of action mediation is the ability to facilitate decision-making and task accomplishment (task/ team performance), and the second is the ability to manage interpersonal relations (maintenance/team development). Fleishman et al. (1991) referred to this stage of the leadership process as managing both material and personnel resources.

Barge (1996) further pointed out that these actions represent only general leadership skills and that the specific action or communication would still need to be formulated and adapted to meet the needs of the specific situation. If a problem is diagnosed as a team performance problem, then the leader needs to determine the appropriate action to solve this task problem, for example, goal focusing, standard setting, or training. If a problem is diagnosed as a team development problem, then the leader needs to determine the appropriate action to solve this maintenance problem, for example, conflict management or building commitment. If a problem is diagnosed as an environmental problem, then the leader needs to determine the appropriate action to solve this context problem, for example, networking, advocating, or sharing information.

The complex nature of team leadership demonstrates that there are no simple recipes for team success. Team leaders must learn to be open and objective in understanding and diagnosing team problems and skillful in selecting the most appropriate actions (or inactions) to help achieve the team's goals.

CHARACTERISTICS OF EFFECTIVE TEAMS

Organizational work groups or teams are judged on their performance outcomes and their achievements. Team leadership theory must focus on what makes teams effective or what constitutes team excellence. Leaders cannot cognitively analyze and then appropriately function to improve groups without a clear focus on team goals or outcomes. Just what makes an excellent team? What do excellent teams have in common? What type of leadership exists in excellent teams?

Researchers have begun to systematically study organizational work teams to better understand what makes them effective or ineffective (Hackman, 1990; Hughes, Ginnett, & Curphey, 1993; LaFasto & Larson, 2001; Larson & LaFasto, 1989; Zaccaro et al., 2001). These studies of real-life teams have provided a research base for the development of criteria or standards of team excellence. The resulting criteria can then be used by leaders in a normative fashion to diagnose the health of any specific team and to take correspondingly appropriate action. Hackman and Walton (1986) suggested criteria necessary for effectiveness of task-performing teams in organizations:

1. Clear, engaging direction

2. An enabling performance situation
    A group structure that fosters competent task work
    An organizational context that supports and reinforces excellence
    Available, expert coaching and process assistance

3. Adequate material resources (p. 87).

Table 10.1 *Comparison of Theory and Research Criteria*

CONDITIONS of Group Effectiveness (Hackman & Walton, 1986)	CHARACTERISTICS of Team Excellence (Larson & LaFasto, 1989)
Clear, engaging direction	Clear, elevating goal
Enabling structure	Results-driven structure
	Competent team members
	Unified commitment
	Collaborative climate
Enabling context	Standards of excellence
Expert coaching	Principled leadership
Adequate material resources	External support

Larson and LaFasto (1989) reported on their grounded approach to understanding team excellence. Rather than developing a set of characteristics a priori regarding effective team functioning, a theoretical sampling of excellent teams was interviewed to gain "insight into what characterizes effectively functioning teams" (Larson & LaFasto, 1989, p. 20). This research has continued to include some 6,000 team members and 600 team leaders from executive, management, and project teams from many different industries, for example, health care, sports, airline, banking, telecommunications, education, and sports (LaFasto & Larson, 2001).

Larson and LaFasto (1989) found that regardless of type of team, there were eight characteristics regularly associated with team excellence. These characteristics are quite consistent with the theoretical components suggested by Hackman and Walton (1986) above, providing grounded research support for the group effectiveness approach (see Table 10.1).

It is important to understand just how these various criteria or characteristics actually affect group effectiveness and just how understanding them relates to team leadership theory.

Clear, Elevating Goal

Team goals need to very clear so that one can tell if the performance objective has been realized. Groups often fail because they are given a vague task and then asked to work out the details (Hackman, 1990). In addition, the goal needs to be involving or motivating so that the members believe it to be worthwhile and important. Teams often fail because they let something else replace their goal such as personal agendas or power issues (Larson & LaFasto, 1989). Research data from numerous teams show that effective leaders keep the team focused on the goal (LaFasto & Larson, 2001).

Results-Driven Structure

Teams need to find the best structure to accomplish their goals. Teams or work groups have different work content with which they deal. Top management teams typically deal with power and influence, task forces deal with ideas and plans, customer service teams deal with clients, and production teams deal with technology (Hackman, 1990). Problem-resolution teams such as task forces need to have a structure that emphasizes trust so that all will be willing and able to contribute. Creative teams such as advertising teams need to emphasize autonomy so that all can take risks and be free from undue censorship. Tactical teams such as emergency room teams need to emphasize clarity so that everyone knows what to do and when. In addition, all teams need to have clear roles for group members, a good communication system, methods to diagnose individual performance, and an emphasis on fact-based judgments (Larson & LaFasto, 1989). Groups with appropriate structures can meet the needs of the group as well as accomplish team goals.

Competent Team Members

Groups should be composed of the right number and mix of members to accomplish all the tasks of the group. In addition, members need to be provided with sufficient information, education, and training to become or to remain competent team members (Hackman & Walton, 1986). As a total group, the members need to possess the requisite technical competence to accomplish the team's goals. Members also need to be personally competent in interpersonal skills or teamwork. A common mistake in forming teams is to assume that people who have all the technical skills necessary to solve a problem also have the interpersonal skills necessary to work together effectively (Hackman, 1990). Team members need to have certain "core competencies" that include the ability to do the job as well as problem-solving ability. In addition, members need to possess certain teamwork factors such as openness, supportiveness, action orientation, and a positive personal style (LaFasto & Larson, 2001). Team members have to not only be able to do their jobs, but they also have to be able to work collaboratively together.

Unified Commitment

A mistake commonly made is to call a work group a "team" but treat it as a collection of individuals (Hackman, 1990). Teams do not just happen; they need to be carefully designed and developed. Excellent teams have developed a sense of unity or identification. Such team spirit can frequently be developed by involving members in all aspects of the process (Larson & LaFasto, 1989).

Collaborative Climate

Trust based on honesty, openness, consistency, and respect seems to be essential for building a collaborative climate in which members can stay problem focused, be open with one another, listen to each other, feel free to take risks, and be willing to compensate for each other (Larson & LaFasto, 1989). Integration of individual actions is seen as one of the funda-mental characteristics of effective teams. Team members "have specific and unique roles, where the performance of each role contributes to collec-tive success. This means that the causes of team failure may reside not only in member inability, but also in their collective failure to coordinate and synchronize their individual contributions" (Zaccaro et al., 2001, p. 451). Research demonstrates that effective team leaders ensure a collaborative climate by making communication safe, by demanding and rewarding collaborative behavior, by guiding the team's problem-solving efforts, and by managing one's own control needs (LaFasto & Larson, 2001).

Standards of Excellence

Effective group norms are important for group functioning. Team mem-bers' performance needs to be regulated so that actions can be coordinated and tasks can be completed (Hackman & Walton, 1986). It is especially important that the organizational context or the team itself set up normative standards of excellence so that members will feel a pressure to perform at their highest levels. The standards need to be clear and concrete, and all team members need to be required to perform to standard (Larson & LaFasto, 1989). A team leader can facilitate this process by (1) requiring results—making expectations clear, (2) reviewing results—providing feedback to resolve performance issues, and (3) rewarding results—acknowledging superior performance (LaFastoi & Larson, 2001). With such standards in place and monitored, members will be encouraged to perform at their highest levels.

External Support and Recognition

Another frequent mistake is to give organizational teams challenging assignments but give them no organizational support to accomplish these assignments (Hackman, 1990). The best goals, team members, and commitment will not mean much if you have no money, equipment, or supplies to accomplish that goal. Also, organizations frequently ask employees to work on a difficult team assignment but then do not reward them in terms of raises or bonuses for that performance. Hyatt and Ruddy (1997), in a recent study, found that having systems in place to support work groups (clear direction, information, data, resources, rewards, and training) enables the group to become more effective and achieve performance goals. Teams that are supported by external sources by being given the resources needed to do their jobs, by being recognized for team accomplishments, and by tying rewards collectively to team member performance rather than individual achievement can achieve excellence (Larson & LaFasto, 1989).

Leadership

Effective team leadership has been found to consistently relate to team effectiveness. Zaccaro et al. (2001) propose that leadership is the central driver of team effectiveness influencing the team through four sets of processes: cognitive, motivational, affective, and coordination. Cognitively the leader helps the team understand the problems confronting the team. Motivationally the leader helps the team become cohesive and capable by setting high performance standards and helping the group to achieve them. Affectively the leader helps the team handle stressful circumstances by providing clear goals, assignments, and strategies. Integratively the leader helps coordinate the team's activities by matching members' skills to roles, providing clear performance strategies, monitoring feedback, and adapting to environmental changes.

Similar findings are revealed from research on more than 600 teams with 6,000 members suggesting that an effective leader performs the following behaviors:

- Keeps the team focused on the goal
- Maintains a collaborative climate
- Builds confidence among members
- Demonstrates technical competence
- Sets priorities
- Manages performance (LaFasto & Larson, 2001)

Leaders can reduce the effectiveness of their team when they are unwilling to confront inadequate performance, when they dilute the team's ability to perform by having too many priorities, and by overestimating the positive aspects of team performance, that is, by being too easy. Effective team leaders possess a personal commitment to the team's goal and give members autonomy to unleash their talents when possible (Larson & LaFasto, 1989).

TEAM LEADERSHIP MODEL

Due to the complicated nature of this phenomenon of team leadership, many models have been developed to integrate what we know about teams, leadership, and team effectiveness. The team leadership model proposed in this chapter places leadership in the driver's seat of team effectiveness. The model is meant to provide a mental road map for the leader to follow to diagnose team problems and to take action steps to correct these problems.

We have discussed the critical functions of team leadership as well as the complexity involved in the process. We have also reviewed the factors associated with team excellence and effectiveness. Figure 10.2 is a model that attempts to integrate the mediation and monitoring concepts (Barge, 1996; Hackman & Walton, 1986) with team effectiveness (Hughes et al., 1993; Larson & LaFasto, 1989; Nadler, 1998). In addition, the model attempts to provide specific actions that leaders can perform to improve team effectiveness (LaFasto & Larson, 2001; Zaccaro et al., 2001). Effective team leaders need a wide repertoire of communication skills to monitor and take action appropriately. The model is designed to simplify and clarify the complex nature of team leadership and to provide an easy tool to aid leadership problem solving.

The team leadership model (Figure 10.2) demonstrates the mediation decisions that a leader (or member acting as leader) needs to make when determining whether to intervene to improve team functioning. The first decision confronting leadership is whether *monitoring* (object mediation) or *action taking* (action mediation) is the most appropriate for the issue at hand. Is it time to gather and interpret information, or is it time to intervene and shape the course of team activity? Hackman and Walton (1986, p. 104) indicated that leaders need to monitor (a) performance conditions (goals, structure, resources), (b) performance processes (effort, knowledge, strategies), and (c) outcome states (satisfaction, performance). Therefore, the first decision confronting the leader is this: Should I continue monitoring these factors, or should I take action based on information already gathered and structured?

If an action or intervention is to be taken, the leader must make the second strategic decision and determine what *level of the team process* needs leadership attention, that is, internal task or relational team dynamics or external environmental dynamics. To determine level, the leader needs to ask himself or herself questions. Is there conflict among members of the group? Then perhaps taking an action to maintain the group and improve interpersonal relationships would be most appropriate. Are the team goals unclear? Then perhaps a task intervention is needed to focus on goals. Is the organization/company not providing proper support to the team to do its job? Then perhaps focusing on obtaining external support for the team might be the most appropriate intervention.

The third decision for leadership is to determine the most *appropriate function or skill* to be performed in the intervention. For example, if the leader decided that the team members were not getting along, than the leader might decide to initiate conflict management. To be an effective leader, one needs to respond with the action that is required of the situation. Therefore, it is the job of the leader to analyze and mediate the situation to make the best decisions for the good of the team. Gouran and Hirokawa (1996) discussed constraints that impede task accomplishment. They indicated that the leader needs to recognize and interpret what is getting in the way of the team's goal accomplishment. The leader needs to make a strategic choice and respond with the appropriate action to minimize the constraint.

Figure 10.2 *Hill's Model for Team Leadership*

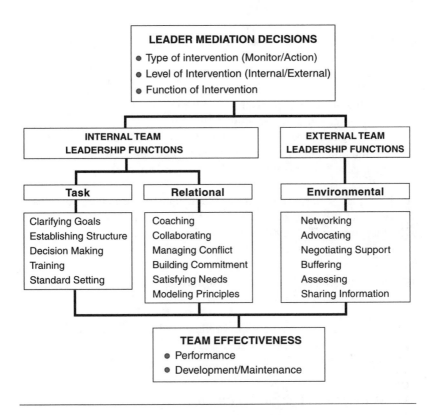

The next section of Figure 10.2 elaborates the skills necessary to internal and external team leadership (internal team leadership functions/external team leadership functions). Researchers have historically focused exclusively on two types of internal team behaviors: task and relational. Recently, with the increased focus on intact work teams, leadership behaviors need to include the external environmental context as well. The model in Figure 10.2 lists a number of leadership skills that can be performed internally (task, relational) and externally (environmental). These skills reflect the ingredients of team excellence described earlier, and it is up to the leader to select the right behavior(s) to meet the demands of the current situation. The leader needs to possess the ability to perform these skills as well as the ability to make a strategic choice about which behavior is needed at the moment.

The first set of skills or behaviors reflects those the leader needs to implement to improve task performance.

Internal Task Leadership Functions

- Goal focusing (clarifying, gaining agreement)
- Structuring for results (planning, organizing, clarifying roles, delegating)
- Facilitating decision making (informing, controlling, coordinating, mediating, synthesizing, issue focusing)
- Training team members in task skills (educating, developing)
- Maintaining standards of excellence (assessing team and individual performance, confronting inadequate performance)

For example, if after monitoring the team's performance, the leader observes that the team members do not have the skills necessary for the task, then the leader might choose an intervention to educate the team members or provide them with necessary skills or professional development (*training*). If the leader determines that some members of the group are not contributing effectively, then this inadequate performance needs to be discussed with the group member (*standard setting*).

The second set of skills/behaviors reflects those that the leader needs to implement to improve team relationships.

Internal Relational Leadership Functions

- Coaching team members in interpersonal skills
- Collaborating (including, involving)
- Managing conflict and power issues (avoiding confrontation, questioning ideas)
- Building commitment and esprit de corps (being optimistic, innovating, envisioning, socializing, rewarding, recognizing)
- Satisfying individual member needs (trusting, supporting, advocating)
- Modeling ethical and principled practices (fair, consistent, normative)

If after monitoring the relationships among team members, the leader observes that some of the group members are in conflict, then perhaps the leader needs to intervene to manage that conflict (*managing conflict and power issues*). Or if the team seems "down in the dumps," the leader might try to build commitment and unity by recognizing team past successes (*building commitment and esprit de corps*).

The third set of skills or behaviors reflects those the leader needs to implement to improve the environmental interface with the team. Real-life teams do not exist in a laboratory but are subsystems of the larger organizational and societal context of which they are a part. To stay viable, the team needs to monitor this environment closely and determine what actions need to be taken to enhance team effectiveness (Barge, 1996; Hyatt & Ruddy, 1997; Zaccaro et al., 2001). If environmental monitoring suggests a leadership intervention, then the leader needs to select from the following functions:

External Environmental Leadership Functions

- Networking and forming alliances in environment (gather information, increase influence)
- Advocating and representing team to environment
- Negotiating upward to secure necessary resources, support, and recognition for team
- Buffering of team members from environmental distractions
- Assessing environmental indicators of team's effectiveness (surveys, evaluations, performance indicators)
- Sharing relevant environmental information with team

If after monitoring the environment, the leader learns that the organizational superiors are unaware of the team's successes, the leader might initiate an "FYI" policy, for example, sending copies of all successes upward as they happen, for example, clippings, articles, and awards (*advocating and representing team to environment*). The leader can also initiate a team newsletter that chronicles team efforts to accomplish the same function but to a broader context. Alternatively, the leader might determine that the team does not have enough secretarial support service to accomplish the goals of the team. The leader then negotiates with upper management to provide the needed support or to alter the goals accordingly (*negotiating upward to secure necessary resources*).

The final section of Figure 10.2 focuses on team effectiveness, or the desired outcome of teamwork. The lower part of the figure represents the two critical functions of team effectiveness: *team performance* (task accomplishment) and *team development* (maintenance of team). For profit-making organizations, team performance clearly means financial stability and financial gain for the team and for the organization. For all types of organizations, team performance also means "quality of decision making, the ability to implement decisions, the outcomes of team work in terms of problems solved and work completed, and finally the quality of institutional leadership provided by the team" (Nadler, 1998, p. 24).

Team development is the second aspect of team effectiveness that focuses on the maintenance of the team as a cohesive and functioning body. Much like a person, a team needs to be a healthy functioning body to be able to produce results and achieve high performance. Team development or "maintenance of effectiveness" means that individual group members can satisfy their own needs by being members of the team. It also means that the members can effectively work together and adapt to changing circumstances (Nadler, 1998). If a leader assesses that one of these critical ingredients of team success is not being achieved, then this weakness of the team needs to be addressed.

The team leadership model (Figure 10.2) provides a tool for understanding the very complex phenomenon of team leadership with its mediation decisions, its critical functions, and its focus on outcomes of team excellence. The model is based on the functional leadership claim that the leader's function or job is to monitor the team and then to take whatever action is necessary to ensure team effectiveness.

HOW DOES THE TEAM LEADERSHIP MODEL WORK?

Team leaders can use the model to help them make decisions about the current state of their teams and what, if any, specific actions they need to take to improve the team's functioning. The model portrays leadership as a team oversight function in which the leader's role is to do whatever is necessary to help the group achieve effectiveness. The model provides the leader with a cognitive map to identify group needs and offers suggestions to the leader as to how to take appropriate corrective actions. The model helps the leader make sense of the complexity of groups and offers practical suggestions based on theory and research as to what actions to take to make the group more effective.

In using the model, the team leader would engage in the leader mediation process in which he or she would decide if monitoring or taking action was most appropriate for the team. If the monitoring reveals that all of the aspects of the team's functioning are satisfactory, then the leader should not take any direct actions but continue to monitor both the internal and external environments in terms of team performance and development. If monitoring reveals that action needs to be taken, then the leader needs to decide at which level or levels an action is needed (internally or externally). Finally, the leader would decide which function(s) or skill(s) would need to be enacted to meet the needs of the team.

Determining the exact intervention is not as easy as it sounds, however, and clearly reflects the difficulty of and high-level skills necessary for team leadership. For example, a leader monitoring the internal functioning of the team notices infighting for control and power. The leader might see this as an *internal relationship problem* because of the authoritative and autocratic behavior of one group member. Or perhaps the leader might see it as an *internal task problem* because the structure of the team is not appropriate and the roles and responsibilities of some group members are unclear. Or perhaps the leader sees the problem as an *external environmental problem* because the team is not given sufficient autonomy from the organization and consequently the members are fighting over what little power and control exist. In any case, the leader can decide to keep monitoring the situation and not take any immediate action. Or the leader can decide at which level to intervene and then decide to enact the most appropriate leadership function at that level. It is also possible that the leader decides to intervene at all three levels—addressing the authoritarian individual (internal/relational), clarifying group roles (internal/task), and negotiating more team autonomy with those higher up in the organization (external).

The team leadership model helps to point the way for constant team analysis and improvement much like that of sports teams. In sports, the coach does not stop working just because the team is currently winning. For example, a football coach keeps working to build commitment, develop young players, share expertise, create new methods and strategies, and generally improve team functioning. The effective football coach never rests on past success but works to improve the team's functioning for the future. Organizational team leaders could learn a great deal from sports team coaches. The team leadership model helps point the way for such constant analysis and improvement. By comparing one's own team to established standards or criteria of team excellence, leaders can determine the areas of greatest weakness for the team that might need critical intervention.

The leader's two primary functions are to monitor and to take action. By using the model to guide the inquiry into whether or not one's team is performing in an effective manner, a leader can diagnose the areas of concern. The leader can then take corrective action outside the team by ensuring necessary resources and contextual supports as well as take corrective action inside the team by strengthening the task and relational functions of the team.

STRENGTHS

One of the strengths of this model is that it is designed to answer many of the questions not answered in earlier small-group research by focusing on the real-life organizational work group and the leadership needed therein. The model places the ongoing work group or team in an environmental context within the organization, industry, or society. In addition, the real-life focus on performance and team effectiveness is one of the strengths enabling leaders and members to diagnose and correct team problems. By learning what constitutes excellent teams and applying these criteria to team performance, leaders can better learn how to lead teams to the highest levels of excellence. This is very important if organizations are to stay competitive in the global economy.

A second strength of the model is that it provides a cognitive guide that helps leaders to design and maintain effective teams especially when performance is below standards. Such an approach is consistent with the emerging theoretical notions of leader as a medium whose job it is to process the complex information inherent within teamwork. "Leadership is a complex process; complexity of actions is thus identifiable as leadership" (Fisher, 1985, p. 185). Any model or theory that would try to simplify such a complex process would be inappropriate and inadequate. The team leadership approach is not simplistic, and it integrates in a manageable and practical form many complex factors that can help a leader be a good "medium" or processor of information.

Another strength of the model is that it takes into account the changing role of leaders and followers in organizations. The model does not focus on the "position power" of a leader but instead focuses on the critical functions of leadership as diagnosis and action taking. Any team member can perform the critical leadership functions to assess the current effectiveness of the team and then take appropriate action(s). This approach is consistent with the current movement in organizations to rethink leadership responsibilities in work groups. The responsibilities or functions of team leadership such as setting goals, coaching, or rewarding have historically rested with the group's formal leader, but now with organizational restructuring these duties and responsibilities are frequently shared and distributed across team members.

In addition, this approach to team leadership can help in selecting team leaders. If you have to name a leader for the team, it might be best to select one who is perceptive, open, objective, analytical, and a good listener who has good diagnostic skills. You might want to select a leader who has a wide repertoire of action-taking skills, that is, who is comfortable intervening in the group process in many ways, such as with negotiation, conflict resolution, problem solving, goal focusing, influencing upward, and so on. Good leaders not only can diagnose the team's problem but also can reach into their bag of tricks and pull out the corresponding appropriate action or actions (requisite variety). For example, if I diagnose that two members of my team are in conflict with one another, I need to be able to determine the root cause of that conflict and select the most appropriate action (or nonaction) to deal with this problem.

CRITICISMS

One of the weaknesses of the present approach is that the entire model is not completely supported or tested. The applied focus on team effectiveness and the organizational work group is a relatively new approach to studying teams. Much of the earlier research on small groups did not directly apply to understanding real-life organizational teams. Many questions still need to be answered regarding team patterns over time, self-fulfilling group cycles, authority issues, and content issues (Hackman, 1990). Do these theoretical relationships hold true in new groups, mature groups, and deteriorating groups? Do these theoretical notions hold true across all types of teams, especially for the new technology-connected virtual teams? Research also needs to focus more on organizational rewards. How can the leadership reinforce the values and behaviors that will perpetuate the functioning of the team rather than rewarding the individual members of the team (Ilgen et al., 1993)? "Clearly, new systems are needed for team-based organizations. No other change will send as powerful a message to employees that the organization values teamwork" (Mankin et al., 1996).

Although one of the strengths of this model is that it takes into account the complex nature of team leadership, this very complexity is also one of this approach's greatest weaknesses. The model is complex and does not provide easy answers to difficult decisions for the leader. With so much distributed and shared leadership in organizations today, such a complicated approach to leadership might not be practical for the growing number of team leaders.

This theoretical, approach in addition to being highly complex, does not offer on-the-spot answers to specific situations for the team leader. What should the leader say back to a team member who is crying? How do you deal with team members who are screaming at each other? What do you do when the organization refuses to reward team performance? The team leadership model does not seem to provide much guidance in everyday interactions and complications of team management. The model assumes that the leader knows about group process and decision making, interpersonal communication, conflict resolution, networking, and so on. The model needs to be expanded to identify specific skills and interventions that could help the group deal with the more critical incidents that arise on a daily basis.

Finally, the fact that the team leadership model suggests new and creative directions for leadership training could be construed as a strength. However, these directions for leadership training currently are vague, complex, and somewhat overwhelming. The long list of team leadership skills makes it very difficult to know where to start. This is compounded by the fact that many teams are empowered and self-directed, necessitating that these skills be taught to everyone who serves in the role of team leader, sometime, somewhere. The roles of leaders and followers can change over time in a planned organizational restructuring or can even change within the course of a day, making it very important for the leader to understand the follower roles and vice versa. More focus and attention need to be given as to how to teach and provide skill development in the areas of diagnosis and action taking so that such leadership skill development can be implemented easily within all levels of the organization.

APPLICATION

There are many ways to apply the team leadership model to increase the effectiveness of organizational teams. The model is useful in helping the leader make decisions: Should I act? If so, how? For example, if the group was not performing effectively (*team effectiveness*), then the leader could make the first strategic choice by monitoring the situation or by acting to improve team functioning. If an action seems warranted, then the leader needs to decide if the action should be directed inward toward team functioning or outward toward the environment or both. Once the context for the action is determined, then the leader needs to choose from his or her repertoire of leadership skills the most appropriate skill to the situation. It is important to continue monitoring the results of the intervention and adapting accordingly depending on these results.

The leader might choose to use a survey like the one included later in this chapter to help conduct the team's diagnosis and set the steps needed for taking action. Team members are asked to fill out the questionnaire, as is the team leader. The results of this information are fed back to the team members and team leader, allowing them to see areas of greatest strength and weakness. It is particularly important that both team leaders and team members fill out the questionnaire. Research suggests that team leaders overestimate their effectiveness on these dimensions and frequently score themselves much higher than do group members (LaFasto & Larson, 2001). By comparing the scores by leaders and by members, the leader can determine which dimensions of team or leadership effectiveness are in need of improvement. The team and leader can then work to prepare action plans to correct the highest-priority problems in the team. Such a team assessment approach is very helpful to monitoring and diagnosis of team problems. It aids in determining the complex factors affecting team excellence to build a committed team involved in action planning.

CASE STUDIES

To facilitate your understanding of the team leadership model, you can refer to the case studies below (Cases 10.1, 10.2, and 10.3). For each case, you will be asked to put yourself in the role of team leader and apply the team leadership model in analyzing and offering solutions to the team problems.

CASE 10.1

Can This Virtual Team Work?

Jim Towne heads up a newly formed information technology team for a major international corporation. The team is composed of about 20 professionals who live and work in Canada, the United States, Europe, South America, Africa, and Australia. All members of the team report to Jim Towne. The team is a virtual team and is connected primarily using technology (videoconference, group decision support ware, e-mail, and telephone). The team has met twice in a face-to-face setting to set goals and plan. All of the team members are quite competent technically in their respective areas. Some team members have a long and valued history with the company; others have recently become members of the company through a corporate merger. The team members have never worked together on any projects previously.

The task of the team is to develop and implement new technology innovations for all of the business units of the corporation globally. The team is excited about the importance and the innovative nature of their assignment. They respect each other and enjoy being part of this team. However, the team is having difficulty getting off the ground, and the members report being extremely overloaded. Most team members travel to business sites at least 2 weeks each month. The travel is important, but it causes team members to get farther and farther behind.

There is one half-time secretary for the team, located in New York. Her responsibility is primarily to organize travel and meetings of team members. Team members are working on several projects at once and have great difficulty finishing any of the projects. One team member has 500 e-mail messages that have yet to be read because each team member sends copies of all messages to everyone on the team. Jim Towne feels under great pressure to prove that this team can work and provide a valuable function to the organization.

Questions

1. Which of the characteristics of team excellence are lacking in this team?
2. At what level(s) should Jim Towne intervene to improve this team (internal task, internal relational, external)? Or should he just keep monitoring the team and not intervene?
3. What specific leadership functions should Jim Towne implement to improve the team?

CASE 10.2

They Dominated the Conversation

The local cancer center has a health team designed to coordinate the care of children with cancer. The team is composed of a physician, Dr. Sherif Hidyat (a clinical oncologist); a radiologist, Dr. Wayne Linett; a nurse practitioner, Sharon Whittling; a social worker, Cathy Ing; a physical therapist, Nancy Crosby; and a child life worker, Janet Lewis. The team members meet on a weekly basis to discuss the 18 children under their care and to come to agreement about the best course of treatment for each child. Cathy Ing, the social worker, is the head of the team and is responsible for the case management of each child. However, when the team meets Drs. Hidyat and Linett dominate the conversation. They feel that their medical background gives them greater knowledge and skill in the treating of cancer in children. They welcome input from the women in the group; however, when it comes to making a decision, they insist on doing it their way for the good of the patient. The social worker, the child life worker, the physical therapist, and the nurse resent this behavior because they are the ones that spend the most time with the children and feel that they know best how to handle their long-term care. The group effectiveness or outcomes of this group are such that the patients feel no one cares or understands them. The team is also having trouble working together, and no one on the team is feeling satisfied with the outcome.

Questions

1. How would you assess the effectiveness of this team both in terms of performance and development?
2. In monitoring this team, at what level do you see the most serious problem(s) of this team? Internal task? Internal relational? External?

3. Would you take action to improve team functioning? If so, how would you choose to intervene? Why?
4. What specific leadership skill or skills would you employ to improve group functioning?

◆

CASE 10.3

Starts With a Bang, Ends With a Whimper

A faculty member, Kim Green from the Management Department, was asked to chair a major university committee to plan the mission of the university for the next 20 years. Three other senior faculty and seven administrators from across the campus were also asked to serve on this committee. The president of the university, Dr. Sulgrave, gave the committee its charge: What should Northcoast University be like in the year 2020? Dr. Sulgrave told the committee that the work of this task force was of utmost importance to the future of the university and the charge of this committee should take precedence over all other matters. The task force was allowed to meet in the president's conference room and use the president's secretary. The report of the committee was due in 2 months.

The task force members felt very good about being selected to such an important team. The team met on a weekly basis for about 2 hours. At first, the members were very interested in the task and participated enthusiastically. They were required to do a great deal of outside research and gathering of information. They would come back to the meetings proud to demonstrate and share their research and knowledge. However, after a while the meetings did not go well. The members could not seem to agree on what the charge to the group meant. They argued among themselves about what they were supposed to accomplish and resented the time the committee was taking from their regular jobs. Week after week the team met but got nothing accomplished. Attendance began to become a problem with people skipping several meetings, showing up late, or leaving early. Group members stopped working on their committee assignments. Kim Green didn't know what to do because she didn't want to admit to the university president that they didn't know what they were doing. She just got more and more frustrated. Meetings became sporadic and eventually stopped altogether. The president was involved in a crisis in the university and seemed to lose interest in Kim Green's committee. The president never called for the report from the committee, and the report was never completed.

Questions

1. Which characteristics of excellence were lacking in this task force?
2. Which characteristics of excellence were evident in this task force?
3. How would you assess Kim Green as a leader?
4. What actions would you take (internally/externally) if you were the leader of this task force?

LEADERSHIP INSTRUMENT

Several different instruments have been used to assess team effectiveness and the leadership within those teams. Larson and LaFasto have developed one such survey (cited in Larson & LaFasto, 1989) to assess a team's health. They developed this survey after studying many different types of excellent organizational teams. Their research has demonstrated eight criteria or factors that are consistently associated with team excellence and high performance. The complete Team Excellence survey contains more than 40 questions across the eight factors that are used to diagnose a team's performance level and to suggest which areas might need corrective action. The eighth factor on this instrument is *principled leadership*. Subsequent research by LaFasto and Larson led to the development of a 42-item questionnaire focusing on this criterion of leadership. The full Collaborative Team Leader instrument and a discussion of its reliability and validity can be found in their latest text (LaFasto & Larson, 2001). The questionnaire included in this chapter provides a sampling of questions from these two surveys so that the reader can see how team and team leadership effectiveness can be evaluated.

The team members are given the questionnaire(s), and their scores are combined and averaged to obtain a group view. At the same time, the leader of the team fills out the same questionnaire(s). The responses from the team leader are then compared with the team members', diagnosing the areas of greatest weakness, if any. Based on all of these comparisons, the team, along with the leader, can then plan the action steps needed to correct and improve the weak areas of team functioning.

The Team Excellence and the Collaborative Team Leader surveys are designed as diagnostic tools for teams to help sort through the complex maze of issues and problems confronting them and to pinpoint areas for action taking. The Team Excellence and Collaborative Team Leader

Questionnaire provided in this chapter contains sample questions from the two instruments developed by LaFasto and Larson. The first seven questions are taken from the Team Excellence Survey developed by LaFasto and Larson in 1987 (cited in Larson & LaFasto, 1989) to measure a team's health in terms of the criteria of team excellence (goal, structure, team members, commitment, climate, standards, and external support). Leadership is measured by the next six questions taken from the Collaborative Team Leader Survey developed by LaFasto and Larson in 1996 (LaFasto & Larson, 2001, pp. 151-154). These final six questions assess the effectiveness of the leader on goal focusing, ensuring a collaborative climate, building confidence, demonstrating know-how, setting priorities, and managing performance. All of these team and leadership factors have been found to relate to team effectiveness (Larson & LaFasto, 1989; LaFasto & Larson, 2001).

As you fill out the sample questionnaire, think about a group or team to which you belong as a member or as the leader. The items that you score *False* (either a 1 or a 2) are the areas of team weakness from your personal perspective. To obtain a team assessment, you would need to compare your scores on this instrument with the scores of the other group members. For example, if most everyone on the team scores *False* to item 3, "Team members possess the essential skills and abilities to accomplish the team's objectives," then the team leader might need to provide training to increase the competence of team members. An instrument such as this that assesses team effectiveness is particularly helpful to the team leader in diagnosing the area of team or leadership weakness and suggesting solutions for improving team effectiveness.

Team Excellence and Collaborative
Team Leader Questionnaire

Instructions: This questionnaire contains questions about your team and the leadership within this team. Indicate whether you feel each statement is true or not true of your team. Use the following scale.

Key: 1 = False   2 = More false than true   3 = More true than false 4 = True

_____   1. There is a clearly defined need—a goal to be achieved or a purpose to be served—that justifies the existence of our team. *(team—clear, elevating goal)*

_____   2. We have an established method for monitoring individual performance and providing feedback. *(team—results-driven structure)*

_____   3. Team members possess the essential skills and abilities to accomplish the team's objectives. *(team—competent team members)*

_____   4. Achieving our team goal is a higher priority than any individual objective. *(team—unified commitment)*

_____   5. We trust each other sufficiently to accurately share information, perceptions, and feedback. *(team—collaborative climate)*

_____   6. Our team exerts pressure on itself to improve performance. *(team—standards of excellence)*

_____   7. Our team is given the resources it needs to get the job done. *(team—external support/recognition)*

_____   8. If it's necessary to adjust the team's goal, our team leader makes sure we understand why. *(leadership—focus on the goal)*

_____   9. Our team leader creates a safe climate for team members to openly and supportively discuss any issue related to the team's success. *(leadership—ensure a collaborative climate)*

_____   10. Our team leader looks for and acknowledges contributions by team members. *(leadership—build confidence)*

_____   11. Our team leader understands the technical issues we must face in achieving our goal. *(leadership—demonstrate sufficient technical know-how)*

_____   12. Our team leader does not dilute our team's effort with too many priorities. *(leadership—set priorities)*

_____   13. Our team leader is willing to confront and resolve issues associated with inadequate performance by team members. *(leadership—manage performance)*

SOURCE: Questions 1-7: Adapted from the Team Excellence Survey (Copyright 1987 LaFasto and Larson. Portions reprinted with permission of Profact). Questions 8-13: Adapted from the Collaborative Team Leader (Copyright 1996 LaFasto and Larson. Portions reprinted with permission).

Scoring Interpretation and Use

In addition to such targeted questions on each of the criteria of excellence, the complete surveys also ask open-ended questions to allow team members the opportunity to comment on issues that might not be specifically covered in the directed questions, such as strengths and weaknesses of the team and its leadership, changes that are needed, norms that are problematic, or issues that need to be addressed. The complete version of the survey is given to team members and the team leader, and all are involved in the diagnosis and in the resulting action planning. Such a method is clearly consistent with the empowerment movement in organizational teams and helps deal with the enormous complexity involved in making teams effective.

---◆---

SUMMARY

The increased importance of organizational teams and the leadership needed within them has produced a renewed interest in team leadership theory. The team leadership model provides a framework within which to study the systematic factors that contribute to a group's outcomes or general effectiveness. Within this approach, the leader's critical function is to assist the group in accomplishing its goals by monitoring/diagnosing the group and taking the requisite action.

A strategic decision model has been developed to reveal the various decisions team leaders must make to improve their group's effectiveness. The model describes the three decisions: What type of intervention should be used (monitoring/action taking)? At what level should the intervention be targeted (internal/external)? What leadership function should be implemented to improve group functioning?

Questionnaires have been developed to ascertain the team's and the leader's general levels of effectiveness. Eight criteria have been found to relate to highly effective teams, and six dimensions have been found to relate to effective team leaders. The questionnaires can be filled out by team members and leaders to measure these team criteria and leadership dimensions. The survey filled out by team members as well as the team leader can aid in diagnosing specific areas of team problems and suggest action steps to be taken by the team.

The strength of this approach includes its focus on real-life organizational teams and their effectiveness. The model also emphasizes the functions of leadership that can be shared and distributed within the work group. The model offers help in selecting leaders and team members with the appropriate diagnostic and action-taking skills. Furthermore, the model is also appropriately complex, providing a cognitive model for understanding and researching organizational teams.

A weakness of this approach is that it is new, and not much research support exists to support the many connections and claims made by the model. The analytical and action-taking leadership skills prescribed by the model need further development. Also, for pragmatists who want immediate answers to every question, this model might be frustratingly complex and long term.

Hackman (1990), in support of this approach, suggested that those who lead organizational teams need to recognize that team effectiveness is a complicated process and that the factors involved are complex and interrelated and must not be studied in isolation. However, the rewards of leading effective teams are well worth the effort involved in such complex problem solving.

REFERENCES

Barge, J. K. (1996). Leadership skills and the dialectics of leadership in group decision making. In R. Y. Hirokawa & M. S. Poole (Eds.), *Communication and group decision making* (2nd ed., pp. 301-342). Thousand Oaks, CA: Sage.

Drecksel, G. L. (1991). Leadership research: Some issues. *Communication Yearbook, 14,* 535-546.

Fisher, B. A. (1985, May). Leadership as medium: Treating complexity in group communication research. *Small Group Behavior, 16*(2), 167-196.

Fleishman, E. A., Mumford, M. D., Zaccaro, S. J., Levin, K. Y., Korotkin, A. L., & Hein, M. B. (1991). Taxonomic efforts in the description of leader behavior: A synthesis and functional interpretation. *Leadership Quarterly, 2*(4), 245-287.

Gouran, D. S., & Hirokawa, R. Y. (1996). Functional theory and communication in decision-making and problem-solving groups: An expanded view. In R. Y. Hirokawa & M. D. Poole (Eds.), *Communication and group decision making* (2nd ed., pp. 55-80). Thousand Oaks, CA: Sage.

Hackman, J. R. (1990). Work teams in organizations: An orienting framework. In J. R. Hackman (Ed.), *Groups that work (and those that don't): Creating conditions for effective teamwork* (pp. 1-14). San Francisco: Jossey-Bass.

Hackman, J. R., & Walton, R. E. (1986). Leading groups in organizations. In P. S. Goodman & Associates (Eds.), *Designing effective work groups* (pp. 72-119). San Francisco: Jossey-Bass.

Hughes, R. L., Ginnett, R. C., & Curphey, G. J. (1993). *Leadership: Enhancing the lessons of experience*. Homewood, IL: Irwin.

Hyatt, D. E., & Ruddy, T. M. (1997). An examination of the relationship between work group characteristics and performance: Once more into the breech. *Personnel Psychology, 50,* 553-585.

Ilgen, D. R., Major, D. A., Hollenbeck, J. R., & Sego, D. J. (1993). Team research in the 1990's. In M. M. Chemers & R. Ayman (Eds.), *Leadership theory and research: Perspectives and directions* (pp. 245-270). San Diego, CA: Academic Press.

Kinlaw, D. C. (1998). *Superior teams: What they are and how to develop them*. Hampshire, UK: Grove.

LaFasto, F. M. J., & Larson, C. E. (1987). *Team Excellence Survey.* Denver, CO: Author.

LaFasto, F. M. J., & Larson, C. E. (2001). *When teams work best: 6000 team members and leaders tell what it takes to succeed.* Thousand Oaks, CA: Sage.

Larson, C. E., & LaFasto, F. M. J. (1989). *Teamwork: What must go right/what can go wrong*. Newbury Park, CA: Sage.

Mankin, D., Cohen, S. G., & Bikson, T. K. (1996). *Teams and technology*. Boston: Harvard Business School Press.

Nadler, D. A. (1998). Executive team effectiveness: Teamwork at the top. In D. A. Nadler & J. L. Spencer (Eds.), *Executive teams* (pp. 21-39). San Francisco: Jossey-Bass.

Parker, G. M. (1990). *Team players and teamwork*. San Francisco: Jossey Bass.

Porter, G., & Beyerlein, M. (2000). Historic roots of team theory and practice. In M. M. Beyerlein (Ed.), *Work teams: Past, present and future* (pp. 3-24). Dordrecht, The Netherlands: Kluwer.

Stewart, G. L., & Manz, C. C. (1995). Leadership for self-managing work teams: A typology and integrative model. *Human Relations, 48*(7), 747-770.

Zaccaro, S. J., Rittman, A. L., & Marks, M. A. (2001). Team leadership. *Leadership Quarterly, 12,* 451-483.

Psychodynamic Approach

Ernest L. Stech

DESCRIPTION

This chapter is aptly named because the psychodynamic approach consists of bits and pieces borrowed from a number of scholars and practitioners. It is truly an approach rather than a coherent theory. However, there are several fundamental propositions underlying the approach. The first of these is that leaders are more effective when they have insight into their own psychological makeup. The specific model or terminology used to obtain insight is less important than having gained an understanding of needs, predispositions, and emotional responses. The second proposition is similar: Leaders are more effective when they understand the psychological makeup of their subordinates. Again the particular labels are less important than having a knowledge of the personality characteristics of the team members.

It is important to distinguish this approach from the trait approach and from the style and situational approaches. In the trait approach, certain characteristics of a person are assumed to be important in attaining leadership status or performing leadership tasks. The style approach suggests that a certain leadership style, particularly the team management (9,9) style, is the best. Situational leadership moves on to suggest that the key element is the match between the leader's style or behaviors and the needs of the subordinates.

The psychodynamic approach makes none of these assumptions. There is no particular personality type that is better than any other in a leadership position. There is no need to match the personality type of the leader to that of the subordinates in order to have an effective work situation. Rather, the important point is that the leader have insight into her or his own emotional responses and habitual patterns of behavior. An authoritarian leader, as an example, can be effective if she understands that her behaviors arise from strong influences in her past (insight) and that her behaviors have very specific effects on the people in the work group. It is even better if that leader understands that the authoritarian behaviors result in vastly different responses from subordinates depending on their personality characteristics. Some will resist directions from an authoritarian leader, while others will be comfortable and even grateful for a strong leader.

The situation improves even more if the team members are aware of their own personality characteristics so that they can understand how they respond to the leader and to each other. Thus, an important function of the leader, using such an approach, is to facilitate the process of having people gain insight and identify their own needs and patterns of emotional reaction to other people.

Thus, the psychodynamic approach focuses more on learned and deep-seated emotional responses that are not in immediate awareness. The leader is not conscious of his or her emotional responses or of their consequences in behavior. This aspect of the approach is unique and results in an entirely different way of dealing with leadership development.

An important underlying assumption in the psychodynamic approach is that the personality characteristics of individuals are deeply ingrained and virtually impossible to change in any significant way. The key is acceptance of one's own personality features and quirks and understanding and acceptance of the features and quirks of others.

To summarize, the psychodynamic approach places emphasis on leaders' obtaining insight into their personality characteristics and understanding the responses of subordinates, based on their personalities. Secondarily, leaders should encourage work group members to gain insight into their personalities so that they can understand their reactions to the leader and to each other.

BACKGROUND

Insight begins, in the psychodynamic approach, with an examination of the roots of the individual in the family. Our first experience with leadership occurs the day we are born. Mom and Dad become our leaders, at least for a few years. That is the most basic premise of the psychodynamic approach to leadership. Our parents create, particularly in the early years of childhood, deep-seated feelings about leadership. The parental image is highlighted in business when we refer to a corporation as "paternalistic." Hill (1984) has written on "the law of the father," a psychodynamic examination of leadership. Members of the U.S. Air Force sometimes refer to their service as the "Big Blue Mother," referring, of course, to the color of the uniforms and the wild blue yonder. The familial metaphor is used frequently in organizations that term themselves "one big happy family," with the natural consequence that the leaders are the parents and the employees the children.

Childhood and adolescent experiences in the family are reflected in reactions to paternalistic, maternalistic, and familial patterns of leadership and management. Some people respect and respond to authority figures. Others rebel. Most important, however, psychological development produces personality types, and the key to effective leadership is to obtain insight into one's own personality and attempt to understand the personality characteristics of followers.

The emergence of the psychodynamic approach to leadership has its roots in the works of Sigmund Freud in his development of psychoanalysis (Freud, 1938). Freud was attempting to understand and help patients who had problems that were not responding to the conventional kinds of treatments. He attempted to use hypnosis to treat patients with hysterical paralysis. Later he discovered that hypnosis was not necessary. Simply having patients talk about their pasts was enough to effect a cure. Freud thereby created what are known as the "talking therapies."

Freud's work spawned a large number of offshoots. One of his well-known disciples was Carl Jung, who eventually developed his own body of psychological writings. Today, Jungian psychology is well accepted, whereas classical psychoanalysis has found less acceptance in recent years. Yet it is from the works of both Freud and Jung that the psychodynamic approach to leadership has been constructed.

A leading proponent of the psychodynamic approach to leadership is Abraham Zaleznik (1977), a management professor at Harvard. The psychodynamic approach is also behind much of the writing about charismatic leaders (Hummel, 1975; Schiffer, 1973; Winer, Jobe, & Ferrono, 1984-1985). One branch of psychodynamic theorizing is termed *psycho-history* and consists of attempts to explain the behavior of historical figures such as Lincoln and Hitler. These studies review the historical record of the leader and delve into the familial background as well. There are some basic general ideas underlying the various psychodynamic approaches to leadership.

Important concepts in the psychodynamic approach to leadership include the family of origin, maturation or individuation, dependence and independence, regression, the shadow self, and archetypes. Each of these plays a unique role in the leadership process.

Family of Origin

The first concept, the *family of origin,* underlies any understanding of the behavior of adults. Each of us is born into a family. The traditional family consists of two parents and one or more children. Today, of course, there are numerous single-parent families as well. No matter which type of family, the role of the parent is to socialize the child into society. The psycho-dynamic view is that the child begins life essentially as a very self-centered being, more animal than human. The parent's role in early infancy is to meet the needs of the child. In one sense, the parent has control over the very dependent child, but at the same time the child has an equal degree of control, through his or her needs, over the parent. Every time the baby cries, the parent responds with food, touch, or a clean diaper.

Such total dependency can and does occur in leadership situations. The leader takes total responsibility for the care and feeding of the subordinate, meeting every need. This is the ultimate version of paternalistic manage-ment, truly becoming the "father" (or "mother") parent of all the employees. Of course, as the leaders and managers realize, they are also at the beck and call of the employees, as much controlled as in control.

Maturation or Individuation

As time goes on, the child becomes more independent of the parent, needing less direct satisfaction of needs. This goes on through the preschool, kindergarten, and elementary and secondary school years. With each succeeding stage of development, the child drifts farther from the parental home. However, the child, properly socialized, carries a parent inside constantly supervising, analyzing, and judging. This is the "parent within"—a conscience.

There is, it is hoped, a process of *maturation* in the life of a child going into adolescence and then adulthood. This is termed *individuation* by psychologists. The child is still attached to and virtually a part of the parent in childhood, bound by a psychological umbilical cord, and not an individual. Toward adulthood, the child becomes an individual, unique and different from either parent, and different from siblings. That is the process of individuation.

Two key issues come up in that process. The first is the relationship to authority figures. A highly authoritarian parent may induce either a very submissive or a very resistant attitude in the child. A laissez-faire parent, on the other hand, can create a confused child who has trouble defining boundaries and limits. When such an individual does confront an authority figure, the reaction can be difficult to predict. All of us have deep-seated feelings about authority figures based on our experiences in the family of origin and then modified by relationships with teachers, counselors, coaches, and other important figures in adolescence and early adulthood.

Reactions to an authoritarian leader are not rational, nor are the reasons for the reactions immediately evident to the follower. The response occurs from one or more traumatic incidents in relationships with parents, teachers, or other authority figures, or it can result from a long series of interactions. In either case, the response "just happens" and cannot be ignored. It is emotional and results, in some cases, in physiological reactions including sweaty palms and shaking hands.

The second issue concerns intimacy and openness. Parents range along a continuum of kindness, tenderness, and nurturance, on the one extreme, and a distant, critical, and unfeeling style, on the other. Every adult, again, has strong tendencies toward one or the other of the extremes based on the maturation process. As an adult, an individual may continue the style of the parent or rebel and choose the opposite style.

Again, the emotional response can be quite strong. A nurturing leader can produce feelings of warmth and even love in a subordinate.

Thus, as leaders and followers, people range from authoritarian to permissive and from nurturing to critical and any combination of those characteristics. As leaders, the adopted style has a major influence on how subordinates respond. The followers' adopted styles dictate how the individual will react to a particular leader.

Dependence and Independence

A leader's style results from the models of leadership exhibited by parents, teachers, coaches, and other adults during the maturation process. Most potent of these is the style of parenting, particularly in the very early and impressionable years. An adult may copy the style of a parent, becoming an authoritarian leader from having been raised in a home with that style. Or the adult may choose to adopt the diametrically opposite style, becoming a laissez-faire leader in contrast to the authoritarian home. Followers are more likely to react strongly to an authoritarian leader.

If adults find themselves in a relationship with an authoritarian leader or one with a more participative style, the reaction of the adult team member to the leader will be a function of the way authority figures, parents in particular, behaved and were dealt with in the past. Psychodynamically, an individual may react to a leader in a *dependent, counterdependent,* or *independent* manner. Dependency is self-explanatory. The counterdependent reaction is rebelliousness, rejecting the directives of the leader. Independence occurs when the subordinate assesses leadership attempts by looking at the situation somewhat objectively. The independent response is one in which the team member decides whether the directive is reasonable, ethical, practical, and so forth. It is neither dependent nor independent.

Repression and the Shadow Self

A difference between the psychodynamic approach and that of others described in this volume is found in the idea of depth psychology. Behavioral psychology takes the position that only behaviors, which can be seen, heard, or felt, are worth studying. Another version of psychology holds that we can also study what people think and feel, the ideas and emotions of which we are conscious. But depth psychology says that some of what impels us to certain acts and feelings is below the conscious level, that is, resides in the subconscious.

Parents, to bring that theme back into the discussion, are charged with the responsibility of socializing the child. That means teaching the young person the difference between right and wrong, between what is acceptable and unacceptable in society. Behaviors that are wrong and unacceptable are punished. For example, most parents teach their child that it is wrong to hit someone and particularly to hit a parent. Yet the child still has the impulse to strike out at someone who has just inflicted pain. Punishment by the parent—which may be a verbal rebuke or some "time out" in a corner—teaches the child not to hit but may, eventually, even teach the child not to feel the anger.

The technical term for the result of this process is *repression.* We put into deep recesses of the mind those thoughts and feelings that are deemed unacceptable by society.

Yet when a person is hurt by someone, the physiological reaction still occurs. Something will eventually happen. It may be in the form of getting indigestion. Or it can take some other form. For example, Maryellen is frustrated by the continual whining of a subordinate, Suzan. If she could recognize it, Maryellen would feel anger, but she has been taught not to feel it. So someone says, "Are you mad at Suzan?" Maryellen replies, "No, of course not. She isn't worth getting angry at!" However, Maryellen does make other sarcastic comments about Suzan to her face and to other employees. Sarcasm is an acceptable way for Maryellen to show her anger.

The only way that Maryellen can deal with this issue is if she sits down, alone or with a facilitator, and begins to review her life in the family of origin. There she would discover that her feelings arise from a relationship with a younger sister who whined all the time and got a lot of attention from the mother. That left Maryellen frustrated and angry but unable to express it. Now the relationship is being repeated at work, and the childhood training is still in effect.

Jungian psychology introduced the *concept of the shadow* (Jung, 1923). This is somewhat related to the idea of repression. An individual's shadow is that part of the personality that is unacceptable consciously and the existence of which is therefore denied. For example, a leader may pride herself on very high ethical standards and impeccable integrity. Yet that woman may also be a very politically astute individual who is able to survive in a complex array of relationships in a corporation by carefully wording her statements and remaining ambiguous on some issues. This side of her personality does not fit with her self-image and will be denied, yet others will see that she is politically adroit and even admire her for it. The shadow is often evident to others although denied by the person.

This leader wonders sometimes, "Why are people so careful about what they say around me?" The answer, of course, is that they are wary of someone who is so good at the political games in the corporation. She is potentially dangerous. Yet she does not see that side of herself. It would be helpful if she could see and accept the political aspect of her personality. Then she would be able to understand some of the reactions of other people to her statements. The only way in which we can become aware of the shadow self is to solicit perceptions of ourselves from other people. That is one of the techniques of contemporary self-development seminars and workshops.

Archetypes

Carl Jung, mentioned earlier for his descriptions of psychological types, also introduced the notion of *archetypes.* An archetype is a strong pattern in the human psyche that persists over time. It can also be considered an original pattern or model of which there are many replicas over space and time. In yet another definition, you can think of an archetype as a kind of template of human behavior and belief.

Pearson (1989, 1991) developed a system of archetypes based on the work of Campbell (1968). Campbell studied myths and stories from a large number of cultures and through that study he developed a single all-encompassing story which he labeled "the hero's journey." That journey, in very simplified form, consists of a call to adventure (sometimes refused at first), then an initiation through a series of trials and temptations, and finally a return. It is exemplified, by the way, in many stories. The oldest in classical Western civilization is that of Odysseus. More recently, *The Hobbit* by J. R. R. Tolkien describes the journey of Bilbo Baggins, the hobbit, through a series of adventures in which he ultimately survives and triumphs.

Pearson set up six archetypes based on the hero's journey: the innocent, orphan, martyr, wanderer, warrior, and magician. The innocent exists before the journey. The orphan moves out of "the home" or comfortable territory into the world. A martyr devotes time and energy to the welfare of others. A person operating in the wanderer mode tends to be very independent or, to use a term from earlier in this chapter, counterdependent. The warrior, as might be expected, goes out into battle, which today would probably consist of professional and corporate skirmishes on the road to success. The final archetype, which is not always attained, is that of the magician. It is important to note that Pearson insists, quite rightly, that the archetypes are not encountered in a straight line or by everyone. People can get "stuck" in one of the archetypes, and most often people cycle back and forth through several of them.

For the purposes of a book on leadership, two archetypes are particularly interesting: the warrior and the magician. Our stereotype of a leader is best captured in the warrior archetype. Pearson describes this archetype as embodying the goals of strength and effectiveness. When faced with danger, the warrior attacks. To illustrate the differences in archetypes, the wanderer flees and the martyr sacrifices self for others in the presence of peril. The warrior is competitive and goal oriented.

As a leader, the warrior imposes her or his will on others, gets them to change in order to accommodate her or his needs. Emotionally, the warrior is controlled—the "poker face"—and represses most feelings. In an organizational setting, the warrior makes the system work for himself or herself—and works for material reward. Aside from material success, the warrior wants to be seen as confident and respected.

The other archetype that applies to leadership is that of the magician. The label here may seem strange. Pearson chooses the term because it represents the notion of changing the lesser into the better. In other words, it is all about transformations that seem magical.

This is an entirely different way of leading. Someone operating out of the magician archetype has gone beyond the aggressive and competitive mode of the warrior. Rather than imposing his or her will, the magician establishes mutuality in the relationship with subordinates. Thus, the magician is willing to change and adapt while also asking team members to do the same. The change and adaptation is required for new or unique circumstances facing the organization or work group. Furthermore, the magician accepts and understands emotional responses to activities. For the magician, it is all right to feel elated when a goal has been reached and to grieve in the event of a failure. Rather than using the system for personal gain, the magician-leader strives to achieve team goals through the rule, regulations, and norms of the organization. Work, for the magician, is its own reward. Monetary or status gains are secondary. Finally, the magician wants to be seen as authentic and balanced. Table 11.1 summarizes the warrior-leader and magician-leader archetypes in tabular form.

As a final note, Pearson's magician stereotype has some of the characteristics of the self-actualized state described by Abraham Maslow, one of the founders of humanistic psychology. Eventually, Maslow developed the idea of D- and B-motivation. The D in D-motivation is for *deficit* or *deficiency* motivation. That is, a person does not have the money, status, resources, or power and is motivated to get them. In B-motivation, the B

Table 11.1 *A Comparison of the Warrior-Leader and Magician-Leader*

WARRIOR-LEADER	MAGICIAN-LEADER
Seeks success for self.	Seeks success for the team.
Wants to be seen as strong and aggressive.	Wants to be seen as solid and centered.
Destroys or conquers competitors.	Motivated by competition. Adapts ideas from them.
Worries about and denies failure.	Learns from failure; moves on.
Emotionally neutral.	Celebrates successes; grieves failures.
Works for status and money.	Works is its own reward.
Accumulates money and resources.	Believes there is enough for everyone; make do with the minimum.

stands for *being*. A person with such motivation believes she or he has enough money, status, resources, or power and thus is able to just be, that is, simply exist as a human being, which frees the individual to be concerned about others, the team, and the organization.

Concepts such as individuation, counterdependence, repression, and archetypes come out of the highly technical literature of psychoanalysis, psychiatry, and psychological counseling and are used by professionals to discuss their clients and clinical techniques. Such discussions can be abstruse and not easily understood by the layperson. There have been attempts to make psychodynamic theory more accessible.

Relational Analysis

A popularized and popular psychodynamic model was created by Eric Berne and titled "transactional analysis" (Berne, 1961; Harris, 1967). It could also have been called "relational analysis." Berne labeled three ego

Figure 11.1 *Ego States of Leader and Subordinate*

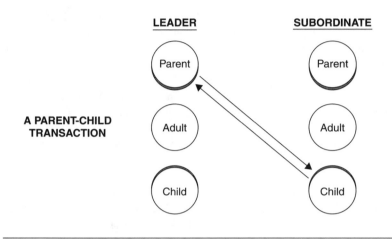

states: *parent, adult,* and *child* (see Figure 11.1). These terms obviously relate to family roles. Every one of us has all three of these ego states. However, they have different levels of effect or significance in individuals.

In Berne's view, the parent ego state can be either critical or nurturing. The critical parent is judgmental, faultfinding, and strict. The nurturing parent, on the other hand, is kind, gentle, and loving. A leader can be parental in attitude and action toward subordinates. The leader may be somewhat autocratic as the critical parent or benevolent as the nurturing parent. The child ego state can be either playful or rebellious. The rebellious child is the counterdependent subordinate. The playful or adaptive child is dependent.

As people mature, they should operate more and more out of the adult ego state. That implies an ability to do reality testing. It means being able to perceive fairly accurately the state of affairs, assign probabilities to various actions, and then select the action that is most likely to produce a desired outcome. People operating out of the adult ego state make tentative decisions and use trial and error to find out what to do. The adult ego state also integrates both the parent and child ego states. That means the guiding, counseling, teaching, and directing aspects of the parental ego state are used when needed, and the spontaneous, sensuous, and joyful facets of the child ego state are called into play when needed.

The importance of transactional analysis is demonstrated in Figure 11.1. A diagram is drawn to represent the ego states of two persons, in this case of a leader and subordinate. The figure illustrates the case where a parental behavior on the part of the leader gets a reaction out of the subordinate from the child ego state. This is a parent-child transaction and relationship. Similarly, a subordinate who acts in a dependent and therefore childlike way will tend to draw out the parental reaction from a leader. The technical term in psychodynamics for this process is *cathecting*. Each person cathects or pulls out of the other person a matching response pattern. This is the very basis for the transactions or deals in transactional analysis.

This analysis suggests that it is not enough to look just at the behavior of a leader. Subordinates may cathect out of a leader a response as much as the opposite. Ideally, a leader and team member will operate adult-to-adult. They will have stated objectives and action plan options, consider the implications and possibilities, and make decisions based on an open process of interaction and discussion. They will consult others who are affected by a decision. And they will follow up to assess what happened and change a project or program as needed.

A good leader will make every effort to operate out of the adult ego state in an effort to cathect adult responses from subordinates. If that does not succeed or there is some kind of parent-child transaction, the leader needs to be able to bring up for discussion the reason for that kind of action and response. The ultimate goal of transactional analysis is to allow the participants in a relationship to talk about what has happened, why it happened, and how to improve matters in the future. A leader's responsibility, in this version of the psychodynamic approach, is to bring to the consciousness of team members the nature of the transactions and also to bring these issues out into the open so that they can be discussed.

HOW DOES THE PSYCHODYNAMIC APPROACH WORK?

From its inception with Freud, the psychodynamic theory and method were intended to produce change in the client. This underpinning has continued throughout the history of the field of psychology, including the advent of social work and pastoral counseling of individuals. In the 1960s, procedures were developed to apply these methods to people without serious mental disturbances, which came to be known as the human potential movement and subsequently as personal growth or personal development. This spawned a whole series of books, seminars, workshops, and lectures so that today there are entire sections of bookstores devoted to the subject.

One assumption underlies all of these psychodynamic and personal growth techniques. The clinician, workshop facilitator, and writer assume that insight into the psychological past of the individual will result in changes in feelings, attitudes, and behaviors. For example, a person who was raised in an authoritarian family of origin can recognize that pattern of child rearing and through understanding it overcome the tendency to become either dependent or counterdependent in relationships with authority figures. Similarly, an individual may have a shadow self that tends to be nurturing and kind, yet the work situation encourages that person to take on a tough, even critical, demeanor. If insight about the shadow self can be brought about, that individual may find it easier to express the nurturing side at work or may wish to find employment in a situation where kindness is accepted as a norm.

The development of insight is a long-term proposition. Adherents to the psychodynamic model would say, in fact, that it is a continuing, life-long endeavor.

Many healthy and "normal" people see counselors, therapists, and guides regularly. These people attend seminars, workshops, and retreats. They read extensively on the subject and continually assess and reassess their own life history, values, emotional reactions, and relationships.

Pearson (1989, 1991) has provided a self-assessment instrument in her books that permits the reader to find which one, two, or three of the archetypes predominate at that time in the individual's life. Again, this provides insight together with the descriptions of the archetypes.

From the viewpoint of the psychodynamic model, all of the various tests and evaluations of leadership style are useful for the insights they produce. A leader who understands his or her style will be more effective than one who is blind to it. Even more important, however, is the leader's ability to understand how that style came about, from the family of origin, from dealings with authoritarian or laissez-faire teachers and coaches, or from social interactions that encouraged the repression of some feelings.

STRENGTHS

The greatest strength of the psychodynamic approach is that it results in an analysis of the relationship between the leader and the follower. This transactional emphasis is important, and it should be emphasized that it is a transaction between the two persons. In some models of leadership, the leader is supposed to exhibit certain appropriate behaviors that will create the desired response in the subordinate. The leader, in that kind of model, is not really an ordinary mortal but someone who can always act in the most appropriate way. The psychodynamic approach takes the position that both leader and subordinate have needs and feelings, not all of which are consciously available, and their relationship will be a result of the mix of those needs and feelings.

A second strength is the universality of the psychodynamic approach. Much of the theory underlying this approach, in contemporary times, is based on a search for a universal truth in human existence, and this is done through a reliance on a study of myth. Jung (1923, 1961), as well as Freud, relied heavily on Greek myths to label psychological actions and reactions such as the Oedipus complex. Subsequently, Joseph Campbell (1968, 1988) spent his lifetime studying mythic stories from cultures around the world, and he was able to show that there are basic themes underlying all of the stories from all of the cultures he studied. This work has been related to the concept of psychological archetypes that presumably are applicable cross-culturally.

Another strength of the psychodynamic approach is that it emphasizes the need for insight on the part of the leader. Insight into self is obtained by bringing into consciousness and dealing with issues from childhood and the family of origin. By talking and writing about these issues, the leader obtains insight that then permits her or him to understand the feelings that emerge in present situations. In turn, the ability to monitor those feelings and the behaviors they produce allows the leader to override them. The leader is also encouraged, in this approach, to gain insight into the reactions of subordinates. Rather than taking their responses at face value, the leader is able to understand why a particular action is taken. This should permit the leader greater tolerance of follower actions.

The psychodynamic approach, following from the preceding comments, encourages the leader to pursue a course of personal growth and development that can result not just in better leadership but also in a more rewarding life. The leader may find satisfaction in more than just the acquisition of power or accomplishment of great goals.

Last, the psychodynamic approach, at least in its most modern form, discourages manipulative techniques in leadership. This is discussed more fully in the section on applications. Effective leadership using the psychodynamic approach is based on self-understanding and empathy with the feelings and reactions of the follower. Ultimately, the effective leader, using this approach, becomes a teacher and counselor as well as a goal setter, directive giver, and all of the other traditional leader roles.

CRITICISMS

There are, of course, criticisms of the psychodynamic approach. One, clearly, is that much of the early work on this approach was based on clinical observation and treatment of persons with serious difficulties. This was a psychology of the abnormal rather than the normal. Psychiatrists work, for the most part, with people who are having problems. Thus, the observations they make are probably biased by the troubles of their clients. In recent times, there has been more emphasis on the psychodynamics of the everyday individual, particularly in the humanistic psychologies and personal growth realm, but the academic and clinical bias is still toward the dysfunctional and problematic.

Even more telling is the subjective nature of the findings of clinical psychologists. The insights obtained by a particular psychiatrist or psychologist will depend, obviously, on the information brought forth by the client or set of clients, but those insights will also be colored by and may even be directed by the unconscious predispositions of the clinician. These professionals prepare for their work by going through a process of insight development, usually by working with a previously trained individual. In other words, every psychoanalyst has undergone psychoanalysis. Every counselor should have undergone rigorous counseling. Those processes do not guarantee that the individual is without biases and predispositions. We all see what we want or need to see, and that includes even the most highly trained and experienced clinician.

Research in the psychodynamic area tends to consist of case study reports from individual psychiatrists. If applied to leadership, such insights may be colored by the biases of the psychiatric observers. A psychiatrist who is herself somewhat counterdependent may describe effective leadership in laissez-faire or democratic terms and denigrate more authoritarian forms.

Closely related to the issue of subjectivity and probably more important are the cultural biases carried by the individual psychologist. Freud's early work was based on the treatment of upper-middle-class Viennese women in a society that was extremely patriarchal. Freud himself, of course, was male, and he associated with well-educated and affluent men. Virtually all psychologists over the years, by definition, are well educated and relatively well off financially. Their patients, for the most part, come from similar backgrounds, particularly the patients who pay for their own treatment. Most of those patients, in the past, have been white and at least middle class, with a Judeo-Christian background. We simply do not know to what extent the picture we have of the human psyche is equally valid for persons with a Hispanic, African American, or Asian cultural background. Thus, any leadership model developed out of the psychodynamic literature or practice is likely to be most applicable to the white, middle-class individual with a Judeo-Christian heritage.

Thus, even though there has been an attempt to achieve universality through the study of mythic stories and psychological archetypes in some studies, a large proportion of the information in the psychodynamic approach is still limited to the white, Anglo-Saxon, Christian or Jewish, middle- or upper-middle-class individual.

Furthermore, much of the early work in psychodynamics was based on the traditional two-parent family of origin. Today, many children are growing up in single-parent families and, perhaps even more common, in families composed of stepparents and stepsiblings. Divorce and remarriage create complex sets of relationships.

The psychodynamic approach is also limited in that it focuses primarily on the psyche of the leader and on the psychological factors that dictate the nature of the relationship between the leader and follower. In other words, it does not take into account organizational factors. These could include the culture of the organization, its structure, and the particular kinds of challenges and tasks it faces. The very nature of the psychodynamic approach also limits its use in practice. Many people simply reject the notion that emotional reactions occur to people or events and that those reactions arise from events and persons in an individual's personal history. Organizational leaders, in particular, subscribe to the view that management and leadership ought to be as rational as possible. Emotional responses are ignored and rejected, even though many an executive has laid awake at night while replaying an emotional situation from that day at work.

A final limitation is that the psychodynamic approach does not lend itself to training in any conventional sense. The leader has to undergo a process of personal growth and insight development, and, ideally, continues that process for as long as he or she is in the leadership position.

APPLICATION

The psychodynamic approach to leadership focuses on the relationship of the leader to his or her subordinates. It does so in the context of general issues of human existence and relationships. As noted previously, the concepts that make up this approach arose out of clinical practice rather than through the standard social science quantitative and qualitative research methods. This approach places a great emphasis on personal growth for leaders. For example, the work of the humanistic psychologists (Maslow, 1968, 1971; Rogers, 1961; Shostrom, 1967) has spawned a wide variety of seminars, workshops, and training sessions devoted to providing individuals with the opportunity to learn about human behavior and experience. More specifically, these experiences provide feedback to the participant on her or his patterns of action and response and the effect of the actions on others.

Because the psychodynamic approach is built on the foundation of deeply embedded emotional responses arising out of infancy, childhood, and adolescence, leaders are encouraged to become aware of those responses in training sessions and then in real-world situations. The additional burden envisioned by the psychodynamic approach is the degree to which certain emotional responses are suppressed together with the events that precipitated them. This requires the leader, in attempting personal growth, to become sensitized to responses that appear weakly in day-to-day interactions. People who become aware of their patterns of emotional response, and are able to articulate them, open up the possibility of change. "Oops, I am starting to get that old feeling of inadequacy when Kirk challenges my statements," brings the feeling into consciousness. There it can be managed. First comes insight, then awareness, and finally change.

The path to insight can come through various experiential training sessions. However, the leader can also approach issues cognitively by reading about emotional responses and how they are formed. There are truly thousands of books on the subject of personal growth, psychology, relationships, and family influences. Many are useful in providing knowledge of how people grow into emotionally mature adults.

There are also ways to intervene directly in an organization to improve relationships between leaders and team members using the psychodynamic approach. One of the methods currently used requires everyone in the organization—managers, supervisors, technical and professional personnel, and line workers—to take a standard psychological inventory such as the Myers-Briggs Type Indicator™ that results in scores on four dimensions of personality. The test outcomes are then made available and discussed by the participants. Each person becomes aware of every other individual's "type." Generally, this results in greater understanding of and tolerance for the way the people work together. The process works because differences are brought out into the open. In some organizations, people are given cards hung on lanyards around their necks with their type shown in bold letters. "Oh, you're an ISTP—life could get interesting here because I'm an ESTJ." In other words, people can even begin to kid around about their types and their differences.

This brings to light an important ethical aspect of the psychodynamic approach. Most modern practitioners encourage clients to bring emotional responses and relational issues out in the open where they can be examined and discussed. Thus, there is an ethic of openness and honesty associated with this approach to leadership and to life in general. Psychological data on a subordinate are not obtained and then used to manipulate that individual. Instead, the follower is encouraged to obtain information or participate in processes that allow him or her to gain insight. Then the follower is asked to share the insights along with other team or organizational members. Nothing is hidden, and the leader is not privy to information that is hidden from everyone else. Most important, the leader shares her or his insights and information with the subordinates. This is in contrast to some of the other leadership approaches, the situational model for an example, where the leader makes an assessment of the subordinate's need structure and then behaves in a way to "motivate" that person in the work situation. This is, in one sense, a manipulative maneuver.

It is very important to understand that there are no evaluative features to the Myers-Briggs or any other psychological inventory. Kroeger and Thuesen (1992) have written a book on the psychological types and their implications for people at work. There is no type that represents a better or worse kind of leader. There is no type that constitutes an ideal subordinate. We should note that type may be related to the kind of education, training, and profession an individual pursues. There are type differences, in general, between accountants, engineers, writers, graphic designers, and so on.

The use of test results to understand and compare styles suggests the ultimate goal of the psychodynamic approach to leadership in practical terms. Humans are able to use language, and one of the more important uses is to talk about relationships. Effective human relationships evolve when the parties are able to talk about the relationship as well as about themselves as individuals and about the work they do. Yet most people find it difficult to bring up this kind of relational communication. The use of the Myers-Briggs or similar questionnaire outcomes is one way to encourage people to discuss their relationships.

CASE STUDIES

In this section, case studies (Cases 11.1, 11.2, and 11.3) of leadership in organizations are provided that can be analyzed using the psychodynamic approach. The questions provided at the end of each case will help you analyze the situations.

CASE 11.1

A Change in Behavior

Jim Ferris is the president and chief executive officer (CEO) of a small manufacturing company that produces metal and plastic components for larger local businesses. Eight months ago, Jim hired an operations manager, who was given responsibility over all of the fabrication, inventory, quality control, and associated functions on the shop floor. Hal, the operations manager, stepped right in and was very effective in improving the efficiency of the whole shop.

Several months after Hal was hired, Jim began having a weekly formal review meeting that included Hal and the supervisors under his direction. The first few meetings went very well. Recently, Hal has begun to act in a very reserved manner in contrast to his very enthusiastic and energetic behavior in the prior months. Jim is smart enough to realize that the change in behavior began just a month or so after he started having the review meetings.

Because Hal was an important factor in the company's current profitability and growth, Jim wanted to identify the problem and deal with it. He retained an industrial psychologist as a consultant, who then came into the plant and interviewed Hal and all of the production supervisors. The psychologist's report pinpointed the problem. Hal had difficulty working for authoritarian leaders. Jim did not see himself that way, but the psychologist pointed out that Jim had shifted from letting Hal go his own way to instituting the review meetings.

Questions

1. What intervention could the industrial psychologist make to minimize the problem?
2. What can Jim do to take Hal's reactions into account and still maintain some control over operations?
3. What would help Hal see, understand, and change his behavior?

CASE 11.2

Not the Type Who Sees the "Big Picture"

Jenny Folsom is the manager of a group of marketing specialists. She has good relationships with most of her team except for Connie Perez. Jenny is on the verge of letting Connie go. Connie just cannot seem to work up to the expectations that Jenny has. Over the past year, Jenny had four quarterly review sessions with Connie. In each one, Jenny pointed out her expectations and where Connie was falling short. Connie continued to act in much the same way even though she felt she was trying to improve.

Before going to the drastic and final step of dismissing an employee, Jenny has gone to the Personnel Department and specifically to the Training and Development Group. She has presented her problem to two training and development specialists. This is what she said: "Connie seems to get bogged down in details. I give her a project to work on and a set of overall objectives. Then, when I talk to her, I find that she is buried in some minor issue, getting all the information she can, talking to other people about that issue. It drives me crazy. I need to get the project completed and have her move on to something else. I want her to see the big picture. We have a lot to do, a whole strategy to implement. I can't afford to have someone getting hung up on minor details."

The training and development specialists sense that there is a big difference in personal styles between Jenny and Connie. They invite Jenny to come back the next day, at which time she is given a briefing on personal styles. It quickly becomes evident that Jenny is an NT (the code is explained later in this chapter) temperament, an "intuitive thinker," in the Jungian personality types. She is good at conceptualizing and systematic planning. She can see the underlying principles of organizations and systems.

With each accomplishment of her group, Jenny can see three or four new big challenges. When the training and development specialists talked this way to Jenny, she agreed readily with their description of her.

Connie, on the other hand, seems to be an SF (sensor-feeler) temperament based on Jenny's description. Connie is very practical and down to earth. She actually is quite good at problem solving in an immediate way. And she is highly resourceful, able to find information and answers. Unfortunately, she simply is not the type to see the "big picture."

Jenny's question to the training and development specialists is, So what do I do?

Questions

1. Should Jenny have a session with Connie on her own?
2. Should she have the session with the training and development specialists?
3. Should Connie be given the analysis results for herself and for Jenny?
4. What kinds of issues should the two women discuss?
5. What kinds of tasks should Jenny assign to Connie in the future?

CASE 11.3

Asking for Feedback

Gerry heads up a team of personnel who staff a large retail copy center. He has an assistant manager, 2 shift leaders, and a staff of 16 well-trained team members. The store is open 7 days a week and 24 hours a day. Gerry is proud of the way his team functions. There is some turnover because the team members are paid a relatively low hourly rate. However, the store engages in a profit-sharing plan that supplements the team members' paychecks fairly well each month. Gerry thought they could do better.

In the prior 6 months, Gerry has tried all of the standard motivational techniques spelled out in textbooks and seminars. Now he decides to take a bold step. On a Sunday afternoon, Gerry holds a team meeting. He talks about their current sales and profitability level and points out that he thinks they could do better. The team members do not respond one way or another to this statement. Gerry then tells them that he wants to do two things that day. First, he wants them to write down, anonymously, their impression of him as a leader and how he could improve his performance. After that is done, he opens up the floor to discussion of how they could improve their overall performance. At first, there is some reluctance on the part of the team members to offer anything beyond the usual suggestions, most of which had been tried at one time or another. Then Gerry says, "Let's be bold. Let's go out on a limb and try some things that we haven't tried before. Does anyone have any ideas?" At first there is silence. Then one team member offers the suggestion that each person be given the opportunity to do some sales work in addition to running the copy machines and staffing the front counter. Some of the people express their doubts, particularly about their own ability to do sales. Gerry points out that whoever wanted to do sales could do it, and others could figure out other ways to find more interesting tasks.

Questions

1. What should Gerry do next in the meeting?
2. What should he do with the suggestions produced by the team?
3. What should he do with the feedback he received?
4. How should he react to anything that he considers negative? Should he compile the feedback and show it to the team members at the next meeting?
5. If so, how should it be handled?

LEADERSHIP INSTRUMENT

The Myers-Briggs Type Indicator, based on Jung's psychological types, is a multiquestion instrument that is usually administered by a clinician or research worker. The test is copyrighted, and its use is limited to persons who have the professional qualifications to administer it and interpret the results. There is another psychological test, the Jungian Type Survey (Gray, Wheelwright, & Wheelwright, n.d.), that is also copyrighted but not restricted to certified practitioners. Both questionnaires are long, too long for use in this book.

There are four dimensions to the Jungian types, which can be combined into 16 personality types. Before getting into more detail on the types, a simplified way of obtaining an estimate of your personality type has been constructed for this chapter.

Psychodynamic Approach Survey

Instructions: Circle one of the two words in each pair below as best describing who you are:

reflective	detached	open
sociable	humane	structured
practical	specific	gregarious
conceptual	general	deep
general	firm	sociable
practical	involved	deep
flexible	involved	planned
planned	detached	open
humane	conceptual	reflective
firm	specific	gregarious
	structured	
	flexible	

Scoring

Count how many times you circled the words sociable or gregarious   _____ E
Count how many times you circled the words reflective or deep   _____ I

Count how many times you circled the words practical or specific   _____ S
Count how many times you circled the words conceptual or general   _____ N

Count how many times you circled the words involved or humane   _____ F
Count how many times you circled the words detached or firm   _____ T

Count how many times you circled the words flexible or open   _____ P
Count how many times you circled the words planned or structured   _____ J

Your score for each letter will range from 0 to 4. For each pair of letters (i.e., E-I, S-N, F-T, and P-J), you will score either 4-0, 3-1, 2-2, 1-3, or 0-4. If you scored 1-3 on the first set of words above, then, for example, you would be classified as an I. The meaning of the letter symbol (I) will be explained below. If you scored 4-0, you would be an E. If you had a score of 2-2, you could be some combination of I and E.

As a result of this scoring, you should end up with four letters, which represent your personality type using the Jungian categories. For example, you could be an ENFP, an INTJ, and so on. If one of your scores was a 2-2, for example, on the I and E as noted above, then you would have two possible codes: INFP or ENFP.

Write your four-letter code(s) here: ___ ___ ___ ___ (or ___ ___ ___ ___)

Scoring Interpretation

Now remember that there is no ideal or preferred code for you as a leader. Rather, you need to compare your code with that of another person or other persons with whom you work (or live or with whom you attend class).

The more similar the codes, the more likely you are to find it easy to communicate and relate with the other person. The more dissimilar the codes, the harder it is to communicate and relate. However, the point is to understand the differences between yourself and the other person. These similarities and differences may help explain misunderstandings and conflicts between individuals including between a leader and one or more team members.

To use the results of this instrument yourself, you need to do more than just obtain an estimate of your psychological type. Remember that there is no preferred or ideal psychological type for a leader. Instead, you need to find someone else who is willing to use the type indicator questionnaire. If you are in a working situation where you interact regularly with someone, try to get that person to help you out in this exercise. Compare your psychological type with that of the other person.

This brings up an important point. In practical problem-solving, decision-making, program-planning, or product-designing processes, diverse styles are needed to make sure that all the options and implications are considered. Outgoing people need to be balanced by others who are more internally oriented. The very practical can be equalized by the conceptual. Humane individuals must sometimes take a more detached and objective view. The highly spontaneous individual can be countered by someone who is more structured.

The code letters stand for specific personality characteristics based on the typology developed by Jung. They are as follows:

E for extravert	**S** for sensor	**F** for feeler	**P** for perceiver
I for introvert	**N** for intuitor	**T** for thinker	**J** for judger

Thus, an INFJ is a combination of introvert, intuitor, feeler, and judger. What do those words mean? Briefly, here is the basis for the categories and labels (see also Figure 11.2). For more complete description and application, you need to consult a book devoted to the subject such as *Type Talk at Work* by Kroeger and Thuesen (1992). The subject is extensive and requires much more space than is available in this chapter.

An extravert (E) is characterized as sociable, externally focused, and gregarious, someone who speaks before thinking. This is similar to our common use of the term. On the other hand, an introvert (I) is someone who is reflective, internally focused, and deep, someone who likes to think things through before speaking. Please note that this does not include our lay definition of an introvert as someone who is shy. The key difference between extravert and introvert is the source of the person's energy: extravert from outside, introvert from within. An extravert team member, "talking with mouth running without brain engaged," will seem reckless to an introvert leader who prepares carefully for any meeting or discussion.

The next dimension, sensor versus intuitor, relates to how people gather information. Sensors (S) tend to be practical, realistic, factual, and specific in the information gathering, whereas intuitors (N) are more conceptual, theoretical, general, and random in the same function. An intuitor leader will be frustrated by a sensor subordinate as described in Case 11.2 where Jenny, the marketing manager, was driven crazy by Connie, who got immersed in details.

The third dimension relates to decision making, and the two types here are labeled thinkers (T) and feelers (F). The former are firm, just, clear, and detached in the decision-making process. Feelers, on the other hand, lean more toward a humane, harmonious, and subjective process using input from several people. This distinction appears, at least on the surface, to be somewhat similar to the styles dimensions of task oriented (thinker) and person oriented (feeler). A thinker leader will have trouble with any process in which a large number of people are involved and thus will probably make decisions by herself after acquiring as much input as possible. Subordinates may feel left out.

The final distinction in the Jungian types is between judgers (J) and perceivers (P). This relates to how people deal with their environment and create their lifestyles. Judgers emphasize control, planning, structure, and schedule in their lives, another aspect of the task-oriented or autocratic leader. Perceivers tend more toward adaptability, flexibility, spontaneity, and openness, which are somewhat similar to the characteristics of a democratic leadership style.

Using these descriptions, you can go back and assess the four-letter code you obtained from the instrument in this chapter. However, if you are really interested in the psychodynamic approach, the Myers-Briggs Type Indicator will provide a more valid and complete assessment. Many counseling centers, counselors, and psychotherapists can administer the questionnaire and get the results scored.

———————————— ◆ ————————————

Figure 11.2 *Dimensions of Personality Types*

Source of one's energy	▶ Extravert	· · · · · · · · · · · · · · Introvert
How one gathers information	▶ Sensor	· · · · · · · · · · · · · · Intuitor
How one makes decisions	▶ Feeler	· · · · · · · · · · · · · · Thinker
How one deals with one's environment	▶ Perceiver	· · · · · · · · · · · · · · Judger

SUMMARY

The psychodynamic approach to leadership arose out of the development of methods for dealing with emotionally disturbed individuals and out of psychological theories of personality development. Freud and Jung were two of the pioneers in this effort.

Clinical work and theorizing led to the development of the concepts of the family of origin, individuation, dependence, counterdependence, independence, regression, repression, the shadow self, and archetypes. Popularized versions of the psychodynamic approach were devised, the best known being transactional analysis.

The essential assumption of the psychodynamic approach is that an individual can change behaviors and feelings by obtaining insight into his or her upbringing, prior relationships, and psychological development. The key is to provide mechanisms such as workshops, counseling sessions, or personality assessments that lead to insight.

The strengths of the psychodynamic approach include the emphasis on analyzing the relationship of the leader to the subordinate, an attempt at universality of human experience, the need for insight development by the leader, the encouragement of personal growth, and a rejection of manipulative techniques in dealing with other humans including subordinates.

A major criticism is that much of the theory is based on the treatment of persons with serious emotional difficulties or crises. A major portion of the psychodynamic theory arises out of the subjective impressions of clinicians and the uses of one-person case studies. There is also a potential for cultural bias in the creation of psychodynamic explanations of behavior, including an assumption of a family of origin consisting of two parents. In addition, much of the theorizing is based on work with upper-middle-class, white, Anglo-Saxon persons within a Judeo-Christian culture. A limitation also occurs in that the psychodynamic approach focuses on the psychology of the individual leader and ignores the culture and social norms of the organization. In practical applications, many people will not accept the notion that emotional reactions affect relationships or decisions and particularly that such reactions result from childhood and adolescent experiences. Finally, this approach limits the ability to train individuals because it emphasizes the need for insight rather than skill development.

In application, the psychodynamic approach suggests that the leader with insight into her or his own personality and into those of the subordinates will function effectively. This is put into practice when the members of an organization are given a personality inventory and the results are shared among all. The participants are then more readily able to understand and accept their differences.

There are numerous personality inventories used in the application of the psychodynamic approach to leadership, but the most common is the Myers-Briggs Type Indicator. Results of this assessment instrument provide distinctions on four dimensions: extravert or introvert, sensor or intuitor, thinker or feeler, and judger or perceiver. As result, there are 16 potential personality types. Sharing of the leader's personality type and those of the members of the team is assumed to improve understanding among the participants.

Thus, the psychodynamic approach is unique because it focuses on the basic personality of the leader and subordinates and not specifically on leadership traits, behaviors, or processes.

REFERENCES

Berne, E. (1961). *Transactional analysis in psychotherapy.* New York: Grove.

Campbell, J. (1968). *The hero with a thousand faces* (2nd ed.). Princeton, NJ: Princeton University Press.

Campbell, J. (with Moyers, B.). (1988). *The power of myth.* Garden City, NY: Doubleday.

Freud, S. (1938). *The basic writings of Sigmund Freud* (A. A. Brill, Ed.). New York: Modern Library.

Gray, H., Wheelwright, J. H., & Wheelwright, J. B. (n.d.). *Jungian Type Survey.* San Francisco: Society of Jungian Analysts.

Harris, T. A. (1967). *I'm OK—You're OK.* New York: Harper & Row.

Hill, M. A. (1984). The law of the father. In B. Kellerman (Ed.), *Leadership: Multidisciplinary perspectives.* Englewood Cliffs, NJ: Prentice Hall.

Hummel, R. P. (1975). Psychology of charismatic followers. *Psychological Reports, 37,* 759-770.

Jung, C. J. (1923). *Psychological types.* New York: Harcourt & Brace.

Jung, C. J. (1961). *Memories, dreams, and reflections.* New York: Vintage.

Kroeger, O., & Thuesen, J. M. (1992). *Type talk at work.* New York: Delacorte.

Maslow, A. (1968). *Toward a psychology of being* (2nd ed.). New York: Van Nostrand.

Maslow, A. (1971). *The farther reaches of human nature.* New York: Penguin.

Pearson, C. S. (1989). *The hero within.* San Francisco: Harper & Row.

Pearson, C. S. (1991). *Awakening the heroes within.* San Francisco: Harper.

Rogers, C. R. (1961). *On becoming a person.* Boston: Houghton Mifflin.

Schiffer, I. (1973). *Charisma: A psychoanalytic look at mass society.* Toronto: University of Toronto Press.

Shostrom, E. L. (1967). *Man, the manipulator.* Nashville, TN: Abingdon.

Winer, J. A., Jobe, T., & Ferrono, C. (1984-1985). Toward a psychoanalytic theory of the charismatic relationship. *Annual of Psychoanalysis, 12-13,* 155-175.

Zaleznik, A. (1977, May-June). Managers and leaders: Are they different? *Harvard Business Review, 55,* 67-68.

Women and Leadership

Julie Indvik

DESCRIPTION

Unlike the other chapters in this book that focus on particular theoretical explanations for leadership behavior and outcomes, this chapter examines broader themes in the ways in which humans interpret the behavior of leaders based on demographic characteristics. Specifically, this chapter explores several ongoing issues for leaders in the largest demographic group of all, women.

Definitions

While the terms *leader* and *manager* will be used interchangeably in this chapter, the terms *sex* and *gender* will not. *Sex* refers to biological differences including anatomy, physiology, and hormones, although some theorists argue that even sex is a continuum rather than a simple bipolar set of categories (e.g., Beemyn & Eliason, 1996; Jagose, 1996). The biological characteristics of males and females imply nothing, in and of themselves, about the cognitive, emotional, or interpersonal abilities relevant to the workplace and leadership. How, then, have men and women developed such different probabilities of becoming leaders in companies and government?

The answer lies in the meanings that most cultures have assigned to the categories of male and female. *Gender* refers to the way in which meaning and evaluations are associated with sex by members of a culture. In other words, masculinity and femininity have various sets of characteristics associated with them, depending on the culture. The degree to which males and females are expected to behave differently, are treated differently, or are valued differently has little to do with *sex* (biology) and everything to do with *gender* (learned beliefs).

Learned beliefs can be especially misleading when there are only two categories in a set (such as female/male or masculine/feminine) because several cognitive distortions arise (Gentile, 1996). First, people's thinking and observations become simplified because of the belief that everyone must fit into either one category or the other. Either-or thinking impedes understanding the nuances and complexities of human interaction and the multifaceted identities that people can develop.

Second, the two categories also seem to imply that everyone within each category is identical. For example, the bipolar categories of *sex* and *gender* often seem to imply that only majority-group members are included when the terms are used. In other words, in the absence of further descriptors, the terms *man* and *woman* are often taken to mean white, heterosexual, healthy, and middle class or above (Bell, Denton, & Nkomo, 1993). This explains why so much organizational research on sex, gender, and leadership does not apply to people of color, people with disabilities, or people with gay sexual orientations (Bell et al., 1993; Hall, 1986; Karambayya, 1997; Muller, 1998; Okimoto, 1998).

The third major distortion with a bipolar category set is the ease with which many people erroneously tend to value one category as superior to the other. In the case of sex and gender, hundreds of studies have documented the variety of ways in which *male* and *masculine* have been valued as superior to *female* and *feminine*. These prejudicial attitudes and discriminatory behaviors have damaged individuals, organizations, and society by limiting the ways in which people can contribute based on their unique, rather than their gender-role-bound, characteristics and talents.

The pervasiveness of the attitudes associated with sex and gender has resulted in workplaces becoming "gendered." This means that the allocation of responsibilities in organizations and nearly all decisions about employees' career progress, resources, salaries, power and authority, and appropriate work behavior are affected by the distinction between *male* and *female, masculine* and *feminine* (Acker, 1992, p. 251). Although many executives and managers prefer to believe that organizations are objective about merit and are gender neutral, the data from many research studies indicate that most workplaces use gender, job-irrelevant as it should be, as a basis for many decisions (Hale, 1996) that ultimately affect who becomes a leader. Just as workplace decision making is gendered, so is much of the distribution of responsibility at home, especially for working parents. Ongoing research has indicated continued dilemmas for women leaders who seek to balance work demands with a personal life (e.g., Ensher, Murphy, & Sullivan, 2002).

With these definitions as a foundation, the next section will provide a framework for the research trends to be explored in this chapter.

OVERVIEW OF RESEARCH TRENDS

Over the past 20 years, researchers of women leaders and managers have built a large body of literature addressing three fundamental questions (Bell & Nkomo, 1992). The earliest question was, *Can women be leaders?* Once this was answered affirmatively, researchers asked, *Do male and female leaders differ in their behavior and effectiveness in organizations?* Trends in the focus of these studies shifted emphasis; depending on the decade, the emphasis was sometimes on establishing differences and sometimes on establishing similarities between men and women leaders (Maier, 1992). A third question has intrigued researchers: *Why do so few women leaders reach the top?* The purpose of this chapter is to review approaches and findings used to answer these three questions.

Can Women Be Leaders?

Despite continued evidence of sex discrimination in many arenas of life, the question in the heading for this section would no longer be posed and most people would agree that the answer is a resounding "Yes!" This section will present comparative demographic data on female and male leaders, as well as an explanation of the benefit of this trend for employers.

Of the approximately 135 million people employed in the United States in 2001, 46.6% were women (Women's Bureau, 2001). These women comprised about 58% of all U.S. women over age 20 (Bureau of Labor Statistics, 2002). Overall, women earned $0.76 for every dollar earned by men in 2001, although women managers earned only $0.66 for every dollar earned by male managers (Women's Bureau, 2001). Women earned 58% of the bachelor's degrees in 2001 (Garofoli, 2002), and by the year 2008 are expected to outnumber men in graduate school as well (Lewis, 1999).

In 2002 women filled 15.7% of corporate officer (top management) positions, including 7.1% of chief financial officers and 16.1% of general counsels in the Fortune 500 composed of America's 500 largest companies (Catalyst, 2002a). While only 5.2% of the top-earning corporate officer slots were filled by women in 2002, they held 9.9% of the "clout titles" in organizations, including chairman, chief executive officer (CEO), and president (Catalyst, 2002a). Women held 12.4% of the seats on Fortune 500 corporate boards of directors in 2001, up from 10% in 1999; 66 of the 500 companies still had no women on their boards (Catalyst, 2002b).

At the very top of major corporations, there are six female CEOs in Fortune 500 companies and an additional five in Fortune 1000 companies (Sellers, 2002). The 11 female CEOs of Fortune 500 and 1000 companies, with the rank of their companies in parentheses, are as follows: Carleton Fiorina of Hewlett-Packard (28), Marce Fuller of Mirant (52), Patricia Russo of Lucent (76), Anne Mulcahy of Xerox (120), Andrea Jung of Avon Products (302), Marion Sandler of Golden West Financial Corporation (371), Patricia Forbes Lieberman of Truserv (513), Cinda Hallman of Spherion (539), Dorrit Bern of Charming Shoppes (699), Pamela Kirby of Quintiles Transnational (808), and Judy Odom of Software Spectrum (979).

However, an increasing number of women own and run their own companies. Over the past 10 years, women have started businesses at twice the rate of men and now own about 44% of the 20.4 million small businesses in the United States despite the fact that only 5% of venture capital and 3% of government contracts are awarded to women-owned businesses (Pofeldt, 2002). In government, women serve in a growing number of leadership capacities, including 12% of state governorships (Women Governors, 2002), 13% of U.S. Senate positions, and 14% of U.S. House of Representatives positions (Ciabattari, 2002).

The growing trend of women filling leadership positions is reflected in the differences between two articles in *Fortune* magazine. In 1996, *Fortune* profiled the strategies of only 7 high-achieving women leaders with a proviso to watch the careers of an additional 15 (Sellers, 1996). By October

1998, however, *Fortune* concluded that a profile of 50 women leaders was warranted because women, at last, were achieving significant power in highly important industries (Sellers, 1998, p. 78). The 2002 list of the 50 most powerful women in business was accompanied by an additional list of 5 women whose careers bear watching (Sellers, 2002).

One question that arises when considering these findings is the degree to which they apply to women of differing racial or ethnic backgrounds. Although women's overall percentage of Fortune 500 executive positions increased from 8.7% in 1995 to 12.5% in 2000, women of color remained at 1.3% during this entire period (Scott, 2001). In 2001 women of color filled 2% of corporate board positions in Fortune 1000 companies; these seats comprised 18.1% of the seats held by all women. Of the 178 board positions held by women of color, 74% were held by African American women, 17% by Latino American women, and 8.4% by Asian American women (Catalyst, 2002b).

A recent review indicated that African American women currently represent the largest group of women of color in management and are surpassing African American men in executive and managerial positions (Bell & Nkomo, 2001). While the three black CEOs of Fortune 500 companies are men, 11 of the 50 most powerful black executives listed in a recent *Fortune* article are women (Daniels, 2002): Oprah Winfrey of Harpo Incorporated, Myrtle Potter of Genentech, Brenda Gaines of Diners Club North America, Paula Sneed of Kraft, Pamela Thomas-Graham of CNBC, Ursula Burns of Xerox, Cathy Hughes of Radio One, Lana Corbi of Hallmark Channel, Jacqueline Woods of Oracle, Kim Crawford of Dell, and Carla Harris of Morgan Stanley.

The data presented above indicate that women's inclusion in leadership roles has increased over the past several decades and yet does not reflect their overall proportion of the labor force or population. Expanded leadership opportunities clearly benefit the individual women sought to fill such roles, but what explains organizational willingness to offer such opportunities (beyond the need to comply with legal requirements)? Enhanced productivity, competitive advantage, and financial performance are three reasons why developing and promoting women leaders are in the best interest of employers.

The resource-based theory of competitive advantage and strategy analysis (Barney, 1997) explains that an organization's primary source of competitive advantage is the capacity to optimize and use its internal resources in uncertain and dynamic contexts. Key among these internal resources are people's capabilities, including varying perspectives on problem solving. Underutilized women and people of color are major sources of untapped value that can enhance an organization's creativity, change efforts, teamwork, and financial performance (Appold, Siengthai, & Kasarda, 1998; Flynn, 1994; Shrader, Blackburn, & Iles, 1997; Thompson, 1999). Consequently, hiring, developing, and promoting women into leadership positions can be one of the most useful strategies an organization can adopt to succeed in an increasingly globalized and uncertain economy.

In summary, recent demographic data on female and male leaders indicate both considerable progress and continued imbalance in the proportion of working women in leader roles. To the degree that women leaders are underutilized, organizations undermine an important source of competitive advantage. The next section will describe studies addressing the second major question posed by researchers.

Do Female and Male Leaders Differ in Their Behavior and Effectiveness?

The purpose of asking and answering this question has shifted several times over the past three decades. Sometimes the purpose of conducting research has simply been to understand the impact of gender on leadership behavior and outcomes; other times, supporting belief systems about equality or one sex's superiority may have motivated researchers to collect data. In recent years, the large number of studies conducted to compare female and male leaders has allowed other researchers to conduct meta-analyses. A meta-analysis consists of a set of statistical procedures for analyzing all studies that include similar variables to determine what the overall trend in results is. This can be especially useful in leadership studies, since some studies have found sex differences whereas others have not. This section will discuss recent meta-analyses as well as recent studies of leadership effectiveness.

Meta-analyses and literature reviews performed over the past 15 years indicate that assuming differences in behavior, cognition, and affect between male and female leaders would lead to erroneous conclusions. More than 160 studies of sex-related differences in leadership style were investigated in a meta-analysis that found only one difference in the studies done in organizations: Women used a more participative or democratic style and a less autocratic or directive style than men did, although this tendency declined in a highly male-dominated setting (Eagly & Johnson, 1990). Both men and women emphasized task accomplishment more when the setting was numerically dominated by leaders of their own sex or when the leadership role was seen as congruent with their gender.

Given the behavioral similarity of male and female leaders, the result of another meta-analysis of 82 studies measuring leader effectiveness (Eagly, Karau, & Makhijani, 1995) should not be surprising: Female and male leaders did not differ overall in effectiveness, although more will be said later about this meta-analysis. Similarly, other reviews have demonstrated essential similarity in leader aptitude, in motivation to be a leader, in job satisfaction, in commitment, and in subordinate satisfaction (e.g., Dobbins & Platz, 1986; Donnell & Hall, 1980; Powell, 1993).

In what ways, then, might male and female leaders differ? Several authors have pointed to sex differences in worldview, in socialization, and in life experience that may result in somewhat different mental models, or "implicit theories," of leadership (e.g., Belenky, Clinchy, Goldberger, & Tarule, 1986; Gilligan, 1982; Lowe & Gardner, 2000; Tannen, 1994). Other authors have illuminated sex differences in the organizational outcomes received by female and male leaders. This chapter has already described the relatively small percentage of women in leader roles relative to their proportion in the labor force and the salary inequities experienced even more sharply by women leaders than by women employees. Several studies have noted the relatively small number of corporate women leaders in line positions, seen as crucial for promotion to executive roles (e.g., Oakley, 2000).

In addition, another meta-analysis found that male and female leaders may be evaluated differently (Eagly, Makhijani, & Klonsky, 1992), which, in turn, can affect the impact of management training (Tharenou, Latimer, & Conroy, 1994), assignments (Ohlott, Ruderman, & McCauley, 1994), and mentors (Dreher & Cox, 1996) on promotion. More specifically, female and male leaders were evaluated equally favorably when they used an equivalent stereotypically feminine leadership style (democratic), but only female leaders were evaluated unfavorably when they used an equivalent stereotypically masculine leadership style (autocratic and directive). Women leaders were particularly devalued when they worked in male-dominated settings and when their evaluators were men, even though women raters did not favor one sex over the other. This finding supports other recent studies that suggest that male and female leaders differ in the lengths to which they must go to be promoted, in the need to adapt their behavior at work, in the amount of support they tend to receive at work, and in the impact of family variables on career advancement (Bell & Nkomo, 2001; Ohlott et al., 1994; Ragins, Townsend, & Mattis, 1998; Tharenou, 2001; Tharenou et al., 1994).

Female and male leaders may also differ in the conditions that prove a good fit for their leadership style. In the meta-analysis on leader effectiveness already mentioned (Eagly et al., 1995), the researchers predicted that the social role theory of sex differences in social behavior would explain the patterns in the literature. This theory proposes that people are generally expected to engage in activities and actions congruent with their culturally defined gender roles (Eagly, 1987). While overall effectiveness did not differ for male and female leaders, comparisons of leader effectiveness favored men more and women less when three conditions were present: when the setting was male dominated (especially in the military); when a high percentage of subordinates were male; and when the role was seen as more congenial to men in terms of self-assessed competence, interest, and low requirements for cooperation with high requirements for control. Effectiveness comparisons favored women leaders to the degree that these conditions were reversed. Additionally, effectiveness comparisons favored women leaders for middle management in business, education, and government or social service, while they favored male leaders in entry-level or supervisory positions, especially in the military.

Eagly and her associates (1992) concluded, "Leadership or managerial roles may be defined in a more masculine or feminine fashion, depending on the organizational context of management. It is the fit between leaders' gender and the specifics of the leadership role that influences leaders' effectiveness" (p. 139). In noting the conditions that seem to favor female or male leaders, the meta-analysis indicated that, across most sectors of the economy other than the military, women's effectiveness increased as they moved up the hierarchy and as cooperation rather than control was required. This pattern in the literature is consistent, not only with another meta-analysis indicating that women's social skills tend to be higher than men's (Eagly & Wood, 1991) but also with studies highlighting that many women leaders' preferred style of cooperative or "web leadership" (e.g., Helgesen, 1990; Lauterbach & Weiner, 1996; Rosener, 1990) provides a good fit with the evolving requirements for 21st-century global leadership (e.g., Bartlett & Ghoshal, 1997; Fisher, 1998; Petrick, Scherer, Brodzinski, Quinn, & Ainina, 1999; Sharpe, 2000).

Finally, three recent studies underscore the pattern that, despite organizational obstacles, women leaders perform effectively. Advanced Teamware, Inc., conducted a study in which more than 6,000 bosses, peers, subordinates, and others were asked to complete comprehensive questionnaires about 915 middle- to senior-level managers and supervisors in large corporations. Of the 31 areas examined, women outperformed men in 28, including conflict resolution, work quality, adaptation to change, productivity, idea generation, and motivation of others. Men handled pressure and coped with their own frustration better than women did, while both groups scored equally on delegating authority (Micco, 1996).

Saville & Holdsworth, a consulting firm in New Zealand, conducted a study with 3,000 managers. While there were no differences between male and female managers on many of the 30 attributes measured, results indicated that women emphasized planning and organizing work and an empathic approach, while they placed less emphasis on the need to win at all costs ("Women May," 1997). Third, Lawrence A. Pfaff & Associates conducted a study in which 1,000 managers' bosses and employees evaluated their performance. Although some performance categories reflected no significant differences between women and men, in the 20 categories reflecting a statistically significant difference, women received higher scores from their bosses and employees. The largest gaps were in areas like planning and decisiveness (Gendron, 1995).

In summary, meta-analyses and individual studies suggest several conclusions about differences between male and female leaders. Although quite similar to men in behavior and effectiveness, women leaders tend to be more participative and less autocratic, a pattern that is well suited to 21st-century global organizations. Since women leaders are evaluated more negatively by men when they behave in stereotypically masculine ways, the range of behavior seen as appropriate for women leaders is more limited. Women leaders were seen as more effective in middle management positions in most sectors other than the military and in situations requiring cooperation, with a balance of men and women. The next section will address the third major question probed in the literature.

Why Do So Few Women Leaders Reach the Top?

This section will describe several popularized explanations and then a number of data-based explanations for women leaders' small numbers in the executive ranks of organizations. Several popularized explanations have been offered for the slow, albeit real, progress of women leaders over the past 30 years. One common explanation offered by theorists and male CEOs is the "pipeline theory," which argues that women's absence from executive positions is simply a function of not having been in managerial positions long enough for natural career progression to occur (Heilman, 1997; Ragins et al., 1998).

A second explanation favored by male CEOs in a recent study was women's lack of general management or line experience (Ragins et al., 1998). A third explanation has proposed that women leaders are themselves the problem, whether because they are simply less suited to executive demands than men (Heilman, 1997), unavailable because so few are sufficiently qualified (Morrison, 1992), or lacking in self-confidence (Morris, 1998). How valid are these explanations?

Before turning to more data-based explanations for women's career advancement, evidence for each of the above popularized explanations will be reviewed. First, the pipeline theory has no data to support it. Heilman (1997) reviewed a number of studies indicating that if simple passage of time were the issue, women's representation at top levels would be many times what it was. McCorduck (1996) noted that since top corporate leaders were 99% male in 1970 and 95% male in 1995, it would take 300 years for U.S. women to achieve parity in business and 500 years to reach it in the U.S. Congress. A study of 70 executive women across the United States found that the average length of time they took to reach executive ranks in their companies was 11.5 years (Gallagher, 1996), a time period that should have easily allowed parity to be reached since, for example, the percentage of women in the Harvard MBA program has plateaued at about 26% since 1983 (Faircloth, 1998).

Only the second popularized explanation of insufficient experience in line positions has any data to support it. This chapter has already noted that corporate women leaders fill a small percentage of line positions (Catalyst, 1998a; Oakley, 2000), and some women leaders (47% of the sample) agreed with male CEOs (82% of the sample) that the absence of line experience was an advancement barrier (Ragins et al., 1998). In another study of 1,366 middle and top managers, however, researchers discovered that top executives were not distinguished from middle managers by their line experience but by the breadth of positions and departments in which they had worked (Hurley, Fagenson-Eland, & Sonnenfeld, 1997). In fact, this study reported that the longer managers had served in a line position, the less likely they were to move into top management. The timing of line and staff (functions without direct profit-making responsibility, such as the

Legal Department or Strategic Planning) positions may be important. Executive women reported that their staff experience tended to occur later in their careers rather than earlier (Gallagher, 1996). Thus, the extent to which extensive line experience is a primary determinant of women's career advancement remains an empirical question for future researchers.

The third popularized explanation of women's unsuitability for leadership has been refuted by the large number of published research findings and meta-analyses of studies detailed in the previous section of this chapter. Women leaders not only have demonstrated a strong achievement record but have also exhibited a number of personal qualities conducive to the executive ranks (e.g., Kelly & Dabul Marin, 1998). While women have reported lower self-confidence (Morris, 1998; Morrison, 1992; Watson & Hoffmann, 1996), it has not been found to affect career advancement directly but only indirectly through the career encouragement and training that women receive (Tharenou et al., 1994).

Data-based explanations for women's slow progress to the top have focused on the intangible, yet effective, barriers known collectively as the "glass ceiling" (Federal Glass Ceiling Commission, 1995). Many authors have listed and documented these barriers in detail (e.g., Eyring & Stead, 1998; Morrison, 1992; Ragins et al., 1998), but this chapter will highlight only some of the major patterns found in recent research. Listed in Table 12.1, barriers to women's advancement may be broadly categorized as organizational, interpersonal, and personal.

Organizational barriers (see Table 12.1) to women leaders' advancement include conditions and practices that put women at a disadvantage compared to equally educated and qualified male peers. *Higher standards of performance and effort for women* have been reported in many studies by both women leaders and male CEOs (Mainiero, 1994a; Morris, 1998; Morrison, 1992; Ragins et al., 1998; Sutton & Moore, 1985). Women can expect this higher standard to continue, based on a recent survey of 1,200 professionals ages 25 to 35 (Catalyst, 2001). Men generally saw women enjoying equal pay for equal effort with highly expanded advancement opportunities, while women generally disagreed.

An *inhospitable corporate culture* (Ragins et al., 1998) refers to a culture in which the values and norms (a) discourage balancing high career aspirations with nonwork obligations (Morrison, 1992), (b) communicate that women do not belong in executive positions (Heilman, 1997), or (c) require that women accomplish major tasks without sufficient resources

Table 12.1 *Common Barriers to Women Leader's Advancement*

Organizational barriers

Higher standards of performance and effort for women
Inhospitable corporate culture
Preference for homophily (gender similarity) as a basis for promotion decisions
Ignorance and inaction by male CEOs and "silent majority" male peers
Imbalance of inadequate recognition and support with excessive difficulties
Lack of definitive developmental opportunities

Interpersonal barriers

Male prejudice, stereotyping, preconceptions
Lack of emotional and interpersonal support
Exclusion from informal networks
Lack of white male mentors

Personal barriers

Lack of political savvy
Work-home conflict

(Morrison, 1992; Ohlott et al., 1994). One recent study found that an inhospitable culture makes a significant difference in the likelihood of women being promoted into lower and middle management positions and therefore being available for the pool of those who will be considered for upper management (Tharenou, 2001). Specifically, a males-only organizational hierarchy hindered women's promotions into lower and middle management, while having female leaders in the hierarchy fostered women's promotions at those levels.

For women of color, the impact of an organization's culture may be complicated by additional strains due to racial preconceptions that may require a bicultural life in order to navigate the roles demanded by culturally distinct contexts at work and home (Bell, 1990; Bell et al., 1993; Muller, 1998; Okimoto, 1998). A recent study, based on extensive interviews with 120 black and white women managers and executives and a survey of 825 black and white women managers, found that African American women "worked from the understanding that they would never truly fit in" (Bell & Nkomo, 2001, p. 129). While earlier research has discussed the debilitating effects of a bicultural life, this study uncovered that the African American women used their insider-outsider status as a means of galvanizing their energies and self-respect regardless of disconfirming corporate messages.

Homophily refers to the tendency to prefer to work or interact with people who are similar demographically and attitudinally. While homophily can be useful for easing initial interaction in a group of people, it can also restrict creative thinking and balanced decision making (Cox, 1993). When top management in an organization is dominated by one demographic group (e.g., European American men) and when decisions about promotion are based, even in part, on their preference for working with people who are demographically similar, then a significant bias has entered the advancement process. The impact of a preference for homophily has been documented in major corporations (Appold et al., 1998; Cox, 1993; Morrison, 1992). Since women of color differ in two demographic characteristics from European American men and in one demographic characteristic from European American women, they may be even more likely to experience marginalization at work (Bell et al., 1993). Related to this unspoken preference are the simple *lack of understanding* that male CEOs may have for the obstacles experienced by women leaders (Catalyst, 2001; Ragins et al., 1998) and the *avoidance of taking a stand* on women's advancement by the many men who do not consciously oppose gender equality (Hale, 1996).

Another organizational barrier found in Table 12.1 refers to a model of leadership development based on interviews with 196 leaders. The model included three components: *challenge, recognition,* and *support* (Morrison, 1992). Challenge refers to assignments that promote learning, while recognition refers to both rewards and resources. Support refers to acceptance, mentoring, and benefit packages that foster work/nonwork balance. Challenging assignments, entailing new situations, broad responsibility, and adverse conditions (McCall, Lombardo, & Morrison, 1988; Morrison, 1992; Ohlott et al., 1994), may become even more stressful when the challenges of the assignment are multiplied by prejudice, isolation, and tokenism. Organizations have often made the mistake of relying entirely on challenge to develop leaders, when challenge would actually create more effective learning if it were balanced with recognition and support. In the case of women leaders, organizations have often sought to address this imbalance by limiting the challenge of assignments given to women, when better alternatives would have been to reduce the impact of prejudice and offer more useful work/nonwork benefits (Morrison, 1992).

The impact of *limiting the level of useful challenge* in assignments for women is to reduce the likelihood of promotion to executive ranks, and the nature of such decisions can be subtle. In a study of 507 managers (Ohlott et al., 1994), both female and male leaders received opportunities to start new ventures and turn around businesses in trouble, but men were given higher levels of responsibility in these positions. This meant that the men's responsibilities entailed higher stakes (more crucial and visible), higher business diversity (managing multiple functions), and higher external pressure (more negotiation and/or international aspects). In contrast, women's responsibilities emphasized the need to influence employees despite having low leverage or formal authority, which suggested the women had been placed in situations known to involve difficult relationships. Thus, even though women leaders appeared to have been given equal opportunities, the features of the responsibilities they were given yielded lower development, thereby reducing their promotional potential.

Overall, women leaders developed via new responsibilities that were characterized by obstacles such as lack of support and resources, while male leaders developed via new responsibilities that were characterized by higher stakes, breadth, and external interface. Even with these differences, developmental opportunities that would decisively place high-potential individuals in the pool for promotion were found to be important, yet gender role had even more impact on women's income and level in the organization than did training, education, and work experience (Kirchmeyer, 1998). As would be expected, training, education, and work experience had far greater impact on men's career advancement than their gender role (Kirchmeyer, 1998; Tharenou et al., 1994).

Another recent study proposed that the conditions hindering or fostering promotions would vary for women and men by the managerial level of the promotion (Tharenou, 2001). A sample of 2,431 white-collar employees completed surveys at three different points in time to capture what affected their promotions to lower, middle, and upper management. For all three managerial levels, both men and women reported that managerial aspirations and an instrumental orientation toward achieving results were helpful, while mentor support made relatively little difference. Both men's and women's promotions to middle management were also fostered by enhancing human capital variables such as education, training, and challenging work. Women's promotions to lower and middle management were fostered by the presence of a woman manager in the hierarchy and hindered by the lack of one, while their promotions to upper management were fostered by career encouragement; men's promotions were unaffected by these additional variables.

The research reviewed in this section points to organizational practices that affect women's entry into leadership roles, but also to a variety of conversations and relationships within the workplace that help to explain sex differences in advancement (Heilman, 1997). Interpersonal barriers (see Table 12.1) refer to those obstacles that occur primarily in the context of working relationships. Supportive relationships can be especially important in women's leadership advancement since women were often more likely to identify individuals rather than organizational practices when asked about what helped their career (Bell & Nkomo, 2001).

Gender *prejudice* can take many forms in organizational life and most often is not conscious. The most basic preconception is that a good manager is inherently masculine. In a comparison of samples drawn in 1999, 1984-1985, and 1976-1977, a recent study found this preconception still operates, although the preference for masculine characteristics decreased somewhat over the past 15 years (Powell, Butterfield, & Parent, 2002). Preconceptions of women leaders as less competent have meant that women must prove themselves repeatedly in each new situation (Ragins et al., 1998) and may not receive assignments with real risk and responsibility until they have excelled in trial situations (Ruderman & Ohlott, 1992). Preconceptions of women leaders as disinterested in challenge have meant that women must identify and explicitly ask for challenging assignments rather than simply having such assignments offered to them as equivalent high-potential men would (Ragins et al., 1998). Racial prejudice remains an additional advancement barrier for women of color (Bell & Nkomo, 2001).

Men's discomfort with women leaders has taken many forms. Research has uncovered that women perceived a need to adapt their behavioral style so that men could avoid feeling intimidated (Ragins et al., 1998) and that a narrower range of acceptable behavior existed for female than for male leaders (Eagly et al., 1992; Ragins et al., 1998). This means that male leaders were positively evaluated when they behaved either cooperatively or autocratically, but that female leaders were evaluated positively only when they behaved cooperatively (Eagly et al., 1992). Whether or not most male employees viewed female employees as behaving inappropriately or as depleting workplace resources meant for men (Hale, 1996), fear of reverse discrimination and backlash have increased (Burke & Black, 1997; Morrison, 1992; Ragins et al., 1998).

Prejudice about women leaders can have direct career ramifications. Women's evaluations of others' performance were not affected by the target's sex, but men tended to evaluate men more positively and women more negatively (Eagly et al., 1992). Women were more likely to be devalued when they composed a small proportion of the applicant pool considered for promotion, when performance standards and information were ambiguous (as often applies to managerial positions), when affirmative action was perceived as influencing selection decisions, and when organizational practices made demographic group membership (e.g., sex) pertinent (Heilman, 1997).

Several studies have documented that women leaders have experienced *lower support* throughout their careers than similarly employed men in terms of collegiality, acceptance, information, feedback, and flexibility (Morrison, 1992; Oakley, 2000; Ohlott et al., 1994; Ragins et al., 1998). Inclusion in *informal networks* provides important resources such as social contact with superiors, networking potential with peers within and beyond the organization, and the potential to influence management (Kelly & Dabul Marin, 1998). Again, several studies have found that women leaders have either tended to be excluded, have had to work harder to be included in informal networks (Morrison, 1992; Ohlott et al., 1994; Ragins et al., 1998), or have had to create formal opportunities for "informal" interaction (Bell & Nkomo, 2001).

One of the most critical types of relationship for career advancement is a *mentor relationship,* in which a senior individual provides task coaching, emotional encouragement, and sponsoring the protégé with top-level decision makers. While a number of studies have documented the prevalence and impact of mentoring relationships for both male and female leaders (e.g., Dreher & Ash, 1990; Ragins et al., 1998), a recent study found that European American male mentors had a dramatic impact on salary and that other European American men were most likely to be their protégés (Dreher & Cox, 1996).

In another sample of 160 executives, women and men were equally likely to be mentors, but women were more likely to have same-sex protégés while men were more likely to have protégés of both sexes (Ragins & Scandura, 1994). While a mentor of any sex, race, or ethnicity can be highly important (Dreher & Cox, 1996; Gallagher, 1996), recent research has demonstrated that bad mentoring may be worse than none at all and that formal mentoring programs may be less effective for women than for men (Ragins, Cotton, & Miller, 2000). Having a supportive boss who can sponsor career advancement has remained a perennial issue for women of color as well (Bell & Nkomo, 2001; Catalyst 1998b, 2002b).

Personal barriers (see Table 12.1) to women leaders' advancement refer to elements of their personal lives or a lack of knowledge that may be an obstacle. Women leaders themselves have reported naïveté and lower *political savvy* as a barrier, particularly in earlier career stages (Bell & Nkomo, 2001; Bierema, 1999; Morrison, 1992; Ragins et al., 1998). The need to build alliances, navigate competing priorities, and develop to a point of functioning as a change agent has been described in several studies (Bell & Nkomo, 2001; Bierema, 1999; Mainiero, 1994b). To mature organizationally, black women leaders have adopted perseverance, a willingness to change employers or functions to gain upward mobility, and self-generated developmental opportunities (Bell & Nkomo, 2001; Catalyst, 2002c).

Perhaps as serious for many women leaders are the *nonwork obligations* for which they remain primarily responsible in a household, although one recent study found that a configuration of multiple work and nonwork roles with positive affect actually enhanced women managers' psychological resources, social support, and management skills (Ruderman, Ohlott, Penzer, & King, 2002). Nonetheless, the need for better balance and the impossibility of "having it all" have been frequent themes in women leaders' descriptions of their lives (Catalyst, 1998a; Faircloth, 1998; Gallagher, 1996; Morris, 1998; Sellers, 1996, 1998), and finding peace with one's life configuration has emerged as a major theme in two recent studies of white and black women executives and managers (Bell & Nkomo, 2001; Ruderman & Ohlott, 2002).

While some women have coped by purchasing domestic services, having a supportive or nonemployed husband, or scaling back their families (Catalyst, 1996; Gallagher, 1996; Kirchmeyer, 1998; Morris, 2002), using organizational supports such as flex-time or parental leave was generally not seen as a genuine option (Catalyst, 1996; Hochschild, 1997). Others have acknowledged that work-home conflict has been an obstacle (Kelly & Dabul Marin, 1998; Morrison, 1992; Tharenou et al., 1994). While a nonemployed spouse was favorable to advancement for both men and women (Kirchmeyer, 1998), homes with families overall proved to be a source of support for male leaders' advancement but a source of demand for female leaders (Tharenou et al., 1994).

In summary, women's career advancement in leadership roles has been hampered by organizational, interpersonal, and personal barriers. Although these barriers may be subtle and have often been enacted unconsciously, they have nonetheless functioned to keep the number of women in leadership positions disproportionately low for both white women and women of color. While one author has concluded that the problem is too systemic to be solved with changes in organizational practice and actually requires changes in federal law (Tharenou, 2001), the studies described above provide the seeds of solutions in both the inner and outer worlds of women leaders. Many of the organizational practices that would increase the flexibility, authority, and recognition available to women leaders have also been suggested as ways that organizations could retain more of the women who might otherwise leave corporate life to start their own businesses (Gordon & Whelan, 1998; Morris, 1995; Royal, 1998; Sellers, 1998).

STRENGTHS

Research on gender dynamics in leadership has made important contributions to a broader understanding of leadership. Improvement in workplaces and in society can occur only when unconscious patterns and beliefs are uncovered and recognized; that is what research on women leaders has provided. Overt and subtle discriminatory behavior and preconceptions about talent being restricted to certain demographic groups have reduced organizations' capacity to make full use of their human resources. Similarly, associating certain behavior patterns with one sex or the other has limited the degree to which a full range of leadership behavior is thought appropriate and is therefore available to leaders of both sexes. To the degree that leaders with talent and experience have the opportunity to apply their skills and choose ethical behavior with flexibility, organizations' customers and employees will benefit. To foster the development of leaders of both sexes, research has clarified the proactive role that organizations must take in addition to the choices that developing leaders must make in order to grow.

Considering the sex of leaders and employees can also yield insights within the major theoretical traditions that are described in other chapters of this book. In contingency theory, for example, the preferred leadership style in a particular situation could be affected by the leader's sex and the sex composition of a group, which in turn could affect how positive the leader-member relations were. In path-goal theory, the sex of the leader and the subordinates could affect the degree to which directive leader behavior was seen as effective, even if the task were ambiguous. In leader-member exchange (LMX) theory, the sex of the vertical dyad members could affect the likelihood of forming an in-group relationship and the particular benefits given by the leader, even if the subordinate's performance were outstanding.

Finally, research on gender dynamics in leadership has contributed to the broader conversation in U.S. society about what the "good life" really means and what values are most important. This conversation, occurring in the media and in offices, in homes, and in classrooms, questions the wisdom of a system primarily focused on material wealth and controlling nature and people. Do we prefer workplaces that reward talent or demographic characteristics? Is merit really objectively applied if one sex has to consistently work harder and receives lower pay and less recognition? Does profit matter more than people's well-being? Does work matter more than personal relationships, including children? How do we really want to allot the 24 hours in each day and how much money do we need to live well? If vision and collaboration now work better than control in workplaces, how has the meaning of leadership changed?

CRITICISMS

The problems with a focus on gender dynamics in leadership are due partly to the consequences of focusing on any demographic characteristic and partly to the oversimplification encouraged by bipolar categories, as already discussed in the introduction to this chapter. As mentioned in the last section, the benefit of studying a demographic characteristic, such as sex, is to recognize unconscious patterns so that new insights can spark improvement in workplaces. The disadvantage of such a focus is that individuals' sex can become the only or the primary attribute identifying them, rather than one of many attributes that may affect their worldview or experience. When individuals are seen only as members of one or the other sex, other distortions are more likely to occur. For example, women may be seen as helpless victims or wily thieves of men's rightful roles; men may be seen as greedy power mongers clutching at the status quo. Such portrayals foster the sense that members of the other sex are adversaries rather than needed collaborators if workplaces are to become more creative and developmental.

As mentioned in the introduction to this chapter, a serious issue with research on sex and gender differences is the implicit assumption that members of each category are identical in race, sexual orientation, and age, to name a few. While more research on women of color has been conducted in the past several years, the vast majority of respondents in the studies reviewed in this chapter were European American women. Similarly, all respondents in the studies reviewed were presumed heterosexual and able-bodied, although that was undoubtedly not the case. To ignore the intersection of sex with other characteristics is to give an incomplete picture of people's experience of work and leadership.

APPLICATION

The findings on women and leadership can be applied by organizations and by men and women, at all levels of an organization. First, the findings can be applied by organizations that have experienced difficulty retaining talented women or difficulty in developing effective leaders. Insights from recent research about the patterns of effective leaders, the barriers to women leaders' advancement, and the necessary components of leadership development can provide the basis for worthwhile organizational initiatives.

Second, research findings on women's effectiveness and on the choices that are necessary for advancement can inform women of what they need to do to develop as leaders. Awareness of the barriers uncovered by recent studies can prepare women to sidestep them as adroitly as possible. Third, the findings on gender dynamics in leadership can inform men of the subtle patterns enacted every day that impede workplace fairness and excellence. Since most men are not proponents of sex inequality at work, these studies provide valuable clues about which preconceptions and decision-making patterns need to change, particularly for men in a position to make developmental or promotion decisions.

CASE STUDIES

In the following section, three case studies (Cases 12.1, 12.2, and 12.3) are presented to provide practice in diagnosing and making recommendations on situations confronting women leaders in organizations. The first case is about a new manager in a pharmaceutical company, the second case is about a meeting of probation managers, and the third case is about a market analyst in a Wall Street firm. After each case, questions are provided to assist your analysis of the case. All cases were adapted from Blank and Slipp (1994).[1]

CASE 12.1

Dispelling the Stereotype

Sue-Jin Kim, a Korean American, came to the United States with her family when she was 5 years old. She is now a financial systems analyst in a large pharmaceutical company. She is assigned by her department head to coordinate work on two budget projects because she has a reputation for being very thorough and is well liked by her peers. Her new assignment involves supervising three male analysts and one woman with whom she had worked as an equal under the direction of the department head.

Sue-Jin is looking forward to the opportunity to demonstrate her abilities as a professional and as a manager dealing with the interpersonal aspects of the project. She knows the stereotype that pegs Asian Americans as excellent technicians but weak managers. She is determined to dispel that notion and to carry out the new assignment in a noticeably superior way, since she wants to be considered for a senior management position in the future.

She knows from working in the unit that several of the analysts are quite lax about completing their projects on time and are not used to stretching their creativity to come up with something really innovative.

Sue-Jin tries to impress on her four supervisees that she has high expectations for the project and wants their cooperation in submitting assignments on time. Because they are professionals as well as former coworkers, she is reluctant to give them specific directives on how to accomplish each task. When she speaks to them about the quality of their work and her concerns about it, she does so in a rather indirect way so as not to embarrass anyone. Yet one of the analysts calls her "uptight" when she describes her expectations.

The work that is subsequently submitted by staff members is mediocre. The department head, Pete Merrill, does not seem pleased with the unit's output under Sue-Jin and says so in a very direct, forceful way. Sue-Jin, however, tells Pete that it will take only a little longer to get things going well and that everything is fine.

She then resolves to make up for the slack performance of others and takes work home several nights a week. Not only does she have high standards, she is used to working very hard. She has occasionally been called a perfectionist by several coworkers and supervisors in the past, but this is her work norm and she expects others to have the same standards.

The stress of this new job is beginning to show. Sue-Jin feels humiliated because the staff does not seem to respect her authority and also because she was criticized so forcefully by the department head. She is afraid that she will fail in this new job.

Questions

1. Which advancement barriers and patterns apply to Sue-Jin's dilemma?
2. What could Pete Merrill do differently to support and develop Sue-Jin more effectively?
3. What could Sue-Jin do differently to improve her team's productivity?
4. What could the organization provide to foster both Pete's and Sue-Jin's effectiveness as managers?

◆

CASE 12.2

"But That's What I Proposed"

Lori Bradley, an experienced probation manager, is meeting with Ted Stolze and Ian Bateson, two other probation managers, and their supervisor, Len Duggan, the assistant chief of probation. They are planning an orientation session for new probation officers on how to prepare investigative reports for the court.

As Lori enters the room, the two other probation managers are throwing paper clips at each other and laughing about a major play in the previous night's NFL championship game. They continue talking as she enters the room, ignoring her. When Len, the assistant chief, enters, the two men include him in their talk about the game.

After a few minutes, Len says, "Okay, let's get down to business and start planning the orientation session. Any ideas?"

Lori says, "I looked again at the session prepared by Columbia County, which was described at our last meeting, and I think we should use that. It worked well for them and seems to fit our county." No one looks at Lori or responds to her, but Ted begins making some suggestions for a different idea and the others follow up with questions to him. After problems arise with Ted's suggestion, Ian then says, "My idea would be to go for the

Columbia County plan; that would work best here." Len, the assistant chief, says, "Ian, I'll go with your judgment." Ted says, "Me too. Great idea, Ian."

Lori breaks in, "But that's what I proposed initially, and you just ignored me." Ian says, "Stop being so sensitive, Lori. We're supposed to be a team here."

Questions

1. Which advancement barriers and patterns apply to Lori's situation?
2. How could Len Duggan have behaved differently to provide a role model for Lori's male colleagues?
3. How could Len Duggan have run the meeting differently to improve the team's decision making and cohesion? What should Len have said after Ian made the same suggestion that Lori did?
4. What could Lori do differently to increase her inclusion in the management team?
5. What could the organization provide to foster all four managers' effectiveness?

◆

CASE 12.3

Others Seek Her Opinions, but the CEO Never Knows

Lisa Weber never doubted that she would be a partner in her Wall Street firm. A graduate of a prestigious business school, with a doctorate in economics, she taught briefly at a major university. She was the first woman hired as a market analyst in her well-regarded firm. Within two years, she had become one of four senior portfolio managers reporting directly to a senior partner. Her clients give her the highest commendations for her outstanding performance, and over the past two years, she has brought in the largest number of new accounts to the firm.

Despite the admiration of her colleagues and their seeming acceptance of her, there is a disturbing, if flattering, aspect to her job. Most of her peers and some of the partners visit her office during the day to discuss in private her opinions on market performance and financial projections. She enjoys these private sessions but is dismayed that at the weekly staff meetings the CEO, Michael Breyer, usually says something like, "Okay, let's get started and bring Lisa up-to-date on some of the trouble spots." None of her peers or the partners mention that Lisa knows as much as they do about what's going on in the firm. She never protests this slight to her competence and knowledge of firm business, nor does she mention the almost daily private meetings where her advice is sought. As the only woman on the executive level, she prefers to be considered a team player and "one of the boys."

During the past year, one of her peers was promoted to partner, although Lisa's performance clearly surpassed his, as measured by the success of her accounts and the amount of new business she brought to the firm. Having heard no mention of partnership for herself, she approached her boss, one of the partners, and asked about the path to a partnership. He replied, "You're doing great, Lisa, but what happens if you are a partner and you make a huge mistake? How would you take it? And what about our clients? There's never been a female partner in the 103 years of our firm."

Shortly thereafter, another woman, Pamela Tobias, was hired as a marketing analyst. Once, when the CEO saw Lisa and Pamela together, he called out to the men, "Hey, guys, two women in one room. That's scary."

During the next six months, Lisa meets several times with the CEO to make her case for a partnership on the basis of her performance. She finally realizes that there is no possibility of change in the foreseeable future and makes a decision to leave and form her own investment firm.

Questions

1. Which advancement barriers and patterns apply to Lisa's situation?
2. What could Michael Breyer do differently to retain and support Lisa more effectively?
3. What could Lisa do differently to foster her own advancement?
4. What could the organization provide to support and develop Lisa's and Pamela's effectiveness?
5. What could the organization provide to raise the gender consciousness of Michael Breyer and Lisa's male colleagues?

——————————————◆——————————————

LEADERSHIP INSTRUMENT

Most of the organizational studies on women leaders have used interviews to obtain richer data or have correlated sex with organizational outcomes or other measures to distinguish males' and females' work experiences. To measure respondents' self-perceptions of gender role, the Bem Sex Role Inventory (BSRI; Bem, 1974) has often been used. The original inventory consisted of 20 masculine, 20 feminine, and 20 neutral psychological traits, although shorter versions have been developed. These items can be scored to determine the extent to which an individual's gender role is primarily masculine, primarily feminine, or androgynous, a combination of the two. To measure respondents' attitudes toward women managers, the Attitudes Toward Women as Managers (ATWAM) scale (Yost & Herbert, 1985) was developed and used in several studies. Many of the items now seem dated because prejudice and sex discrimination in the workplace have become far subtler since this instrument was developed.

The following 20 items were developed specifically for this chapter to allow readers to observe their own attitudes about workplace issues for female and male leaders.

Gender Consciousness Questionnaire

Instructions: Indicate the degree to which each statement reflects your personal beliefs or expectations. Use the following scale.

Key: 1 = False   2 = More false than true   3 = More true than false   4 = True

1. _____ If my child were to become ill during workday hours, I would expect my working spouse to take care of the situation.
2. _____ I prefer to work with a boss who has the same sex as mine.
3. _____ If I had a son and a daughter who were equally educated and qualified for a position, it makes sense that my son would earn more money than my daughter for doing the same work.
4. _____ Organizations should focus on controlling costs and maximizing profits, not on accommodating nonwork responsibilities.
5. _____ If my spouse were offered a career opportunity that exceeded my current job, I would not expect to relocate in order to foster my spouse's career.
6. _____ People of the other sex are generally less suited or qualified to be leaders than members of my own sex.
7. _____ I expect my working spouse to take primary responsibility for household chores.
8. _____ Individuals should be expected to adapt themselves to organizational policies and practices, rather than the other way around.
9. _____ I expect to earn more than my spouse, and I would not be comfortable if my spouse earned more than I did.
10. _____ Members of my sex are easier to work with than members of the other sex.
11. _____ If members of the other sex want to be promoted, they should pay attention to making their work behavior nonthreatening for members of my sex.
12. _____ Being in control of any situation should be the top priority for a leader.
13. _____ It seems natural for people at work to listen without interrupting me and to include my ideas in most decisions that are made.
14. _____ When members of the other sex are promoted into leadership positions, I usually think that some form of favoritism was part of the decision.
15. _____ I expect to work in an organization where members of my sex make most of the decisions.
16. _____ When people or groups have competing goals, my priority as a leader is to make sure the outcome reflects my priorities.
17. _____ Members of the other sex who seek leader positions should be careful not to reduce opportunities for members of my sex.
18. _____ Members of the other sex are too sensitive and tend to misinterpret interpersonal situations at work.
19. _____ Finding an influential mentor to help me with my career should be easy.
20. _____ Leaders should not expect to live balanced lives; work must come first.

Scoring

The Gender Consciousness Questionnaire is designed to measure your beliefs in three areas: expectation of privilege, preference for similarity, and preference for control. Score the questionnaire by doing the following:

- *Expectation of privilege:* Sum your responses on all the odd-numbered items.
- *Preference for similarity:* Sum your responses on items 2, 6, 10, 14, and 18.
- *Preference for control:* Sum your responses on items 4, 8, 12, 16, and 20.

Scoring Interpretation

Several basic beliefs underlie many of the statements in this questionnaire. There are no correct answers to any question. Your responses simply indicate the degree to which you hold a particular belief.

- *Expectation of privilege*
High score	30-40
Moderate score	16-29
Low score	1-15

A high score on this group of items indicates that you tend to expect that your perspective or your needs will take precedence in your work and home life. The alternative would be a recognition that others' concerns and perspectives have as much validity as one's own.

- *Preference for similarity*
High score	15-20
Moderate score	6-14
Low score	1-5

A high score on this group of items indicates that you tend to more positively evaluate people whose sex is the same as yours. A preference for similarity need not be limited to sex but can also apply to other demographic characteristics such as race, age, or social class. The alternative would be a recognition that individuals can make valuable contributions whether they are demographically similar or different from oneself.

- *Preference for control*
High score	15-20
Moderate score	6-14
Low score	1-5

A high score on this group of items indicates that you tend to subscribe to an organizational value set with an emphasis on monetary outcomes, control of individuals, and more autocratic decision-making processes. The alternative would be a balance of individual and organizational priorities, a balance between profit and human or planetary needs, and a more collaborative approach to problem solving and decision making.

◆

SUMMARY

Over the past 20 years, researchers of women leaders have addressed several fundamental questions: Can women be leaders? Do female and male leaders differ in their behavior and effectiveness? Why do so few women leaders reach the top? The purpose of this chapter was to review recent studies addressing each of these questions and to offer guidelines to potential leaders and organizations.

While both white women and women of color have made significant progress in attaining leadership roles in business and government, the number of women leaders still remains far below their proportions in the labor force. The resource-based theory of competitive advantage would suggest that organizations could increase their competitive advantage by optimizing the underutilized intellectual and social capital of women with leadership potential.

Several meta-analyses and reviews of leadership research indicated very few differences between male and female leaders. The only behavioral difference was women leaders' use of a more participative and less autocratic style in most environments, an approach found better suited for 21st-century global leadership. Female and male leaders did not differ overall in effectiveness but tended to be evaluated differently, particularly by male evaluators. To the degree that a particular leadership role and setting were gender congruent for male or female leaders, they were seen as more effective.

Despite the array of studies indicating that women possess the behavioral skills and inner qualities that qualify them for effective leadership, they remain underrepresented in such positions. Organizational, interpersonal, and personal barriers to women leaders' advancement have been identified by researchers. Prejudice, male executives' preference for gender similarity, nonequivalent developmental assignments, lack of support, and work-home conflict were among the major barriers to women leaders' progress.

Other studies have traced the career paths of successful women leaders and have identified a number of organizational, interpersonal, and personal strategies that may be useful to potential women leaders. To make better use of the talent of high-potential women, organizations must identify, track, develop, and support potential women leaders at the same time that gender consciousness throughout the organization is raised. Women need to develop their competence and build effective alliances and partnerships, both within and beyond their organizations. On a personal level, resilience, perseverance, and initiative can be invaluable to women leaders as they sidestep barriers and meet challenges.

The strengths of this approach to leadership include a greater understanding of subtle organizational exclusion and effective career development for leaders as well as the insights offered about the impact of sex and gender in other leadership theories. This approach can be critiqued for the simplistic and adversarial thinking resulting from a primary identification of people as male or female. While a small amount of material on women leaders of color was presented in this chapter, they have largely been neglected by researchers and by organizations. Nonetheless, the growth of organizational acceptance and research interest in women leaders bodes well for all those who celebrate the full use of individuals' talents in the workplace.

NOTE

1. Adapted from *Voices of Diversity.* Copyright © 1994 by Renee Blank and Sandra Slipp. Reprinted by permission of AMACOM, a division of American Management Association International, New York, NY. All rights reserved. http://www.amanet.org.

REFERENCES

Acker, J. (1992). Gendering organizational theory. In A. Mills & P. Tancred (Eds.), *Gendering organizational analysis* (pp. 248-260). Newbury Park, CA: Sage.

Appold, S., Siengthai, S., & Kasarda, J. (1998). The employment of women managers and professionals in an emerging economy: Gender inequality as an organizational practice. *Administrative Science Quarterly, 43,* 538-565.

Barney, J. (1997). *Gaining and sustaining competitive advantage.* Reading, MA: Addison-Wesley.

Bartlett, C., & Ghoshal, S. (1997). The myth of the generic manager: New personal competencies for new management roles. *California Management Review, 40,* 92-116.

Beemyn, B., & Eliason, M. (Eds.). (1996). *Queer studies: A lesbian, gay, bisexual, and transgender anthology.* New York: New York University Press.

Belenky, M., Clinchy, B., Goldberger, N., & Tarule, J. (1986). *Women's ways of knowing.* New York: Basic Books.

Bell, E. (1990). The bicultural life experience of career-oriented black women. *Journal of Organizational Behavior, 11,* 459–477.

Bell, E., Denton, T., & Nkomo, S. (1993). Women of color in management: Toward an inclusive analysis. In E. Fagenson (Ed.), *Women in management* (pp. 105-130). Newbury Park, CA: Sage.

Bell, E., & Nkomo, S. (1992). Re-visioning women managers' lives. In A. Mills & P. Tancred (Eds.), *Gendering organizational analysis* (pp. 235-247). Newbury Park, CA: Sage.

Bell, E., & Nkomo, S. (2001). *Our separate ways: Black and white women and the struggle for professional identity.* Boston: Harvard Business School Press.

Bem, S. (1974). The measurement of psychological androgyny. *Journal of Counseling and Clinical Psychology, 42,* 155-162.

Bierema, L. (1999). A model of executive women's learning and development. *Adult Education Quarterly, 49*(2), 107-122.

Blank, R., & Slipp, S. (1994). *Voices of diversity.* New York: AMACOM.

Bureau of Labor Statistics, U.S. Department of Labor. (2002). *Labor force statistics from the current population survey.* Retrieved December 8, 2002, from http://www.bls.gov

Burke, R., & Black, S. (1997). Save the males: Backlash in organizations. *Journal of Business Ethics, 16,* 933-942.

Catalyst. (1996). *Women in corporate leadership: Progress and prospects.* Retrieved June 4, 1999, from http://www.catalystwomen.org

Catalyst. (1998a). *Fact sheet.* Retrieved June 4, 1999, from http://www.catalyswomen.org

Catalyst. (1998b). *Women of color in corporate management: Dynamics of career advancement.* Retrieved June 4, 1999, from http://www.catalystwomen.org

Catalyst. (2001). *Catalyst study dispels myths about Generation X professionals and sheds light on what this new generation of leaders seek at work.* Retrieved December 6, 2002, from http://www.catalystwomen.org

Catalyst. (2002a). *Catalyst census marks gains in numbers of women corporate officers in America's largest 500 companies.* Retrieved December 6, 2002, from http://www.catalystwomen.org

Catalyst. (2002b). *Catalyst charts growth of women on America's corporate boards.* Retrieved December 6, 2002, from http://www.catalystwomen.org

Catalyst. (2002c). *Catalyst finds women of color are taking charge of their careers and moving up the corporate ladder.* Retrieved December 6, 2002, from http://www.catalystwomen.org

Ciabattari, J. (2002, June 2). Who would you vote for? *Parade Magazine,* pp. 4-6.

Cox, T., Jr. (1993). *Cultural diversity in organizations.* San Francisco: Berrett-Koehler.

Daniels, C. (2002, July 22). The most powerful black executives in America. *Fortune,* pp. 60-76.

Dobbins, G., & Platz, S. (1986). Sex differences in leadership. *Academy of Management Review, 11,* 118-127.

Donnell, S., & Hall, J. (1980, Spring). Men and women as managers: A significant case of no significant difference. *Organizational Dynamics,* pp. 60-77.

Dreher, G., & Ash, R. (1990). A comparative study of mentoring among men and women in managerial, professional, and technical positions. *Journal of Applied Psychology, 75,* 539-546.

Dreher, G., & Cox, T. (1996). Race, gender, and opportunity: A study of compensation attainment and the establishment of mentoring relationships. *Journal of Applied Psychology, 81,* 297-308.

Eagly, A. (1987). *Sex differences in social behavior.* Hillsdale, NJ: Lawrence Erlbaum.

Eagly, A., & Johnson, B. (1990). Gender and the emergence of leaders: A meta-analysis. *Psychological Bulletin, 108,* 233-256.

Eagly, A., Karau, S., & Makhijani, M. (1995). Gender and the effectiveness of leaders: A meta-analysis. *Psychological Bulletin, 111,* 3-22.

Eagly, A., Makhijani, M., & Klonsky, B. (1992). Gender and the evaluation of leaders: A meta-analysis. *Psychological Bulletin, 117,* 125-145.

Eagly, A., & Wood, W. (1991). Explaining sex differences in social behavior: A meta-analytic perspective. *Journal of Personality and Social Psychology, 17,* 306-315.

Ensher, E., Murphy, S., & Sullivan, S. (2002). Reel women: Lessons from female TV executives on managing work and reel life. *Academy of Management Executive, 16*(2), 106-121.

Eyring, A., & Stead, B. A. (1998). Shattering the glass ceiling: Some successful corporate practices. *Journal of Business Ethics, 17,* 245-251.

Faircloth, A. (1998, October 12). The class of '83. *Fortune,* pp. 126-132.

Federal Glass Ceiling Commission. (1995). *Good for business: Making full use of the nation's human capital.* Washington, DC: U.S. Department of Labor.

Fisher, A. (1998, September 28). Overseas, U.S. businesswomen have the edge. *Fortune,* p. 304.

Flynn, G. (1994). Women managers rate higher than male counterparts. *Personnel Journal, 73,* 17.

Gallagher, C. (1996). *Windows in the glass ceiling: The importance of professional relationships.* Unpublished dissertation, California School of Professional Psychology, Alameda.

Garofoli, J. (2002, August 26). On college campuses, it's a woman's world. *San Francisco Chronicle,* pp. B1, B3.

Gendron, G. (1995, April). The real female advantage. *Inc., 17*(5), 16.

Gentile, M. (1996). *Managerial excellence through diversity.* Prospect Heights, IL: Waveland.

Gilligan, C. (1982). *In a different voice: Psychological theory and women's development.* Cambridge, MA: Harvard University Press.

Gordon, J., & Whelan, K. (1998). Successful professional women in midlife: How organizations can more effectively understand and respond to the challenges. *Academy of Management Executive, 12*(1), 8-27.

Hale, M. (1996). Gender equality in organizations: Resolving the dilemmas. *Public Personnel Administration, 16*(1), 7.

Hall, M. (1986). The lesbian corporate experience. *Journal of Homosexuality, 12*(3-4), 59-75.

Heilman, M. (1997). Sex discrimination and the affirmative action remedy: The role of sex stereotypes. *Journal of Business Ethics, 16,* 877-889.

Helgesen, S. (1990). *The female advantage: Women's ways of leadership.* New York: Doubleday Currency.

Hochschild, A. (1997). *The time bind: When work becomes home and home becomes work.* New York: Metropolitan Books.

Hurley, A., Fagenson-Eland, E., & Sonnenfeld, J. (1997, Autumn). An investigation of career attainment determinants. *Organizational Dynamics, 26*(2), 65-71.

Jagose, A. (1996). *Queer theory.* New York: New York University Press.

Karambayya, R. (1997). In shouts and whispers: Paradoxes facing women of color in organizations. *Journal of Business Ethics, 16,* 891-897.

Kelly, R., & Dabul Marin, A. (1998). Position power and women's career advancement. *Women in Management Review, 13*(2), 53-67.

Kirchmeyer, C. (1998). Determinants of managerial career success: Evidence and explanation of male/female differences. *Journal of Management, 24,* 673-692.

Lauterbach, K., & Weiner, B. (1996). Dynamics of upward influence: How male and female managers get their way. *Leadership Quarterly, 7*(1), 87-107.

Lewis, D. (1999, June 11). Degreed women may alter workplace. *San Francisco Chronicle,* p. B3.

Lowe, K., & Gardner, W. (2000). Ten years of the *Leadership Quarterly:* Contributions and challenges for the future. *Leadership Quarterly, 11*(4), 459-514.

Maier, M. (1992). Evolving paradigms of management in organizations: A gendered analysis. *Journal of Management Studies, 17,* 288-317.

Mainiero, L. (1994a). Getting anointed for advancement: The case of executive women. *Academy of Management Executive, 8*(2), 53-67.

Mainiero, L. (1994b, Spring). On breaking the glass ceiling: The political seasoning of powerful women executives. *Organizational Dynamics,* pp. 5-20.

McCall, M., Jr., Lombardo, M., & Morrison, A. (1988). *The lessons of experience: How successful executives develop on the job.* New York: Lexington Books.

McCorduck, P. (1996). *The futures of women: Scenarios for the 21st century.* Reading, MA: Addison-Wesley Longman.

Micco, L. (1996). Women outmuscle men in management tasks, study finds. *HR News Online.* Retrieved September 30, 1996, from http://www.shrm.org/hrnews/

Morris, B. (1995, September 18). Executive women confront midlife crisis. *Fortune,* pp. 60-86.

Morris, B. (1998, October 12). The trailblazers: Women of Harvard's MBA Class of '73. *Fortune,* pp. 106-125.

Morris, B. (2002, October 14). Trophy husbands. *Fortune,* pp. 79-98.

Morrison, A. (1992). *The new leaders.* San Francisco: Jossey-Bass.

Muller, H. (1998). American Indian women managers. *Journal of Management Inquiry, 7*(1), 4-29.

Oakley, J. (2000). Gender-based barriers to senior management positions: Understanding the scarcity of female CEOs. *Journal of Business Ethics, 27*(4), 321-334.

Ohlott, P., Ruderman, M., & McCauley, C. (1994). Gender differences in managers' developmental job experiences. *Academy of Management Journal, 37*(1), 46-67.

Okimoto, R. (1998). *Chinese American and Japanese American women professionals: A comparative study of their organizational communication behavior and underlying cultural values and attitudes in the workplace.* Unpublished dissertation, California School of Professional Psychology, Alameda.

Petrick, J., Scherer, R., Brodzinski, J., Quinn, J., & Ainina, M. F. (1999). Global leadership skills and reputational capital: Intangible resources for sustainable competitive advantage. *Academy of Management Executive, 13*(1), 58-69.

Pofeldt, E. (2002). *Jumping off the corporate ladder.* Retrieved December 8, 2002, from http://www.fortune.com

Powell, G. (1993). *Women and men in management* (2nd ed.). Newbury Park, CA: Sage.

Powell, G., Butterfield, D. A., & Parent, J. (2002). Gender and managerial stereotypes: Have the times changed? *Journal of Management, 28*(2), 177-193.

Ragins, B., Cotton, J., & Miller, J. (2000). Marginal mentoring: The effects of type of mentor, quality of relationship, and program design on work and career attitudes. *Academy of Management Journal, 43*(6), 1177-1194.

Ragins, B., & Scandura, T. (1994). Gender differences in expected outcomes of mentoring relationships. *Academy of Management Journal, 37,* 957-971.

Ragins, B., Townsend, B., & Mattis, M. (1998). Gender gap in the executive suite: CEOs and female executives report on breaking the glass ceiling. *Academy of Management Executive, 12*(1), 28-42.

Rosener, J. (1990, November-December). Ways women lead. *Harvard Business Review,* pp. 119-125.

Royal, W. (1998, July 20). Vanishing execs: Women. *Industry Week,* pp. 32-37.

Ruderman, M., & Ohlott, P. (1992). *Managerial promotions as a diversity practice.* Paper presented at the annual meeting of the Academy of Management, Las Vegas, NV.

Ruderman, M., & Ohlott, P. (2002). *Standing at the crossroads: Next steps for high-achieving women.* San Francisco: Jossey-Bass.

Ruderman, M., Ohlott, P., Penzer, K., & King, S. (2002). Benefits of multiple roles for managerial women. *Academy of Management Journal, 45*(2), 369-377.

Scott, M. (2001, August 1). For women, the glass ceiling persists. *Black Enterprise,* p. 30.

Sellers, P. (1996, August 5). Women, sex and power. *Fortune,* pp. 42-56.

Sellers, P. (1998, October 12). The 50 most powerful women in American business. *Fortune,* pp. 76-98.

Sellers, P. (2002, October 14). True grit. *Fortune,* pp. 101-112.

Sharpe, R. (2000, November 20). As leaders, women rule. *Business Week,* pp. 75-84.

Shrader, C., Blackburn, V., & Iles, P. (1997). Women in management and firm financial performance: An exploratory model. *Journal of Managerial Issues, 9*(3), 355-372.

Sutton, C., & Moore, K. (1985, September-October). Executive women 20 years later. *Harvard Business Review,* pp. 42-66.

Tannen, D. (1994). *Talking from 9 to 5.* New York: William Morrow.

Tharenou, P. (2001). Going up? Do traits and informal social processes predict advancing in management? *Academy of Management Journal, 44*(5), 1005-1017.

Tharenou, P., Latimer, S., & Conroy, D. (1994). How do you make it to the top? An examination of influences on women's and men's managerial advancement. *Academy of Management Journal, 37,* 899-931.

Thompson, R. (1999, April). Diversity among managers translates into profitability. *HR Magazine,* p. 10.

Watson, C., & Hoffman, L. (1996). Managers as negotiators: A test of power versus gender as predictors of feelings, behavior and outcomes. *Leadership Quarterly, 7*(1), 63-85.

Women Governors. (2002). Retrieved December 8, 2002, from http://www.gender-gap.com/government

Women may make better managers—Study. (1997, April). *Management, 44*(3), 14.

Women's Bureau, U.S. Department of Labor. (2001). *20 leading occupations of employed women: 2001 annual averages.* Retrieved December 8, 2002, from http://www.dol.gov/wb

Yost, E., & Herbert, T. (1985). *Attitudes Toward Women as Managers (ATWAM) scale.* San Diego, CA: Pfeiffer/Jossey-Bass.

Leadership Ethics

DESCRIPTION

This chapter is different from most chapters in this book. Generally, the other chapters focus on one unified leadership theory or approach (e.g., trait approach, path-goal theory, or transformational leadership), whereas this chapter is multifaceted and presents a broad set of ethical viewpoints. The chapter is not intended as an "ethical leadership theory" but rather as a guide to some of the ethical issues that arise in leadership situations.

Probably as long ago as the cave dwellers, human beings have been concerned with the ethics of our leaders. Later, our history books are replete with descriptions of good kings and bad kings, great empires and evil empires, and strong presidents and weak presidents. But in spite of a wealth of biographical accounts of great leaders and their morals, very little research has been published on the theoretical foundations of leadership ethics. While there have been many studies on business ethics in general since the early 1970s, these studies have been only tangentially related to leadership ethics. Even in the literature of management, written primarily for practitioners, there are very few books on leadership ethics. This suggests that theoretical formulations in this area are still in their infancy.

One of the earliest writings that specifically focused on leadership ethics appeared as recently as 1996. It was a set of working papers generated from a small group of leadership scholars, brought together by the W. K. Kellogg Foundation. These scholars examined how leadership theory and practice could be used to build a more caring and just society. The ideas of the Kellogg group are now published in a volume titled *Ethics, the Heart of Leadership* (Ciulla, 1998).

Since the last edition of this book, interest in the nature of ethical leadership has grown exponentially, particularly because of the many scandals in corporate America. On the academic front there has also been a strong interest in exploring the nature of ethical leadership (cf. Ciulla, 2003; Johnson, 2001).

The present chapter addresses leadership ethics by defining ethics, giving an overview of ethical theories, discussing why ethics is central to leadership, and describing the unique perspectives of Heifetz, Burns, and Greenleaf. The chapter continues with a discussion of five principles of ethical leadership: respect, service, justice, honesty, and community. Finally, some strengths and weaknesses of present-day leadership ethics are noted, followed by a summary.

ETHICS DEFINED

From the perspective of Western tradition, the development of ethical theory dates back to Plato (427-347 B.C.) and Aristotle (384-322 B.C.). The word *ethics* has its roots in the Greek word *ethos,* which means "customs," "conduct," or "character." Ethics is concerned with the kinds of values and morals an individual or society finds desirable or appropriate. Furthermore, ethics is concerned with the virtuousness of individuals and their motives. Ethical theory provides a system of rules or principles that guide us in making decisions about what is "right or wrong" and "good or bad" in a particular situation. It provides a basis for understanding what it means to be a morally decent human being.

In regard to leadership, ethics has to do with what leaders do and who leaders are. It is concerned with the nature of leaders' behavior and their virtuousness. In any decision-making situation, ethical issues are either implicitly or explicitly involved. The choices that leaders make and how they respond in a given circumstance are informed and directed by their ethics.

Table 13.1 *Domains of Ethical Theories*

CONDUCT	CHARACTER
Consequences (Teleological Theories)	Virtue-based Theories
▶ Ethical Egoism	
▶ Utilitarianism	
Duty (Deontological Theories)	

ETHICAL THEORIES

For the purposes of studying ethics and leadership, ethical theories can be thought of as falling within two broad domains: theories about leaders' *conduct* and theories about leaders' *character* (see Table 13.1). Stated another way, ethical theories are about the actions of leaders, on the one hand, and who they are as people, on the other. Throughout the chapter, our discussions about ethics and leadership will always fall within one of these two domains.

Ethical theories that deal with the conduct of leaders are in turn divided into two kinds: theories that stress the *consequences* of leaders' actions, and those that emphasize the *duty* or *rules* governing leaders' actions (see Table 13.1). Teleological theories, from the Greek word *telos,* meaning "ends" or "purposes," try to answer questions about right and wrong by focusing on whether an individual's conduct will produce desirable consequences. The question, "What is right?" from the teleological perspective is answered by looking at results—at the outcomes. In effect, the consequences of an individual's actions determine the goodness or badness of a particular behavior.

In assessing consequences, there are three different approaches to making decisions regarding moral conduct (see Figure 13.1). One is *ethical egoism,* which states that an individual should act so as to create the greatest good for herself or himself. A leader with this orientation would take a job or career that he or she selfishly enjoys (Avolio & Locke, 2002). Self-interest is an ethical stance closely related to transactional leadership theories (Bass & Steidlmeier, 1999). Ethical egoism is common in some business contexts in which a company and its employees make decisions in ways

Figure 13.1 *Ethical Theories Based on Self-Interest Versus Interest for Others*

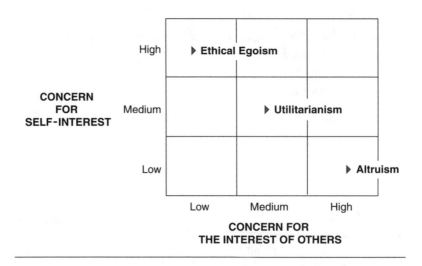

that will achieve its goal of maximizing profits. For example, a midlevel, upward-aspiring manager who wants her team to be the best in the company could be described as acting out of ethical egoism.

A second teleological approach is *utilitarianism,* which states that we should behave so as to create the greatest good for the greatest number. From this viewpoint, the morally correct action is the action that maximizes social benefits while minimizing social costs (Schumann, 2001). When the U.S. government allocates a large part of the federal budget for preventive health care rather than for catastrophic illnesses, it is acting from a utilitarian perspective—putting money where it will have the best result for the largest number of citizens. Closely related to utilitarianism, and opposite of ethical egoism, is *altruism,* an approach that suggests that actions are moral if their primary purpose is to show concern for the best interests of others. From this perspective, a leader may be called on to act in the interests of others, even when it runs contrary to his or her own self-interests (Bowie, 1991). Authentic transformational leadership is based on altruistic principles (Bass & Steidlmeier, 1999; Kanungo & Mendonca, 1996). The strongest example of altruist ethics can be found in the work of Mother Teresa, who gave her entire life to help poor people.

Quite different from looking at which actions will produce which outcomes, deontological theory is derived from the Greek word *deos,* which means "duty." Whether or not a given action is ethical rests not only with its consequences (teleological) but with whether the action itself is good. Telling the truth, keeping promises, being fair, and respecting others are all examples of actions that are inherently good, independent of the consequences. The deontological perspective focuses on the actions of the leader and his or her moral obligations and responsibilities to do the right thing. A leader's actions are moral if the leader has a moral right to do them, if the actions do not infringe on others' rights, and if the actions further the moral rights of others (Schumann, 2001).

During the late 1990s, the president of the United States, Bill Clinton, was brought before Congress for misrepresenting under oath an affair he had maintained with a White House intern. For his actions he was impeached by the U.S. House of Representatives and then acquitted by the U.S. Senate. At one point during the long ordeal, the president appeared on national television and gave what is now a famous speech declaring his innocence. Because subsequent hearings provided information that suggested that he may have lied during his television speech, there were many Americans who felt President Clinton had violated his duty and responsibility (as a person, leader, and president) to tell the truth. From a deontological perspective, it could be said that he failed his ethical responsibility to do the right thing—to tell the truth.

While teleological and deontological theories approach ethics by looking at the behavior or conduct of a leader, a second set of theories approaches ethics from the viewpoint of a leader's character (see Table 13.1). These theories are called virtue-based theories, and they focus on who leaders are as people. In this perspective, virtues are rooted in the heart of the individual and in his or her disposition (Pojman, 1995). Furthermore, it is believed that virtues and moral abilities are not innate but can be acquired and learned through practice. People can be taught by their families and communities to be morally appropriate human beings.

Although virtue theories have only recently regained their popularity, their origin can be traced back in the Western tradition to the Greek period and the works of Plato and Aristotle. The Greek term associated with these theories is *aretaic,* which means "excellence" or "virtue." Consistent with Aristotle, current advocates of virtue-based theory stress that more attention should be given to the development and training of moral values (Velasquez, 1992). Rather than tell people what to *do,* attention should be directed toward telling people what to *be*—by helping them to become more virtuous.

What, then, are the virtues of an ethical person? There are many, all of which seem to be important. Based on the writings of Aristotle, a moral person demonstrates the following virtues: courage, temperance, generosity, self-control, honesty, sociability, modesty, fairness, and justice (Velasquez, 1992). For Aristotle, virtues allowed individuals to live well in communities. Applying ethics to leadership and management, Velasquez has suggested that managers should develop virtues such as perseverance, public-spiritedness, integrity, truthfulness, fidelity, benevolence, and humility.

In essence, virtue-based ethics is about being and becoming a good, worthy human being. While people can learn and develop good values, this theory maintains that virtues are present within the individual's disposition. When practiced over time, from youth to adulthood, good values become habitual and part of the persons themselves. From telling the truth, people become truthful; from giving to the poor, people become benevolent; and from being fair to others, people become just. Our virtues are derived from our actions and our actions manifest our virtues (Frankena, 1973; Pojman, 1995).

CENTRALITY OF ETHICS TO LEADERSHIP

As discussed in Chapter 1, leadership is a process whereby the leader influences others to reach a common goal. The *influence* dimension of leadership requires the leader to have an impact on the lives of those being led. To make a change in other people carries with it an enormous ethical burden and responsibility. Because leaders usually have more power and control than followers, they also have more responsibility to be sensitive to how their leadership affects followers' lives.

Whether in group work, organizational pursuits, or community projects, leaders engage subordinates and use them in their efforts to reach common goals. In all of these situations, leaders have the ethical responsibility to treat followers with dignity and respect—as human beings with unique identities. This "respect for persons" demands that leaders be sensitive to followers' own interests, needs, and conscientious concerns (Beauchamp & Bowie, 1988). While all of us have an ethical responsibility to treat other people as unique human beings, leaders have a special responsibility because the nature of their leadership puts them in a special position, where they have a greater opportunity to influence others in significant ways.

Ethics is central to leadership, and leaders help to establish and reinforce organizational values. Every leader has a distinct philosophy and point of view. All leaders "have an agenda, a series of beliefs, proposals, values, ideas, and issues that they wish to 'put on the table'" (Gini, 1998). The values promoted by the leader have a significant impact on the values exhibited by the organization (cf. Carlson & Perrewe, 1995; Schminke, Ambrose, & Noel, 1997; Trevino, 1986). Again, because of their influence, leaders play a major role in establishing the ethical climate of their organizations.

In short, ethics is central to leadership because of the nature of the process of influence, the need to engage followers to accomplish mutual goals, and the impact leaders have on establishing the organization's values.

The following section provides a discussion of some of the work of several prominent leadership scholars who have addressed issues related to ethics and leadership. Although many additional viewpoints exist, those presented are representative of what is currently the predominant thinking in the area of ethics and leadership.

HEIFETZ'S PERSPECTIVE
ON ETHICAL LEADERSHIP

Based on his work as a psychiatrist and his observations and analysis of many world leaders (e.g., President Lyndon Johnson, Mohandas Gandhi, and Margaret Sanger), Ronald Heifetz (1994) has formulated a unique approach to ethical leadership; it emphasizes how leaders help followers to confront conflict and to effect changes from conflict. Heifetz's perspective is related to ethical leadership because it deals with values—values of workers, and the values of the organizations and communities in which they work. According to Heifetz, leadership involves the use of authority to help followers deal with the conflicting values that emerge in rapidly changing work environments and social cultures. It is an ethical perspective because it speaks directly to the values of workers.

For Heifetz (1994), leaders must use authority to mobilize people to face tough issues. The leader provides a "holding environment" in which there is trust, nurturance, and empathy. Within a supportive context, followers can feel safe to confront and deal with hard problems. Specifically, leaders use authority to get people to pay attention to the issues, to act as a reality test regarding information, to manage and frame issues, to orchestrate conflicting perspectives, and to facilitate the decision-making process (Heifetz, 1994, p. 113). The leader's duties are to assist the follower in struggling with change and personal growth.

BURNS'S PERSPECTIVE
ON ETHICAL LEADERSHIP

As discussed in Chapter 9, Burns's theory of transformational leadership places a strong emphasis on followers' needs, values, and morals. Transformational leadership involves attempts by leaders to move followers to higher standards of moral responsibility. This emphasis sets transformational leadership apart from most other approaches to leadership because it clearly states that leadership has a moral dimension (cf. Bass & Steidlmeier, 1999).

Similar to that of Heifetz, Burns's (1978) perspective argues that it is important for leaders to engage themselves with followers and help them in their personal struggles regarding conflicting values. In the process, the connection between the leader and the follower raises the level of morality in both the leader and the follower.

The origins of Burns's position on leadership ethics are rooted in the works of such writers as Abraham Maslow, Milton Rokeach, and Lawrence Kohlberg (Ciulla, 1998). The influence of these writers can be seen in how Burns emphasizes the leader's role to attend to the personal motivations and moral development of the follower. For Burns, it is the responsibility of the leader to help followers assess their own values and needs in order to raise them to a higher level of functioning, to a level that will stress values such as liberty, justice, and equality (Ciulla, 1998).

Burns's position on leadership as a morally uplifting process has not been without its critics. It has raised many questions. How do you choose what is a better set of moral values? Who is to say that some decisions represent higher moral ground than others? If leadership, by definition, requires raising individual moral functioning, does this mean that the leadership of a leader such as Adolf Hitler is not actually leadership? Notwithstanding these very legitimate questions, Burns's perspective on leadership is unique in how it makes ethics the central characteristic of the process. His writing has placed ethics at the forefront of scholarly discussions of what leadership means and how leadership should be carried out.

GREENLEAF'S PERSPECTIVE
ON ETHICAL LEADERSHIP

In the early 1970s, Robert Greenleaf developed a somewhat paradoxical approach to leadership called *servant leadership*. It is an approach that has gained increased popularity in recent years (cf. Block, 1993; De Pree, 1989, 1992). With its strong altruistic ethical overtones, servant leadership emphasizes that leaders should be attentive to the concerns of their followers and empathize with them; they should take care of them and nurture them.

Greenleaf (1970, 1977) argued that leadership was bestowed on a person who was by nature a servant. In fact, the way an individual emerges as a leader is by first becoming a servant. A servant leader focuses on the needs of followers and helps them to become more knowledgeable, more free, more autonomous, and more like servants themselves. They enrich others by their presence.

In addition to serving, the servant leader has a social responsibility to be concerned with the "have-nots" and to recognize them as equal stakeholders in the life of the organization. Where inequalities and social injustices exist, a servant leader tries to remove them (Graham, 1991). In becoming a servant leader, a leader uses less institutional power and less control, while shifting authority to those who are being led. Servant leadership values everyone's involvement in community life because it is within a community that one fully experiences respect, trust, and individual strength. Greenleaf places a great deal of emphasis on listening, empathy, and unconditional acceptance of others.

In the novel *The Journey to the East,* by Herman Hesse (1956), there is an example of leadership that was the inspiration behind Greenleaf's formulation of servant leadership. The story is about a group of travelers on a mythical journey who are accompanied by a servant who does menial chores for the travelers but also sustains them with his spirits and song. The servant's presence has an extraordinary impact on the group, but when the servant becomes lost and disappears, the group of travelers falls into disarray and abandons their journey. Without the servant, they are unable to carry on. It was the servant who was leading the group. He emerged as a leader by caring for the travelers.

A common theme running through all three of the perspectives (i.e., Heifetz, Burns, and Greenleaf) is that the leader-follower relationship is central to ethical leadership. In addition, they all emphasize that it is critically important for leaders to pay close attention to the unique needs of their followers.

In many ways, the ideas presented by these leadership scholars are parallel to and consonant with the *ethic of caring* set forth by Gilligan (1982), who contended that personal relationships should be the beginning point of ethics. In the past 20 years, the "caring principle" has become recognized by scholars as one of the predominant moral principles. From a caring perspective, a leader's actions are morally correct if they express care in protecting the people with whom the leader has special relationships (Schumann, 2001). An ethic of caring is extremely important in organizations because it is the main ingredient in building trust and cooperative relationships (Brady, 1999).

PRINCIPLES OF ETHICAL LEADERSHIP

In this section, we turn to a discussion of five principles of ethical leadership, the origins of which can be traced back to Aristotle. The importance of these principles has been discussed in a variety of disciplines including biomedical ethics (Beauchamp & Childress, 1994), business ethics (Beauchamp & Bowie, 1988), counseling psychology (Kitchener, 1984), and leadership education (Komives, Lucas, & McMahon, 1998), to name a few. Although not inclusive, these principles provide a foundation for the development of sound ethical leadership: *respect, service, justice, honesty,* and *community* (see Figure 13.2).

Ethical Leaders Respect Others

Philosopher Immanuel Kant (1724-1804) argued that it is our duty to treat others with respect. To do so means always to treat others as ends in themselves and never as means to ends. As Beauchamp and Bowie (1988) pointed out, "Persons must be treated as having their own autonomously established goals and must never be treated purely as the means to another's personal goals" (p. 37). They go on to suggest that treating others as ends rather than as means requires that we treat other people's decisions and values with respect because failing to do so would signify that we were treating them as a means to our own ends.

Leaders who respect others also allow them to be themselves, with creative wants and desires. They approach other persons with a sense of unconditional worth and valuable individual differences (Kitchener, 1984). Respect includes giving credence to others' ideas and confirming them as human beings. At times, it may require that leaders have to defer to others. As Burns (1978) suggested, leaders should nurture followers in becoming

Figure 13.2 *Principles of Ethical Leadership*

aware of their own needs, values, and purposes and assist them in integrating these with the leader's.

Respect for others is a complex ethic that is similar to but goes deeper than the kind of respect that parents teach children when they are little. Respect means that a leader listens closely to his or her subordinates, is empathic, and is tolerant of opposing points of view. It means treating subordinates in ways that confirm their beliefs, attitudes, and values. When a leader exhibits respect to subordinates, subordinates can feel competent about their work. In short, leaders who show respect in fact treat others as worthy human beings.

Ethical Leaders Serve Others

Earlier in this chapter, we contrasted two ethical theories—one based on a concern for self (ethical egoism) and another based on the interests of others (ethical altruism). The service principle is clearly an example of altruism. Leaders who serve are altruistic; they place their followers' welfare foremost in their plans. In the workplace, altruistic service behavior can be observed in activities such as mentoring, empowerment behaviors, team building, and citizenship behaviors, to name a few (Kanungo & Mendonca, 1996).

The leader's ethical responsibility to serve others is very similar to the ethical principle in health care of beneficence. Beneficence is derived from the Hippocratic tradition, which implies that health professionals ought to make choices that benefit patients. In a general way, beneficence asserts that providers have a duty to help others pursue their own legitimate interests and goals (Beauchamp & Childress, 1994). Similar to health professionals, ethical leaders have a responsibility to attend to others, be of service to them, and make decisions pertaining to them that are beneficial and not harmful to their welfare.

In the past decade, the service principle has received a great deal of emphasis in the leadership literature. It is clearly evident in the writings of Greenleaf (1977), Gilligan (1982), Block (1993), Covey (1990), De Pree (1989), and Kouzes and Posner (1995), all of whom maintained that attending to others is the primary building block of moral leadership. Further emphasis on service can be observed in the work of Senge (1990) in his well-recognized writing on learning organizations. Senge contended that one of the important tasks of leaders in learning organizations is to be the steward (servant) of the vision within the organization. Being a steward means clarifying and nurturing a vision that is greater than one's self. This means not being self-centered but integrating one's self or vision with others in the organization. Effective leaders see their own personal vision as an important part of something larger than themselves—a part of the organization and the community at large.

In short, whether it be Greenleaf's notion of waiting on the have-nots or Senge's notion of giving oneself to a larger purpose, the idea behind service is contributing to the greater good of others. In practicing the principle of service, ethical leaders must be willing to be follower centered, must place others' interests foremost in their work, and must act in ways that will benefit others.

Ethical Leaders Are Just

Ethical leaders are concerned about issues of fairness and justice. They make it a top priority to treat all of their subordinates in an equal manner. Justice demands that leaders place issues of fairness at the center of their decision making. As a rule, no one should receive special treatment or special consideration except when their particular situation demands it. In instances where individuals are treated differently, the grounds for differential treatment need to be clear, reasonable, and based on sound moral values.

For example, many of us can remember being involved with some type of athletic team while we were growing up. The coaches we liked were the ones we thought were fair with us. No matter what, we did not want the coach to treat anyone differently than the rest. In situations where someone came late to practice with a poor excuse, we wanted that person disciplined just as we would have been disciplined. If a player had a personal problem and needed a break, we wanted the coach to give it. Without question, the good coaches were those who never had favorites and those who made a point of playing everyone on the team. In essence, what we wanted was that our coach be fair and just.

When resources and rewards or punishments are distributed to employees, the leader plays a major role. The rules that are used and how they are applied say a great deal about whether the leader is concerned about justice and how he or she approaches issues of fairness.

Rawls (1971) stated that a concern with issues of fairness is a requirement for all people who are cooperating together to promote their common interests. It is similar to the Golden Rule: Do unto others as you would have them do unto you. If we expect fairness from others in how they treat us, then we should treat others fairly in our dealings with them. Issues of fairness become problematic because there is always a limit on goods and resources, and there is often competition for those limited things available. Because of the real or perceived scarcity of resources, conflicts often occur between individuals about fair methods of distribution. It is important for leaders to clearly establish the rules for distributing rewards. The nature of these rules says a lot about the ethical underpinnings of the leader and the organization.

Beauchamp and Bowie (1988) have outlined several of the common principles that serve as guides for leaders in how to distribute the benefits and burdens fairly in an organization (see Table 13.2). Although not inclusive, these principles point to the reasoning behind why leaders choose to distribute things the way they do in organizations. In a given situation, a leader may use a single principle or a combination of several principles in treating subordinates.

To illustrate the principles described in Table 13.2, consider the following hypothetical example. Imagine you are the owner of a small trucking company, which employs 50 drivers. You have just opened a new route, and it promises to be one that pays well and has an ideal schedule. Only one driver can be assigned to the route, but seven drivers have applied for it. Each feels he or she should have an *equal opportunity* to get the route. One of the

Table 13.2   *Principles of Distributive Justice*

These principles are applied in different situations

To each person

‣ an equal share

‣ according to individual need

‣ according to that person's rights

‣ according to individual effort

‣ according to societal contribution

‣ according to merit

drivers recently lost his wife to breast cancer and is struggling to care for three young children (*individual need*). Two of the drivers are minorities and one of them feels strongly that he has a *right* to the job. One of the drivers has logged more driving hours for 3 consecutive years and she feels her *effort* makes her the logical candidate for the new route. One of the drivers serves on the National Safety Board and has a 20-year accident-free driving record (*societal contribution*). Two drivers have been with the company since its inception and their *performance* has been meritorious year after year.

As the owner of the company, your challenge is to assign the new route in a fair way. Although many other factors could influence your decision (e.g., seniority, wage rate, or employee health), the principles described in Table 13.2 provide a set of guides for deciding who is to get the new route.

Ethical Leaders Are Honest

When we were children, a phrase we frequently heard from grownups was "never tell a lie." To be good meant we must tell the truth. For leaders the lesson is the same. To be a good leader, leaders need to be honest.

The importance of being honest can be understood more clearly when we consider the opposite of honesty: dishonesty (cf. Jaksa & Pritchard, 1988). Dishonesty is a form of lying, a way of misrepresenting reality. Dishonesty may bring with it many objectionable outcomes, and foremost is the distrust it creates. When leaders are not honest, others come to see them as undependable and unreliable. People lose faith in what leaders say and stand for; their respect for leaders is diminished. As a result, the leader's impact is compromised because others no longer trust and believe in the leader.

When we relate to others, dishonesty also has a negative impact. It puts a strain on how people are connected to each other. When we lie to others, we are in essence saying that we are willing to manipulate the relationship on our own terms. We are saying that we do not trust the other person in the relationship to be able to deal with information we have. In reality, we are putting ourselves ahead of the relationship by saying that we know what is best for the relationship. The long-term effect of this type of behavior is that it weakens relationships. Dishonesty, even when used with good intentions, contributes to the breakdown of relationships.

But being honest is not just about telling the truth. It has to do with being open with others and representing reality as fully and completely as possible. However, this is not an easy task because there are times when telling the complete truth can be destructive or counterproductive. The challenge for leaders is to strike a balance between being open and candid while at the same time monitoring what is appropriate to disclose in a particular situation. It is important for leaders to be authentic but at the same time it is essential that they be sensitive to the attitudes and feelings of others. Honest leadership involves a wide set of behaviors.

Dalla Costa (1998) made the point clearly in his book *The Ethical Imperative* that being honest means more than "not deceiving." For leaders within organizations, being honest means "do not promise what you can't deliver, do not misrepresent, do not hide behind spin-doctored evasions, do not suppress obligations, do not evade accountability, do not accept that the 'survival of the fittest' pressures of business release any of us from the responsibility to respect another's dignity and humanity" (p. 164). In addition, Dalla Costa suggested that it is imperative that organizations recognize and acknowledge the necessity of honesty and reward honest behavior within the organization.

Ethical Leaders Build Community

In Chapter 1, we defined leadership as the process of influencing others to reach a common or communal goal. This definition has a clear ethical dimension because it refers to a *common* goal. A common goal requires that the leader and followers agree on the direction to be taken by the group. Leaders need to take into account their own and followers' purposes, while working toward goals that are suitable for both of them. This factor, concern for others, is the distinctive feature that delineates *authentic* transformational leaders from *pseudo*-transformational leaders (Bass & Steidlmeier, 1999). Concern for the common good means that leaders cannot impose their will on others. They need to search for goals that are compatible with everyone.

Burns (1978) placed this idea at the center of his theory on transformational leadership. A transformational leader tries to move the group toward a common good that is beneficial for both the leaders and the followers. In moving toward mutual goals, both the leader and follower are changed. It is this feature that makes Burns's theory unique. For Burns, leadership has to be grounded in the leader-follower relationship. It cannot be controlled by the leader, such as Hitler's influence in Germany when Hitler coerced people to meet his own agenda—and followed goals that did not advance the goodness of humankind.

An ethical leader takes into account the purposes of everyone involved in the group and is attentive to the interests of the community and the culture. Such a leader demonstrates an ethic of caring toward others (Gilligan, 1982) and does not force others or ignore the intentions of others (Bass & Steidlmeier, 1999).

Rost (1991) went a step further and suggested that ethical leadership demands attention to a civic virtue. By this he means that leaders and followers need to attend to more than their own mutually determined goals. They need to attend to the *community's* goals and purpose. As Burns (1978, p. 429) wrote, transformational leaders and followers begin to reach out to wider social collectivities and seek to establish higher and broader moral purposes. All of our individual and group goals are bound up in the common good and public interest. We need to pay attention to how the changes proposed by a leader and followers will affect the larger organization, the community, and society. An ethical leader is concerned with the common good—in the broadest sense.

STRENGTHS

The present chapter discusses a broad set of ideas regarding ethics and leadership. This general field of study has several strengths. First, it provides a body of timely research on ethical issues. There is a high demand for moral leadership in our society today. Beginning with the Nixon administration in the 1970s and continuing on into the Clinton administration in the 1990s, people have been insisting on higher levels of moral responsibility from their leaders. At a time when there seems to be a vacuum in ethical leadership, this research offers us some direction on how to think about ethical leadership and how to practice it.

Second, this body of research suggests that ethics ought to be considered as an integral part of the broader domain of leadership. Except for Burns's transformational leadership, none of the other leadership theories discussed in this book includes ethics as a dimension of the leadership process. This chapter suggests that leadership is not an amoral phenomenon. Leadership is a process of influencing others; it has a moral dimension that distinguishes it from other types of influence, such as coercion or despotic control. Leadership involves values, including showing respect for followers, being fair to others, and building community. It is not a process that can be demonstrated without showing our values. When we influence, we have an effect on others—and that means we need to pay attention to our values and our ethics.

Third, this body of research highlights several principles that are important to the development of ethical leadership. The virtues discussed in this research have been around for more than 2,000 years, and they are reviewed in this chapter because of their significance for today's leaders.

CRITICISMS

Although the area of ethics and leadership has many strengths, it also has some weaknesses. First, it is an area of research in its early stage of development and therefore it lacks a strong body of traditional research findings to substantiate it. As was pointed out in the beginning of the chapter, very little research has been published on the theoretical foundations of leadership ethics. Although many studies have been published on business ethics, these studies have not been directly related to ethical leadership. The dearth of research on leadership ethics makes speculation about the nature of ethical leadership difficult. Until a greater number of research studies have been conducted that deal directly with the ethical dimensions of leadership, theoretical formulations about the process will remain tentative.

Another criticism is that leadership ethics today relies primarily on the writings of just a few individuals who have written essays and texts that are strongly influenced by their personal opinions about the nature of leadership ethics and their view of the world. Although these writings, such as Greenleaf's and Burns's, have stood the test of time, they have not been tested using traditional quantitative or qualitative research methodologies. They are primarily descriptive and anecdotal in nature. As such, leadership ethics lacks the traditional kind of empirical support that usually accompanies accepted theories of human behavior.

APPLICATION

Although issues of morality and leadership are discussed more frequently in society today, this interest has not resulted in a large number of programs in training and development designed to teach ethical leadership. Many new programs are oriented toward helping managers become more effective people at work and in life in general, but these programs do not directly target the area of ethics and leadership.

Yet the ethics and leadership research in this chapter can be applied to individuals at all levels of organizations and in all walks of life. At a very minimum, it is crucial to state that *leadership involves values,* and one cannot be a leader without being aware and concerned about one's own values. Because leadership has a moral dimension, being a leader demands awareness on our part of the way our ethics defines our leadership.

Managers and leaders can use the information in this research to better understand themselves and strengthen their own leadership. Ethical theories can remind leaders to ask themselves, "What is the right and fair thing to do?" or "What would a good person do?" Leaders can use the ethical principles described in this research as benchmarks for their own behavior. Do I show respect to others? Do I act with a generous spirit? Do I show honesty and faithfulness to others? Do I serve the community? Finally, we can learn from the overriding theme in this research that the leader-follower relationship is central to ethical leadership. To be an ethical leader, we must be sensitive to the needs of others, treat others in ways that are just, and care for others.

CASE STUDIES

The following section contains three case studies (Cases 13.1, 13.2, and 13.3) based on actual situations in which ethical leadership was required. Case 13.1 describes the owner of a small business and the ethical problems he faces during a difficult period of consolidation. Case 13.2 is concerned with one manufacturing company's unique approach to safety standards. Case 13.3 deals with the ethical issues surrounding how a human resource service company established the pricing for its services. At the end of each case, there are questions that point to the intricacies and complexities of practicing ethical leadership.

CASE 13.1

A Struggling Company With Not Enough Cash

Joe Woodman bought a small struggling computer company. After several difficult years, revenues started to grow and it seemed, according to the financial statements, that profits were growing as well. But in reality, the business did not have enough cash.

The company's key stakeholders, such as the bank, vendors, and investors, were applying pressure on Joe to improve earnings and cash flow. They threatened to take over the business if major changes were not made. About the same time and making matters worse, Joe was notified that several contracts, constituting about 25% of his top-line revenues would be lost to the competition.

Joe responded by laying off employees, freezing wages, and closing several marginal operations, but these efforts were not enough. Joe was still badly in need of more cash and professional management. To remain viable, he had three options.

1. He could negotiate a "capital for control" type exchange with the investor and the banks. If he did this, the banks could help recruit new talent and also offer interim financing to support the company while restructuring occurred. On the downside, with this option his status within the organization would significantly change; instead of being the owner, Joe would become more of a senior manager.

2. Joe could maintain control and pursue hiring turn-around management, explaining to them that the company was in a critical turn-around phase and that the organization's future depended on the new managers' ability to generate credibility and positive performance in 1 year's time. He would have to disclose the wage freezes of the past 2 years and explain that he could not initially

offer competitive salaries or certain traditional benefits. If he took this option, Joe would have difficulty recruiting skilled managers because they would not want to come into a situation with failing operations, no operating cash, and the prospects of a dramatically dwindling revenue base. If it succeeds, this option would allow Joe to keep control and save his reputation.

3. Joe could remain in control and pursue hiring turn-around management but he would not fully explain the serious situation. He might say that the company is one of the fastest-growing companies in the industry, that it just completed an operational turn-around, had regained profitability, and was now upgrading staff to take the company to the next level. He could support this positive picture by representing pro forma financial information as though it were actual. This approach would probably be successful initially in gaining new qualified staff, but the new managers might join only to leave soon afterward. They would probably not develop into loyal, long-term employees because of Joe's breach of trust. This option would give Joe the opportunity to maintain control and keep all his workers employed.

Questions

1. Of the three options available to Joe, which is the most ethical?
2. How does egoism come into play in this case? In which of the three options is altruism most apparent?
3. Which option would provide the greatest good for the greatest number? From an ethical perspective, what is Joe's *duty* in this situation?
4. What pressures does Joe face regarding honesty and telling the truth about his situation?

CASE 13.2

How Safe Is Safe?

Perfect Plastics Incorporated (PPI) is a small injection molding plastics company that employs 50 people. The company is 10 years old and has a healthy balance sheet, and it is doing about $4 million a year in sales. The company has a good safety record, and the insurance company that has PPI's liability policy has not had to pay any claims to employees for several years. There have been no major injuries of any kind since the company began.

The owner takes great pride in the interior design and working conditions at PPI. He describes the interior of the plant as being like a hospital compared with his competitors. Order, efficiency, and cleanliness are top priorities at PPI. It is a remarkably well-organized manufacturing company.

PPI has a very unique approach to guaranteeing safe working conditions. Each year, management brings in outside consultants from the insurance industry and the Occupational Safety and Health Administration (OSHA) to audit the plant for any unsafe conditions. Each year, the inspections reveal a variety of concerns, which are then addressed through new equipment, repairs, and changed work-flow designs. Although the inspectors continue to find opportunities for improvement, the overall safety improves each year.

The attorneys for PPI are very opposed to the approach to safety that the company takes. The lawyers are vehemently against the procedure of having outside auditors. If a lawsuit were to be brought against PPI, the attorneys argue that any previous issues could be used as evidence of a historical pattern and knowledge of unsafe conditions. In effect, the audits that PPI is voluntarily having conducted could be used by plaintiffs to strengthen a case against the company.

The president and management recognize the potential downside of outside audits, but they point out that the periodic reviews are critical to the ongoing improvement of the safety of everyone in the plant. The purpose of the audits is to make the shop a secure place, and that is what has occurred. Management also points out that PPI employees have responded positively to the audits and to the changes that result.

Questions

1. As a company, would you describe PPI as having an identifiable set of moral values? How does its policies contribute to this philosophy?
2. Which ethical perspective best describes PPI's approach to safety issues? Would you say PPI takes a utilitarian, duty, or virtue-based approach?
3. Regarding safety issues, how does management see its responsibilities toward its employees? How do the attorneys see their responsibilities toward PPI?
4. Why does it appear that the ethics of PPI and its attorneys are in conflict?

CASE 13.3

Reexamining a Proposal

After working 10 years as the only minority manager in a large printing company, David Jones decided he wanted to set out on his own. Because of his experience and prior connections, David was confident he could survive in the printing business but he wondered if he should buy an existing business or start a new one.

As part of his planning, David contacted a professional employer organization (PEO), which had a sterling reputation, to obtain an estimate for human resource services for a start-up company. The estimate was to include costs for payroll, benefits, workers' compensation, and other traditional human resource services. Because David had not yet started his business, the PEO generated a "generic" quote applicable for a small company in the printing industry. In addition, because the PEO had nothing tangible to quote, it gave David a quote for human resource services that was unusually high.

In the meantime, David Jones found an existing small company that he liked, and he bought it. Then he contacted the PEO to sign a contract with the PEO to provide human resource services at the previously quoted price. David was ready to take ownership and begin his new venture. He signed the original contract as presented.

After David signed the contract, the PEO reviewed the earlier proposal based on the actual figures of the company he had purchased. This review raised many concerns for management. While the goals of the PEO were to provide quality service, be competitive in the marketplace, and make a reasonable profit, the quote it had provided David appeared to be too high and way out of line. It was not comparable in any way with the other service contracts the PEO had with similar companies of similar size and function.

During the review process, it became apparent that several concerns needed to be addressed—first, the original estimate made the PEO appear as if it was gouging the client. Although the client had signed the original contract, was it fair to charge such a high price for the proposed services? Would charging such high fees mean that the PEO would lose this client or similar clients in the future? Another concern was related to the PEO's support of minority businesses. For years, the PEO had prided itself in having strong values about affirmative action and fairness in the workplace, but this contract appeared to be somewhat unfair and actually hurt a minority client. Finally, the PEO was concerned with the implications of the contract for the salesperson who drew up the proposal for David. Changing the estimated costs in the proposal would have a significant impact on the commission of the salesperson, and in effect, this would negatively affect the morale of others in the PEO's sales area.

After a reexamination of the original proposal, a new contract was drawn up for David's company with lower estimated costs. While lower than the original proposal, the new contract remained much higher than the average contract in the printing industry. David Jones willingly signed the new contract.

Questions

1. What role should ethics play in writing a proposal such as this? Did the PEO do the ethical thing for David Jones? How much money should the PEO have tried to make? What would you have done in this situation?
2. From a deontological (duty) perspective versus a teleological (consequences) perspective, how would you describe the ethics of the PEO?
3. Based on what the PEO did for David Jones, how would you evaluate the PEO on the ethical principles of respect, service, justice, honesty, and community?
4. How would you assess the ethics of the PEO if you were David Jones? If you were among the PEO management? If you were the salesperson? If you were a member of the community?

LEADERSHIP INSTRUMENT

Ethics and morals are often regarded as very personal, and we resist having others judge us about them. We also resist judging others. Perhaps for this reason, there have been very few questionnaires designed to measure ethical leadership. To address this problem, Craig and Gustafson (1998) developed the Perceived Leader Integrity Scale (PLIS), which is based on utilitarian ethical theory. The PLIS attempts to evaluate leaders' ethics by measuring the degree to which subordinates see them as acting in ways that would produce the greatest good for the greatest number of people.

By taking the PLIS, you can try to assess the ethical integrity of one of your supervisors. At the same time, the PLIS will allow you to apply the ideas we discussed in the chapter to a real-world setting. The PLIS represents one way to assess the principle of ethical leadership.

In addition, the PLIS can be used for feedback to employees in organizations and as a part of leadership training and development. Finally, if used as part of an organizational climate survey, the PLIS could be useful as a way of identifying areas within an organization that may need an ethics intervention (Craig & Gustafson, 1998).

Perceived Leader Integrity Scale (PLIS)

Instructions: The following items concern your immediate supervisor. You should consider your immediate supervisor to be the person who you feel has the most control over your daily work activities. Circle responses to indicate how well each item describes your immediate supervisor.

Key: 1 = Not at all   2 = Somewhat   3 = Very much   4 = Exactly

1.	Would use my mistakes to attack me personally	1 2 3 4
2.	Always gets even	1 2 3 4
3.	Gives special favors to certain "pet" employees, but not to me	1 2 3 4
4.	Would lie to me	1 2 3 4
5.	Would risk me to protect himself/herself in work matters	1 2 3 4
6.	Deliberately fuels conflict among employees	1 2 3 4
7.	Is evil	1 2 3 4
8.	Would use my performance appraisal to criticize me as a person	1 2 3 4
9.	Has it in for me	1 2 3 4
10.	Would allow me to be blamed for his/her mistakes	1 2 3 4
11.	Would falsify records if it would help his/her work situation	1 2 3 4
12.	Lacks high morals	1 2 3 4
13.	Makes fun of my mistakes instead of coaching me as to how to do my job better	1 2 3 4
14.	Would deliberately exaggerate my mistakes to make me look bad when describing my performance to his/her superiors	1 2 3 4
15.	Is vindictive	1 2 3 4
16.	Would blame me for his/her own mistake	1 2 3 4
17.	Avoids coaching me because (s)he wants me to fail	1 2 3 4
18.	Would treat me better if I belonged to a different ethnic group	1 2 3 4
19.	Would deliberately distort what I say	1 2 3 4
20.	Deliberately makes employees angry at each other	1 2 3 4
21.	Is a hypocrite	1 2 3 4
22.	Would limit my training opportunities to prevent me from advancing	1 2 3 4
23.	Would blackmail an employee if (s)he thought (s)he could get away with it	1 2 3 4
24.	Enjoys turning down my requests	1 2 3 4
25.	Would make trouble for me if I got on his/her bad side	1 2 3 4
26.	Would take credit for my ideas	1 2 3 4
27.	Would steal from the organization	1 2 3 4
28.	Would risk me to get back at someone else	1 2 3 4
29.	Would engage in sabotage against the organization	1 2 3 4
30.	Would fire people just because (s)he doesn't like them if (s)he could get away with it	1 2 3 4
31.	Would do things which violate organizational policy and then expect his/her subordinates to cover for him/her	1 2 3 4

SOURCE: Based on a version of the PLIS that appeared in *Leadership Quarterly, 9*(2), S. B. Craig and S. B. Gustafson, "Perceived Leader Integrity Scale: An Instrument for Assessing Employee Perceptions of Leader Integrity," pp. 143-144, 1998. Used with permission of the authors.

Scoring Interpretation

The PLIS measures subordinates' perceptions of their leaders' integrity in organizational settings. Your responses on the PLIS indicate the degree to which you see your supervisor's behavior as ethical.

Score the questionnaire by doing the following. Sum the responses on all 31 items. A low score on the questionnaire indicates that you perceive your supervisor to be highly ethical. A high score indicates that you see your supervisor to be very unethical. The interpretation of what the score represents is given below.

Total score: _____

Interpretation: Your score is a measure of your perceptions of your supervisor's ethical integrity. Based on previous findings (Craig & Gustafson, 1998), the following interpretations can be made about your total score.

31-35	High ethical	If you scored in this range, it means that you see your supervisor as highly ethical. Your impression is that your supervisor is very trustworthy and highly principled.
36-66	Moderate	Scores in this range mean that you see your supervisor as moderately ethical. Your impression is that he or she sometimes engages in slightly unethical behaviors.
67-124	Low ethical	This range is descriptive of supervisors who are seen as very unethical. Your impression is that they do things which are dishonest, unfair, and unprincipled.

———————————————◆———————————————

SUMMARY

Although there has been an interest in ethics for thousands of years, very little theoretical research exists on the nature of leadership ethics. This chapter presents an overview of ethical theories as they apply to the leadership process.

Ethical theory provides a set of principles that guides leaders in making decisions about how to act and how to be a morally decent person. In the Western tradition, ethical theories are typically divided into two kinds:

theories about *conduct* and theories about *character.* Theories about conduct emphasize the consequences of leader behavior (teleological approach) or the rules that govern their behavior (deontological approach). Virtue-based theories focus on the character of leaders, and they stress qualities such as courage, honesty, fairness, and fidelity.

Ethics plays a central role in the leadership process. Because leadership involves influence and leaders often have more power than followers, they have an enormous ethical responsibility for how they affect other people. Leaders need to engage followers to accomplish mutual goals; hence it is imperative that they treat followers and their ideas with respect and dignity. Leaders also play a major role in establishing the ethical climate within their organization, and that role requires leaders to be particularly sensitive to the values and ideals they promote.

Several prominent leadership scholars (Heifetz, Burns, and Greenleaf) have made unique contributions to our understanding of ethical leadership. The theme common to all three writers is an ethic of caring, which pays attention to followers' needs and the importance of leader-follower relationships.

This chapter suggests that sound ethical leadership is rooted in respect, service, justice, honesty, and community. It is the duty of leaders to treat others with *respect*—to listen to them closely and be tolerant of opposing points of view. Ethical leaders *serve* others by being altruistic, placing others' welfare ahead of their own in an effort to contribute to the common good. *Justice* requires that leaders place fairness at the center of their decision making, including the challenging task of being fair to the individual while simultaneously being fair to the common interests of the community. Good leaders are *honest.* They do not lie nor do they present truth to others in ways that are destructive or counterproductive. Finally, ethical leaders are committed to building *community,* which includes searching for goals that are compatible with the goals of followers and the society as a whole.

Research on ethics and leadership has several strengths. At a time when the public is demanding higher levels of moral responsibility from its leaders, this research provides some direction in how to think about ethical leadership and how to practice it. In addition, this research reminds us that leadership is a moral process. Scholars should include ethics as an integral part of the leadership studies and research. Third, this area of research describes basic principles that we can use in developing real-world ethical leadership.

On the negative side, this research area of ethical leadership is still in an early stage of development. Few studies have been done that directly address the nature of ethical leadership; as a result, the theoretical formulations about the process remain tentative. Second, this area of research relies on the writings of a few individuals whose work has been primarily descriptive and anecdotal. As a result, the development of theory on leadership ethics lacks the traditional empirical support that usually accompanies theories of human behavior. In spite of these weaknesses, the field of ethical leadership is wide-open for future research. There remains a strong need for research that can advance our understanding of the role of ethics in the leadership process.

REFERENCES

Avolio, B. J., & Locke, E. E. (2002). Contrasting different philosophies of leader motivation: Altruism versus egoism. *Leadership Quarterly, 13,* 169-191.

Bass, B. M., & Steidlmeier, P. (1999). Ethics, character, and authentic transformational leadership behavior. *Leadership Quarterly, 10*(2), 181-217.

Beauchamp, T. L., & Bowie, N. E. (1988). *Ethical theory and business* (3rd ed.). Englewood Cliffs, NJ: Prentice Hall.

Beauchamp, T. L., & Childress, J. F. (1994). *Principles of biomedical ethics* (4th ed.). New York: Oxford University Press.

Block, P. (1993). *Stewardship: Choosing service over self-interest.* San Francisco: Berrett-Koehler.

Bowie, N. E. (1991). Challenging the egoistic paradigm. *Business Ethics Quarterly, 1*(1), 1-21.

Brady, F. N. (1999). A systematic approach to teaching ethics in business. *Journal of Business Ethics, 19*(3), 309-319.

Burns, J. M. (1978). *Leadership.* New York: Harper & Row.

Carlson, D. S., & Perrewe, P. L. (1995). Institutionalization of organizational ethics through transformational leadership. *Journal of Business Ethics, 14*(10), 829-838.

Ciulla, J. B. (1998). *Ethics, the heart of leadership.* Westport, CT: Greenwood.

Ciulla, J. B. (2003). *The ethics of leadership.* Belmont, CA: Wadsworth/Thomson Learning.

Covey, S. R. (1990). *Principle-centered leadership.* New York: Fireside.

Craig, S. B., & Gustafson, S. B. (1998). Perceived Leader Integrity Scale: An instrument for assessing employee perceptions of leader integrity. *Leadership Quarterly, 9*(2), 127-145.

Dalla Costa, J. (1998). *The ethical imperative: Why moral leadership is good business.* Reading, MA: Addison-Wesley.

De Pree, M. (1989). *Leadership is an art.* New York: Doubleday.

De Pree, M. (1992). *Leadership jazz.* New York: Dell.

Frankena, W. (1973). *Ethics* (2nd ed.). Englewood Cliffs, NJ: Prentice Hall.

Gilligan, C. (1982). *In a different voice: Psychological theory and women's development.* Cambridge, MA: Harvard University Press.

Gini, A. (1998). Moral leadership and business ethics. In J. B. Ciulla (Ed.), *Ethics, the heart of leadership* (pp. 27-46). Westport, CT: Greenwood.

Graham, J. W. (1991). Servant-leadership in organizations: Inspirational and moral. *Leadership Quarterly, 2*(2), 105-119.

Greenleaf, R. K. (1970). *The servant as leader.* Newton Centre, MA: Robert K. Greenleaf Center.

Greenleaf, R. K. (1977). *Servant leadership: A journey into the nature of legitimate power and greatness.* New York: Paulist.

Heifetz, R. A. (1994). *Leadership without easy answers.* Cambridge, MA: Harvard University Press.

Hesse, H. (1956). *The journey to the East.* London: P. Owen.

Jaksa, J. A., & Pritchard, M. S. (1988). *Communication ethics: Methods of analysis.* Belmont, CA: Wadsworth.

Johnson, C. R. (2001). *Meeting the ethical challenges of leadership.* Thousand Oaks, CA: Sage.

Kanungo, R. N., & Mendonca, M. (1996). *Ethical dimensions of leadership.* Thousand Oaks, CA: Sage.

Kitchener, K. S. (1984). Intuition, critical evaluation and ethical principles: The foundation for ethical decisions in counseling psychology. *The Counseling Psychologist, 12*(3), 43-55.

Komives, S. R., Lucas, N., & McMahon, T. R. (1998). *Exploring leadership: For college students who want to make a difference.* San Francisco: Jossey-Bass.

Kouzes, J. J., & Posner, B. Z. (1995). *The leadership challenge: How to keep getting extraordinary things done in organizations* (2nd ed.). San Francisco: Jossey-Bass.

Pojman, L. P. (1995). *Ethical theory: Classical and contemporary readings* (2nd ed.). Belmont, CA: Wadsworth.

Rawls, J. (1971). *A theory of justice.* Boston: Harvard University Press.

Rost, J. C. (1991). *Leadership for the twenty-first century.* New York: Praeger.

Schminke, M., Ambrose, M. L., & Noel, T. W. (1997). The effect of ethical frameworks on perceptions of organizational justice. *Academy of Management Journal, 40*(5), 1190-1207.

Schumann, P. L. (2001). A moral principles framework for human resource management ethics. *Human Resource Management Review, 11,* 93-111.

Senge, P. M. (1990). *The fifth discipline: The art and practice of the learning organization.* New York: Doubleday.

Trevino, L. K. (1986). Ethical decision making in organizations: A person-situation interactionist model. *Academy of Management Review, 11*(3), 601-617.

Velasquez, M. G. (1992). *Business ethics: Concepts and cases* (3rd ed.). Englewood Cliffs, NJ: Prentice Hall.

Author Index

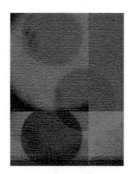

331

Subject Index

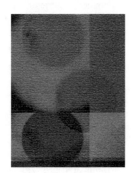

About the Author

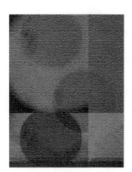

Peter G. Northouse (Ph.D., University of Denver) is Professor of Communication at Western Michigan University. For more than 20 years, he has taught leadership and organizational communication on both the undergraduate and graduate levels. In addition to several book chapters, he has published many articles in professional journals and is coauthor of *Health Communication: Strategies for Health Professionals* (3rd ed.). He serves on the editorial board of the *Journal of Health Communication*. His research interests include leadership ethics, transformational leadership, and conflict resolution. He has worked as a consultant in a variety of areas, including leadership development, conflict management, cancer communication, and organizational communication. He holds a doctorate in speech communication from the University of Denver, and a master's and bachelor's degree in communication education from Michigan State University.

About the Contributors

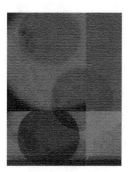

Susan E. Kogler Hill (Ph.D., University of Denver, 1974) is Associate Professor and Chair of the Communication Department at Cleveland State University. Her research and consulting have been in the areas of interpersonal and organizational communication, specializing in group leadership, teamwork, empowerment, and mentoring. She is author of a text titled *Improving Interpersonal Competence.* In addition, she has published in many professional journals and has written chapters in several books.

Julie Indvik (Ph.D., University of Wisconsin–Madison, 1985) is Professor and former Chair of the Department of Management at California State University, Chico. For the past 17 years, she has developed curriculum and taught both undergraduate and graduate students in the areas of workplace diversity, international organizational behavior, transpersonal leadership, and team facilitation. Her research interests, many publications, and consulting work have centered on workplace spiritual issues, emotional issues, diversity, and leadership.

Ernest L. Stech (Ph.D., University of Denver, 1970) is President of Chief Mountain Consulting and adjunct Professor of Communication at Northern Arizona University. He is former Chairman of the Board and CEO of Documents on Demand, Inc., and former President and CEO of Frost Engineering Development Corp. He has authored numerous articles in professional journals and several textbook chapters. He is author of *Leadership Communication* and coauthor of *Working in Groups* and *Effective Group Communication.* His research interests have concentrated on the analysis of human interaction in various organizational and social settings.